ActionScript Graphing Cookbook

Learn how to create appealing and interactive visual presentations of your data in ActionScript

Peter Backx

Dominic Gélineau

PUBLISHING

BIRMINGHAM - MUMBAI

ActionScript Graphing Cookbook

First published: November 2012

Production Reference: 1091112

Published by Packt Publishing Ltd.
Livery Place
35 Livery Street
Birmingham B3 2PB, UK.

ISBN 978-1-84969-320-2

www.packtpub.com

Cover Image by Asher Wishkerman (wishkerman@hotmail.com)

Credits

Authors
Peter Backx
Dominic Gélineau

Reviewers
Carlos Estebes
Prashanth Hirematada
Do The Thuan

Acquisition Editor
Joanna Finchen

Lead Technical Editor
Arun Nadar

Technical Editor
Jalasha D'costa

Project Coordinator
Abhishek Kori

Proofreaders
Maria Gould
Lawrence A. Herman
Aaron Nash

Indexer
Tejal Soni

Graphics
Valentina D'silva
Aditi Gajjar

Production Coordinator
Shantanu Zagade

Cover Work
Shantanu Zagade

About the Authors

Peter Backx has a MoS and a PhD in Computer Sciences from Ghent University. He is a software developer and architect. He uses technology to shape unique user experiences and build rock-solid scalable software. ActionScript is his favorite tool for creating highly interactive and deeply engaging user interfaces.

Peter currently works as a freelance consultant and shares his knowledge and experiments on his blog www.streamhead.com.

Most importantly, I would like to thank Isa and my family for understanding my long days and nights at the computer.

Many of the recipes in this book would not have been possible without the terrific work of all developers in the open source community.

And finally, I'd like to thank everyone at Packt Publishing for giving me this opportunity and supporting me with advice and careful follow-up.

Dominic Gélineau has been developing Flash websites and applications for the last five years, including two years at B-Reel New York, worldwide leader in producing rich web experiences. He has a degree in Communications and one in Computer Science. His areas of expertise are animations, interfaces, and analytics. Dominic writes about these subjects on his blog http://www.zedia.net.

About the Reviewers

Carlos Estebes is the founder of Ehxioz (http://ehxioz.com/), a Los Angeles-based software development startup that specializes in developing modern web applications and utilizing the latest web development technologies and methodologies. He has over 10 years of web development experience and holds a BSc in Computer Science from California State University, Los Angeles.

Carlos previously collaborated with Packt Publishing as a technical reviewer in the third edition of *Learning jQuery*.

Prashanth Hirematada is the CTO and co-founder of Kwestr and has over 15 years of experience in building e-commerce, gaming platforms, social games, and apps. Previously, he co-founded (2007) "In Game Ad Interactive", invested by WPP. He's also the founder of Gamantra in 2006, a game technology company. Before that he was a Chief Architect at Shanda Interactive Entertainment Ltd. [NASDAQ: SNDA]. He had joined Shanda in 2004 through Shanda's acquisition of Zona, Inc., a game technology company in Silicon Valley, California, USA. Prashanth started his career in the valley working for various technology start-up companies involved in NeXT technologies.

Inventor of the spin buffer (Dr. Dobbs's Journal, 2007), he also is a published author of *Flash 10 Multiplayer Game Essentials* (by *Packt Publishing*, UK), and a technical reviewer of game-related books.

Do The Thuan is a passionate self-taught Senior Flash Developer who has been in love with programing since the age of MS-DOS and Turbo Pascal. He inadvertently discovered the beauty and power of Flash and started to learn 2D Animation and Actionscript, then got his first professional job in 2007. During his career, he has built numerous interactive websites, media players, galleries, and rich internet applications, and started several open source projects on `http://github.com/thienhaflash`. He also did some Unity3D works, mostly mini games for iOS devices and unity editor extensions.

With a special interest in optimization and a sound mathematics background, he is always looking for better ways to improve the performance and memory usage of Flash. He occasionally puts experiments and tutorials on his personal blog at `http://thienhaflash.wordpress.com`.

I would like to give a special thanks to my father for being such a wise guider of all my life.

www.PacktPub.com

Support files, eBooks, discount offers and more

You might want to visit www.PacktPub.com for support files and downloads related to your book.

Did you know that Packt offers eBook versions of every book published, with PDF and ePub files available? You can upgrade to the eBook version at www.PacktPub.com and as a print book customer, you are entitled to a discount on the eBook copy. Get in touch with us at service@packtpub.com for more details.

At www.PacktPub.com, you can also read a collection of free technical articles, sign up for a range of free newsletters and receive exclusive discounts and offers on Packt books and eBooks.

 PACKTLiB®

http://PacktLib.PacktPub.com

Do you need instant solutions to your IT questions? PacktLib is Packt's online digital book library. Here, you can access, read and search across Packt's entire library of books.

Why Subscribe?

- ▶ Fully searchable across every book published by Packt
- ▶ Copy and paste, print and bookmark content
- ▶ On demand and accessible via web browser

Free Access for Packt account holders

If you have an account with Packt at www.PacktPub.com, you can use this to access PacktLib today and view nine entirely free books. Simply use your login credentials for immediate access.

Table of Contents

Preface

The cookbook that you are reading will show you how to draw a myriad of graphs in ActionScript. ActionScript is one of the easiest ways to represent graphical information to users across browsers and platforms. It allows you to add a wide range of dynamic effects and interactions to your graphs and charts.

We'll start from the humble beginnings, explaining a little about the ActionScript display list and end at full-blown interactive 3D graphs. In between, you will get to see what goes into animating graphs, adding interaction, and much, much more.

What this book covers

Chapter 1, *Getting Started with Graph Drawing*, goes over the basics of drawing in ActionScript. We cover everything needed to draw graphs, such as the display list and transformations.

Chapter 2, *Working with Data*, will explain how you can import data into your ActionScript program. There are many types of graphs, but all of them are based on data.

Chapter 3, *Creating Bar Charts*, gives us all the tools to create multiple bar charts. Be it vertical, horizontal, comparison, or histograms, this chapter will provide solid bases to improve those charts even more.

Chapter 4, *Drawing Different Types of Graphs*, will go through an array of different charts, each presented in different recipes, some common such as the Venn diagram, some less common such as the Treemap.

Chapter 5, *Adding Interaction*, covers how you can give the user various options to interact with the graph. Selecting, zooming, and panning will be explained as well as a few other options.

Chapter 6, *Mapping Geographical and Spatial Data*, will show how to bring data and maps together to derive further meaning. We will start with simple recipes just showing a map and points of interest and ending up generating heat maps.

Chapter 7, Animating a Graph, explores how to animate graphs using different techniques and animation libraries.

Chapter 8, Creating a Relational Network, shows how to create a relational network, a data visualization that is used to represent a tree data structure, from scratch.

Chapter 9, Creating Three-Dimensional Graphs, lays the groundwork for drawing 3D graphs. Although this is not for the faint of heart, 3D graphs can add a tremendous "wow" factor to your application. This is the first chapter on 3D that gives a high-level overview of everything involved in drawing in 3D, and shows how you can draw some basic graphs.

Chapter 10, Working with Various 3D Graph Types, goes all out on 3D. We'll show you why 3D can add real value to your graphs by applying data to models of real life objects.

What you need for this book

In order to compile and run the examples in this book, you need an ActionScript compiler, which was most likely included with the ActionScript IDE that you are using. You can also use the freely available Flex SDK (`http://www.adobe.com/devnet/flex/flex-sdk-download.html`).

You can create the ActionScript files in any text editor you want, but the example code uses FlashDevelop (`http://www.flashdevelop.org/`). The code will also work verbatim with any other Flash editor, but you may need to use slightly different menu options than the ones mentioned in the *How to do it...* sections. However, the differences will be minimal.

Most of the book's code can run with any ActionScript 3 player, but the 3D chapters require at least version 11. You may also want to install the debug version of the players, because these add some useful features for development. They can be downloaded from `http://www.adobe.com/support/flashplayer/downloads.html`.

Who this book is for

This book is for anyone interested in creating interactive and dynamic graphs in ActionScript. Some programming knowledge is required to understand the examples, preferably in ActionScript 3, but you will be able to understand most of the code if you know any modern object-oriented programming language (for example, Java or C#).

Although an understanding of the ActionScript 3 display list will be very useful, it is not a requirement. The parts needed for drawing graphs are all explained in the first chapter and throughout the book whenever something new is introduced.

Conventions

In this book, you will find a number of styles of text that distinguish between different kinds of information. Here are some examples of these styles, and an explanation of their meaning.

Code words in text are shown as follows: "The _keyData object and the addKey method use coordinates and sizes that were obtained in a drawing program (such as Adobe Photoshop)."

A block of code is set as follows:

```
private function addKey(x:Number, z:Number, usage:Number):Mesh
    {
        var keyGeometry:CubeGeometry = new CubeGeometry(54,usage,54);
        var key:Mesh = new Mesh(keyGeometry, _material);

        key.x = -1 * (x + 27 - 512);
        key.y = usage / 2 + 3;
        key.z = z + 27 - 256;

        addChild(key);

        return key;
    }
```

New terms and **important words** are shown in bold. Words that you see on the screen, in menus or dialog boxes for example, appear in the text like this: "In FlashDevelop, right-click on greensock.swc and choose **Add To Library**."

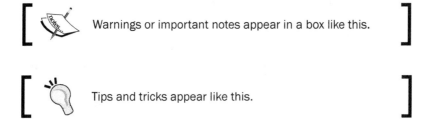

> Warnings or important notes appear in a box like this.

> Tips and tricks appear like this.

Reader feedback

Feedback from our readers is always welcome. Let us know what you think about this book—what you liked or may have disliked. Reader feedback is important for us to develop titles that you really get the most out of.

To send us general feedback, simply send an e-mail to feedback@packtpub.com, and mention the book title through the subject of your message.

If there is a topic that you have expertise in and you are interested in either writing or contributing to a book, see our author guide on www.packtpub.com/authors.

Customer support

Now that you are the proud owner of a Packt book, we have a number of things to help you to get the most from your purchase.

Downloading the example code

You can download the example code files for all Packt books you have purchased from your account at `http://www.packtpub.com`. If you purchased this book elsewhere, you can visit `http://www.packtpub.com/support` and register to have the files e-mailed directly to you.

Downloading the color images of this book

We also provide you a PDF fle that has color images of the screenshots/diagrams used in this book. The color images will help you beter understand the changes in the output. You can download this file from `http://www.packtpub.com/sites/default/files/downloads/3202_Images.pdf`.

Errata

Although we have taken every care to ensure the accuracy of our content, mistakes do happen. If you find a mistake in one of our books—maybe a mistake in the text or the code—we would be grateful if you would report this to us. By doing so, you can save other readers from frustration and help us improve subsequent versions of this book. If you find any errata, please report them by visiting `http://www.packtpub.com/support`, selecting your book, clicking on the **errata submission form** link, and entering the details of your errata. Once your errata are verified, your submission will be accepted and the errata will be uploaded to our website, or added to any list of existing errata, under the Errata section of that title.

Piracy

Piracy of copyright material on the Internet is an ongoing problem across all media. At Packt, we take the protection of our copyright and licenses very seriously. If you come across any illegal copies of our works, in any form, on the Internet, please provide us with the location address or website name immediately so that we can pursue a remedy.

Please contact us at `copyright@packtpub.com` with a link to the suspected pirated material.

We appreciate your help in protecting our authors, and our ability to bring you valuable content.

Questions

You can contact us at `questions@packtpub.com` if you are having a problem with any aspect of the book, and we will do our best to address it.

1
Getting Started with
Graph Drawing

In this chapter, we will cover:

- ▶ Drawing in two dimensions
- ▶ Building point charts
- ▶ Creating a line graph based on a function
- ▶ Adding labels and axes
- ▶ Graphing a spreadsheet
- ▶ Area charts
- ▶ Multiple area charts
- ▶ Styling a graph
- ▶ Adding legends
- ▶ Using Flex for charts

Introduction

In this chapter, we will see a number of recipes that go into the very basics of drawing in ActionScript. The recipes will explain the coordinate system, so that you know where you are drawing. A quick overview of the ActionScript `DisplayList` object and other ActionScript drawing functions is given.

A final recipe shows how Flex can be used to generate many standard graphs with virtually no actual programming. Flex is not the focus of the recipes, but the book wouldn't be complete without at least some coverage of the framework and its functions related to graph drawing.

Although we do not expect you to be an ActionScript expert, some basic knowledge will help you in quickly understanding and applying the recipes presented. Also, we will not go into the details of the tools used.

Drawing in two dimensions

This recipe goes into the very basics of what it takes to draw in two dimensions. There's a little math in there to explain the coordinate system and transformations. It's not the most interesting read, but it is very important that you understand this for all the following recipes.

We also extensively use the ActionScript 3.0 display list concept. We will explain the principles, but if you've never heard of it, you may want to read up on it in other ActionScript tutorials or books. A few of these are mentioned in the *See also* section of this recipe.

Getting ready

All recipes in this book are completely editor-agnostic; you can use them in any ActionScript editor you like. The samples are provided for the free FlashDevelop IDE available at `http://www.flashdevelop.org/`, because it is completely free and of a very high quality.

If you want to follow along with FlashDevelop, now is the time to download and install it. Make sure you also configure the Flex SDK, if FlashDevelop does not do this for you. The Flex SDK is the part that will be responsible for compiling and executing your programs. More information can be found on the FlashDevelop wiki found at `http://www.flashdevelop.org/wikidocs/index.php?title=Configuration#Configuring_the_Flex_SDK`.

In FlashDevelop, create a new AS3 project. You can create one for each chapter, or re-use the same one for most of the recipes. Most recipes will require you to set the document class. This is done by right-clicking on the class in the project view and picking **set document class** from the options.

If you are using Flash Professional, we will not use the timeline that you may be used to. Information on setting up the document class can be found in the following blog article: `http://active.tutsplus.com/tutorials/actionscript/quick-tip-how-to-use-a-document-class-in-flash/`.

How to do it...

The first three steps will need to be performed for virtually all the recipes in this book, so we won't repeat them, unless they differ:

1. Create a new class (in this case it's called `Recipe1`).
2. Have it extend `flash.display.Sprite`.

3. Set it as the *Document Class*.

    You should have the following piece of code:

```
package
{
  import flash.display.Sprite;
  public class Recipe1 extends Sprite
  {
    public function Recipe1()
    {
    }
  }
}
```

4. Now run the code. You should get a blank screen with no warnings or errors.

5. In order to draw a nice looking point, we will actually draw a small circle. The following piece of code creates a shape, draws a circle, moves the center point, and displays it:

```
package
{
  import flash.display.Shape;
  import flash.display.Sprite;

  public class Recipe1 extends Sprite
  {
    public function Recipe1()
    {
            var point:Shape = new Shape( );
            point.graphics.beginFill( 0xff9933 , 1 );
            point.graphics.drawCircle( 0 , 0 , 3 );
            point.x = 20;
            point.y = 20;
            addChild( point );
    }
  }
}
```

6. To more easily draw points inside graph coordinates of our choosing, we can introduce `graph:Sprite`, which will perform a transformation on all points we draw inside it:

```
package
{
    import flash.display.Shape;
    import flash.display.Sprite;
    import flash.geom.Matrix;

    public class Recipe1 extends Sprite
    {
        public function Recipe1()
        {
            var graph:Sprite = new Sprite();
            graph.x = 20;
            graph.y = 20;
            addChild(graph);

            var point:Shape = new Shape();
            point.graphics.beginFill( 0xff9933 , 1 );
            point.graphics.drawCircle( 0 , 0 , 3 );
            point.x = 0;
            point.y = 0;
            graph.addChild(point);
        }
    }
}
```

The visual result is exactly the same as the previous piece of code, but now the point is at the coordinates (0,0).

7. To obtain the transformation presented in the *How it works...* section of this recipe, we just need to apply the right transformation to the graph sprite:

```
package
{
    import flash.display.Shape;
    import flash.display.Sprite;
    import flash.geom.Matrix;

    public class Recipe1 extends Sprite
    {
        public function Recipe1()
        {
            var graph:Sprite = new Sprite();
```

```
        graph.x = 400;
        graph.y = 300;
        graph.scaleY = -1;
        addChild(graph);

        var point:Shape = new Shape();
        point.graphics.beginFill( 0xff9933 , 1 );
        point.graphics.drawCircle( 0 , 0 , 3 );
        point.x = 0;
        point.y = 0;
        graph.addChild(point);
    }
  }
}
```

How it works...

ActionScript 3.0 uses a concept called a display list. A **display list** is a collection of visual elements. The most important display list is your main class. This is the list that will be displayed (that is the reason why it extends `Sprite`).

This list is organized as a tree. It has a root node, to which various display objects are attached. Some of these display objects can also contain more display objects, hence the tree structure.

For instance, if you add a `Sprite` child to your main class, it will be displayed. If you add yet another `Sprite` child to that child, it too will be drawn on the screen.

However this isn't the end of the story. You can apply transformations to objects in the display list. A transformation can be scaling, rotating, and moving, or all at once. If you apply a transformation to one object, this transformation will also apply to all its children. This is how we displayed a point at (0,0) that was in the center of the screen.

When drawing a point, we do this by adding a shape to the display list:

1. First a shape is created, which will hold all data related to our point (location, color, size).
2. The ActionScript `Graphics` class is used to draw a solid circle into the shape.
3. Next we change the location of the shape.

We could also draw the circle at the position, but because the (0,0) coordinates of the circle sprite are at the top-left corner, this would not place the point in the center of the shape. This will complicate any transformation on the shape as we'll see later on. That's because the pivot point for scaling and rotating is the (0,0) coordinate.

4. Finally we add the point object to the display list. Without this last line, the point would not be visible.

To understand the transformation that takes place, you should take note of two different coordinate systems that are used:

1. **Screen coordinates**: If you used the default FlashDevelop settings, you will have a screen that goes from $x = 0$, $y = 0$ in the upper-left corner to $x = 800$, $y = 600$ in the bottom-right corner.

   This means that the X-axis of the coordinate system goes from the left of the screen to the right. The Y-axis goes from the top, down to the bottom.

   Usually the coordinates are given as a pair, so $x = 0$, $y = 0$ is written as (0,0). The following diagram demonstrates the screen coordinates:

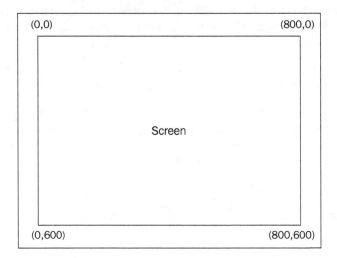

2. Most graphs however are not drawn in screen coordinates. For instance, if you want to plot a function, you may want to put the (0,0) coordinates in the center of the screen. This might look something like the following screenshot. The graph coordinates are in blue; we show only the direction and origin for the graph axes:

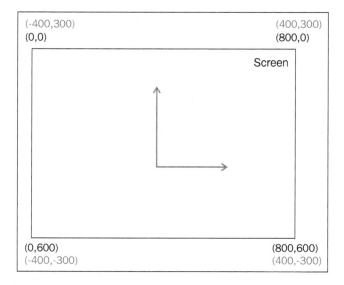

So if you want to draw a graph point at (0,0), you would in effect have to draw it on the screen coordinates (400,300).

To create such a transformation, we first translate the (0,0) point to the center of the screen. And second, the *Y*-axis is scaled by -1. This inverts the *Y* direction (up is down, and down is up).

In the next recipe, we will see a transformation matrix. This matrix is a mathematical shorthand notation for a coordinate transformation.

There's more...

Although this recipe seems simple; there's much you can learn from it. Let's look at some more features.

Graphics drawing

We've only covered the very basics of drawing with the `Graphics` class. Further recipes will show more details. But if you can't wait, try experimenting with the color and the size. The ActionScript 3.0 reference pages have the information you need:

```
http://help.adobe.com/en_US/FlashPlatform/reference/actionscript/3/
flash/display/Graphics.html.
```

Coordinate systems and transformations

A great exercise is to experiment with the transformations. Try to obtain various results. If you modify the `scaleX` and `scaleY` variables, you can zoom in or out of the graph. You can even rotate your system.

Or if you're into maths, you can directly manipulate the transformation matrix of the graph sprite. Again, the ActionScript 3.0 reference guide will help you out:

```
http://help.adobe.com/en_US/FlashPlatform/reference/actionscript/3/
flash/geom/Matrix.html.
```

See also

If you want to read up on the display list, most of the ActionScript 3.0 fundamental books have a dedicated chapter about it. For instance, *Learning ActionScript 3* or *Essential ActionScript 3* (both published by *O'Reilly*) are good references.

If you want to read up on coordinate systems and transformations, you can find the best coverage in any vector maths book. Wikipedia is also a very informative source: `http://en.wikipedia.org/wiki/Coordinate_system`.

Building point charts

This recipe builds on the previous one. The previous recipe placed all the codes into one big method. This is fine for the first experiment, but when things get more complicated, you'll lose track of what goes where.

This recipe brings structure into the code and shows how to graph multiple points without repeating yourself.

Getting ready

Make sure you at least glanced over the previous recipe. You'll need it here.

Create a new, blank `Recipe2` class, set it as the document class, and copy and paste the code inside the `Recipe1` constructor placed inside it. To be sure, run the class and verify that everything looks the same as in the previous recipe.

How to do it...

We will tackle the generalization of the code in a few steps. If you take a look at the code, you'll notice that there are actually two important blocks: one that creates the graph shape and one that draws a point.

1. In the first step we will extract these blocks into two methods:

    ```
    package
    {
      import flash.display.Shape;
      import flash.display.Sprite;
    ```

```
public class Recipe2 extends Sprite
{
  private var graph:Sprite;

  public function Recipe2()
  {
    createGraph();
    drawPoint();
  }

  private function createGraph():void
  {
    graph = new Sprite();
    graph.x = 400;
    graph.y = 300;
    graph.scaleY = -1;
    addChild(graph);
  }

  private function drawPoint():void
  {
    var point:Shape = new Shape();
    point.graphics.beginFill( 0xff9933 , 1 );
    point.graphics.drawCircle( 0 , 0 , 3 );
    point.x = 0;
    point.y = 0;
    graph.addChild(point);
  }
}

}
```

The end result should still be exactly the same.

2. The coordinates of the current graph are chosen for this one example; it would be much better to parameterize this. As parameters, we'll include the top-left and bottom-right coordinates we'd like to have:

```
createGraph(-400, 300, 400, -300);
```

 See the images of the *Drawing in two dimensions* recipe in this chapter for the coordinate system that we are using.

To make sure the method works with all possible choices of coordinates, we need to do some calculations in the `createGraph` method:

❑ Translating the graph to the new center point (keeping in mind the scale).

❑ Scale the graph to the right size. This can be done by comparing the current width and height against the values we want. The current width and height are fixed when you enter your project properties. But you can also obtain them from the stage object.

❑ Lastly, if the coordinates are reversed, we must mirror the image.

All these calculations together form this reusable method:

```
private function createGraph(left:Number, top:Number,
right:Number, bottom:int):void
    {
        var width:Number = Math.abs(right - left);
        var height:Number = Math.abs(bottom - top);
        var scaleWidth:Number = stage.stageWidth / width;
        var scaleHeight:Number = stage.stageHeight / height;
        var flipX:Boolean = (left > right);
        var flipY:Boolean = (top > bottom);

        graph = new Sprite();
        graph.x = scaleWidth * Math.abs(left);
        graph.y = scaleHeight * Math.abs(top);
        graph.scaleX = (flipX ? -1 : 1) * scaleWidth;
        graph.scaleY = (flipY ? -1 : 1) * scaleHeight;
        addChild(graph);
    }
```

3. Now that we've got the hard part out of the way, let's make the `drawPoint` method a little more reusable. For now, we want to set all the points to the same style and size, so the only parameters to the method are the location.

The resulting code is as follows:

```
package
{
    import flash.display.Shape;
    import flash.display.Sprite;

    public class Recipe2 extends Sprite
    {
        private var graph:Sprite;
```

```
    public function Recipe2()
    {
      createGraph(-400, 300, 400, -300);
      drawPoint(0, 0);
      drawPoint(20, 20);
      drawPoint(-40,-40);
    }

    private function createGraph(
left:Number, top:Number, right:Number, bottom:Number):void
    {
      var width:Number = Math.abs(right - left);
      var height:Number = Math.abs(bottom - top);
      var scaleWidth:Number = stage.stageWidth / width;
      var scaleHeight:Number = stage.stageHeight / height;
      var flipX:Boolean = (left > right);
      var flipY:Boolean = (top > bottom);

      graph = new Sprite();
      graph.x = scaleWidth * Math.abs(left);
      graph.y = scaleHeight * Math.abs(top);
      graph.scaleX = (flipX ? -1 : 1) * scaleWidth;
      graph.scaleY = (flipY ? -1 : 1) * scaleHeight;
      addChild(graph);
    }

    private function drawPoint(x:Number, y:Number):void
    {
      var point:Shape = new Shape();
      point.graphics.beginFill( 0xff9933 , 1 );
      point.graphics.drawCircle( 0 , 0 , 3 );
      point.x = x;
      point.y = y;
      graph.addChild(point);
    }
  }
}
```

This code also shows that the method can be reused to draw several different points. If everything went well, you should see three points along a diagonal, with the bottom-left point being a little farther away from the others.

How it works...

To see how the transformation actually works, add the following line to the end of the graph constructor:

```
trace(graph.transform.matrix);
```

 If you have issues viewing the trace statements output, it may be due to the Flash player you are using or the FlashDevelop configuration. The FlashDevelop wiki has troubleshooting instructions right here: http://www.flashdevelop.org/wikidocs/index. php?title=AS3:Debugging.

This `trace` statement will display the transformation matrix in use. If you still remember your math, you may find this other way of looking at the process enlightening (see http://en.wikipedia.org/wiki/Transformation_matrix for an in-depth discussion on the topic).

The `createGraph` method sets up the following transformations:

> ▶ It calculates the required scaling based on the target width and height.

> ▶ The `flipX` and `flipY` variables are used to calculate whether the target coordinate system is mirrored or not. For instance, in this example, the Y- axis of the screen coordinates points down (0 is at the top and positive numbers are at the bottom), while the coordinate system in which we draw the graph works the other way around. This means we need to mirror the Y coordinates.

The `drawPoint` method draws a new point and can be called repeatedly to draw multiple points.

It creates a new shape for every point. This is not strictly necessary and might even cause a degraded performance when drawing many points. In the coming chapters, we'll see some uses for this approach, but if you have issues with performance, you can directly draw on the `Recipe2` sprite and not instantiate new shapes for every point.

There's more...

Again, this basic program is very powerful. And with a few changes, it allows for lots of experimentation.

Coordinate system

Try to change the parameters of the `createGraph` method and see if you can predict the results.

Typically, scientific graphs will have their origin (0,0) in the center of the graph. Most business-type charts will have their origin somewhere in the bottom-left corner. All of these can be easily achieved by changing the parameters of the `drawGraph` method.

Scaling woes

If you change the coordinate system, you may notice that the point scales with the coordinate system. You can fix this by scaling back the point to the original size. Or you can transform all the operations, instead of the shape (refer to the next recipe for the solution).

Adding more parameters

If you like multiple points with different colors, then why not add another parameter to the `drawPoint` method.

See also

This recipe closely relates to many of the others in this chapter. So if something isn't clear, go back to the previous one, or skip ahead and come back to it later.

Creating a line graph based on a function

Now that we have our coordinate system and we know how to draw points, it's time to look a little further. This recipe introduces some other Graphics functions that will allow you to draw lines.

This recipe uses one of the most typical line graphs, namely the display of a function.

Getting ready

Before starting this recipe, we will go through one final iteration of our code in order to have a proper object-oriented structure that we can easily and quickly extend in this and later recipes.

Start by creating a `Recipe3` class, set it as document class, and have it extend `Sprite`.

Next create a `Graph` class (in a new file, with name `Graph.as`) where we will centralize all graph drawing methods:

```
package
{
  import flash.display.Shape;
  import flash.display.Sprite;
  import flash.events.Event;

  public class Graph extends Sprite
```

```
{
  private var left:Number;
  private var top:Number;
  private var right:Number;
  private var bottom:Number;

  private var matrix:Matrix;

  public function Graph(left:Number, top:Number, right:Number,
bottom:Number)
    {
      this.left   = left;
      this.top    = top;
      this.right  = right;
      this.bottom = bottom;

      addEventListener(Event.ADDED_TO_STAGE, createGraph);
    }

  private function createGraph(event:Event):void
    {
      removeEventListener(Event.ADDED_TO_STAGE, createGraph);

      var width:Number = Math.abs(right - left);
      var height:Number = Math.abs(bottom - top);
      var scaleWidth:Number = stage.stageWidth / width;
      var scaleHeight:Number = stage.stageHeight / height;
      var flipX:Boolean = (left > right);
      var flipY:Boolean = (top > bottom);

      matrix = new Matrix(
        (flipX ? -1 : 1) * scaleWidth,
        0,
        0,
        (flipY ? -1 : 1) * scaleHeight,
        scaleWidth * Math.abs(left),
        scaleHeight * Math.abs(top)
      );
    }

  public function drawPoint(x:Number, y:Number):void
    {
      var transformedLocation:Point = matrix.transformPoint(new
Point(x, y));
```

```
    var point:Shape = new Shape();
        point.graphics.beginFill( 0xff9933 , 1 );
        point.graphics.drawCircle( 0 , 0 , 3 );
    point.x = transformedLocation.x;
    point.y = transformedLocation.y;
        addChild(point);
  }
 }
}
```

You'll notice two major changes from the previous recipe:

1. Due to the way the display list works, we don't have access to the stage until the graph is attached to it. This means we have to create the graph after the `ADDED_TO_STAGE` event is fired. This detail is not important for the rest of the recipe, so if you don't understand it at this point, don't worry.

2. Instead of transforming the graph shape (via its `x`, `y`, `scaleX`, and `scaleY` parameters), we transform the coordinates of the point. The result is that the circle is always as we expected and is not scaled with your coordinates system (see the *Scaling woes* section in the previous recipe).

How to do it...

1. We now start with the same program as the *Building point charts* recipe, but using the new `Graph` class:

```
package
{
  import flash.display.Sprite;

  public class Recipe3 extends Sprite
  {
    private var graph:Graph;

    public function Recipe3()
    {
      graph = new Graph( -400, 300, 400, -300);
      addChild(graph);

      graph.drawPoint(0, 0);
      graph.drawPoint(20, 20);
      graph.drawPoint(-40,-40);
    }

  }
}
```

If everything went right, you should see, once again, the exact same result. Only now, our main program (`Recipe3`) only shows what we want to do (that is, to create a graph and draw points). How those actions are performed, is written inside the `Graph` class.

2. Now to create this recipe. We need a way to draw lines. Add the following method to the `Graph` class:

```
public function drawLine(x1:Number, y1:Number, x2:Number,
y2:Number):void
{
  var transformedLocation1:Point = matrix.transformPoint(new
Point(x1, y1));
  var transformedLocation2:Point = matrix.transformPoint(new
Point(x2, y2));

  graphics.lineStyle(2, 0x000000);
  graphics.moveTo(transformedLocation1.x, transformedLocation1.y);
  graphics.lineTo(transformedLocation2.x, transformedLocation2.y);
}
```

3. Now let's do something useful with this. Say you want to draw the sine function in the range starting from $-\pi/2$ and ending at $\pi/2$. The result will go from -1 to 1. So we use $(-\pi/2, 1)$ and $(\pi/2)$ as the upper-left and lower-right corners of our graph.

But a sine is not a linear function, so we can't just draw one line from $(-\pi/2, -1)$ to $(\pi/2, 1)$. What we will do, is approximate the sine curve by splitting it into smaller parts and drawing a number of shorter lines.

Take a look at the following code:

```
package
{
  import flash.display.Sprite;
  import flash.geom.Point;

  public class Recipe3 extends Sprite
  {
    private var graph:Graph;

    public function Recipe3()
    {
      graph = new Graph( -Math.PI/2, 1, Math.PI/2, -1);
      addChild(graph);

      var i:Number = -Math.PI/2;
      var step:Number = 0.1;
      var previousPoint:Point = new Point(i, Math.sin(i));
```

```
for (i += step; i <= Math.PI/2; i += step)
{
   var point:Point = new Point(i, Math.sin(i));
   graph.drawLine(previousPoint.x, previousPoint.y , point.x,
point.y);
   previousPoint = point;
}
}


}
}
```

The result is the sine curve, as shown in the following screenshot:

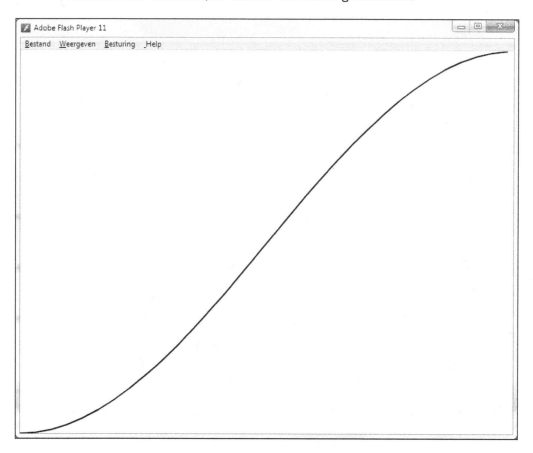

Because we used many small lines (the program uses π / 0.1 or 31 pieces), the segments are hardly distinguishable.

4. Change the step variable to 1 and you'll immediately see the separate lines, as shown in the following screenshot:

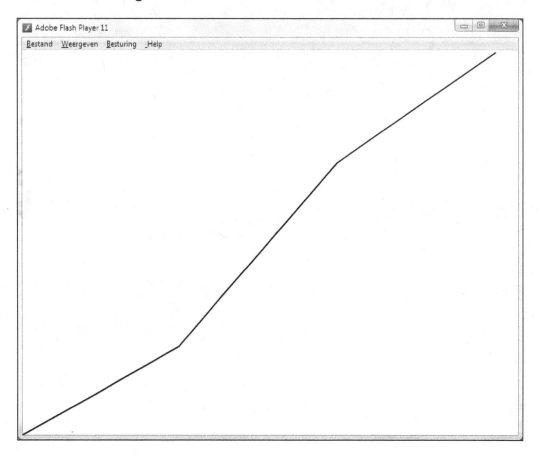

You can still see the sine curve, but it's clear that the three segments don't have a very good approximation.

How it works...

To draw a line, we use the `Graphics` methods as follows:

▶ We calculate the correct position of the beginning and the end points of the line

▶ The ActionScript `Graphics` methods are used to set a line style and draw the line

You can try this out with any data, not just a function. Replace the `drawPoint` method calls in `Recipe3` with the following piece of code:

```
graph.drawLine(0, 0, 20, 40);
```

You should see a short line appear. Once we can draw a line, drawing a function just builds on top of that:

- To change the way the transformation is handled, instead of scaling the entire shape, we just scale the coordinates. The result is that the graphics element, such as circles and line widths, don't scale with the coordinate system.

- To approximate the actual sine curve, we take samples and fill in the holes with a straight line. This is linear interpolation and if it's done right, it's hardly distinguishable from the real thing.

There's more...

If function drawing is the main aim of your program, there are quite a few ways this code can be extended and improved.

Improving the Graph class

Until now, our two graph methods (`drawPoint` and `drawLine`) have taken number arguments. A better interface would probably have point classes as arguments. Why not try this refactoring yourself? It will give you more insight into the code. The result will be used in the next recipes.

Using points to draw functions

There are many ways to draw a function. One thing you may have thought about using is the `drawPoint` method, just placing many points. You can quite easily adapt the program to do this. However, you'll notice you need quite a lot more points to obtain the same result.

Curves

The ActionScript `Graphics` class can also draw so called **Bézier** curves with the `curveTo` method. You'll only need two well-chosen curves to get a very convincing result. This is not for the faint of heart, but you can find code that should get you started at these sites:

http://www.cartogrammar.com/blog/actionscript-curves-update/

http://gskinner.com/blog/archives/2008/05/drawing_curved_.html

See also

If you want to read up on linear interpolation, a good starting point is Wikipedia http://en.wikipedia.org/wiki/Linear_interpolation or your old, math books.

The sine function is also well explained on Wikipedia:
`http://en.wikipedia.org/wiki/Sine`.

Adding labels and axes

Before diving into some more graph types, it's about time we started adding axes and scales. If we don't have those, there really is no way to properly interpret our nice charts.

In this recipe we will add a horizontal and vertical axis to the sine graph we created in the previous recipe. We will also add markers and labels.

Getting ready

This recipe continues to expand the `Graph` class presented in the previous recipe. So if you haven't written that yet, copy it from the provided sources.

Next, create a `Recipe4` class, just as we did in the previous recipes.

How to do it...

To create axes, we will add two methods to the `Graph` class. They are as follows:

- `public function drawVerticalAxis(x:Number, y1:Number, y2:Number)`
- `public function drawHorizontalAxis(y: Number, x1:Number, x2:Number)`

Calling the methods will draw a straight line from (x,y1) to (x,y2) and (x1,y) to (x2,y), respectively.

1. For our first implementation we can simply reuse the `drawLine` method.

   Add the following methods to the `Graph` class:

   ```
   public function drawVerticalAxis(x:Number, y1:Number,
   y2:Number)
   {
     drawLine(x, y1, x, y2);
   }


   public function drawHorizontalAxis(y: Number, x1:Number,
   x2:Number)
   {
     drawLine(x1, y, x2, y);
   }
   ```

2. Now you can try them out in the `Recipe4` class:

```
package
{
  import flash.display.Sprite;
  import flash.geom.Point;

  public class Recipe4 extends Sprite
  {
    private var graph:Graph;

    public function Recipe4()
    {
      graph = new Graph( -Math.PI/2, 1, Math.PI/2, -1);
      addChild(graph);

      graph.drawVerticalAxis(0, 1, -1);
      graph.drawHorizontalAxis(0, -Math.PI / 2, Math.PI /
2);

      var i:Number = -Math.PI/2;
      var step:Number = 0.1;
      var previousPoint:Point = new Point(i,
Math.sin(i));
      for (i += step; i <= Math.PI/2; i += step)
      {
        var point:Point = new Point(i, Math.sin(i));
        graph.drawLine(previousPoint.x, previousPoint.y ,
point.x, point.y);
        previousPoint = point;
      }
    }

  }
}
```

The result should be the same graph as before, but now with two lines forming an axis.

A typical axis has at least two features that make it actually useful:

    i.   Regularly spaced tick marks.

    ii.   Labels associated with those marks.

3. We will first draw the marks. In order to do this, we first create a separate `drawAxisLine` method. This will also allow you to style the axes differently than the actual graph.

    A first revision of the `drawHorizontalAxis` method looks like the following code:

    ```
    public function drawHorizontalAxis(y: Number, x1:Number,
    x2:Number):void
    {
      var transformedLocation1:Point = matrix.transformPoint(new
    Point(x1, y));
      var transformedLocation2:Point = matrix.transformPoint(new
    Point(x2, y));
      drawAxisLine(transformedLocation1, transformedLocation2);
    }

    private function drawAxisLine(p1: Point, p2: Point):void
    {
      var line:Shape = new Shape();
      line.graphics.lineStyle(1, 0x000000);
      line.graphics.moveTo(p1.x, p1.y);
      line.graphics.lineTo(p2.x, p2.y);
      addChild(line);
    }
    ```

4. Now we add marks. This uses a stepping algorithm very similar to the one we used for drawing a function. First we calculate the mark position on the axis and next a short line is drawn, perpendicular to the axis:

    ```
    public function drawHorizontalAxis(y: Number, x1:Number,
    x2:Number):void
    {
      var transformedLocation1:Point = matrix.transformPoint(new
    Point(x1, y));
      var transformedLocation2:Point = matrix.transformPoint(new
    Point(x2, y));
      drawAxisLine(transformedLocation1, transformedLocation2);

      var step:Number     = 50;
      for (var markX:Number = transformedLocation1.x;
        markX <= transformedLocation2.x;
        markX += step)
      {
        var markPoint1:Point = new Point(markX,
    transformedLocation1.y);
        var markPoint2:Point = new Point(markX, transformedLocation1.y
    + 10);
        drawAxisLine(markPoint1, markPoint2);
      }
    }
    ```

5. And finally we add labels. To display a label we use the ActionScript `TextField` class. This class has a tremendous amount of parameters that allow you to customize how the text is displayed. We will look at a few parameters in the later recipes, but for now, we use the standard formatting.

    We don't want to clutter the display too much, so we only add a text label every four markers:

```
public function drawHorizontalAxis(y: Number, x1:Number,
x2:Number):void
{
   var transformedLocation1:Point = matrix.transformPoint(new
Point(x1, y));
   var transformedLocation2:Point = matrix.transformPoint(new
Point(x2, y));
   drawAxisLine(transformedLocation1, transformedLocation2);

   var labels:Array   = ["-PI/2","-PI/4","0","PI/4","PI/2"];
   var step:Number = 50;
   var labelCount:int = 0;
   for (var markX:Number = transformedLocation1.x;
     markX <= transformedLocation2.x;
     markX += step)
   {
     var markPoint1:Point = new Point(markX,
transformedLocation1.y);
     var markPoint2:Point = new Point(markX, transformedLocation1.y
+ 10);
     drawAxisLine(markPoint1, markPoint2);

     if (int(markX) % 200 == 0)
     {
       //place a label every 4 markers
       var textField:TextField = new TextField();
       textField.text = labels[labelCount++];
       textField.x = markX;
       textField.y = transformedLocation1.y + 12;
       addChild(textField);
     }
   }
}
```

6. Run the program again, and you'll see a horizontal axis with values.

How it works...

This recipe is probably one of the least spectacular ones. It just builds on top of ActionScript methods for drawing lines and displaying text. There's a lot of mechanical work involved in getting everything in the right location, but nothing complicated.

The best way to understand the recipe is to play with the various parameters:

- ▶ Increase and decrease the marker step size
- ▶ Change the size of the markers
- ▶ Change the number of labels (make sure you have enough label values in the labels array; if not, you'll end up receiving error messages)

There's more...

Now let's talk about some other options, or possibly some pieces of general information that are relevant to this task.

Vertical axis

Only the code for the horizontal axis was shown. The code for the vertical axis is, of course, very similar and a great exercise.

Screen versus graph coordinates

All the axes drawing code was written in screen coordinates. This simplified a few things, but it could also make it more complex to correctly place the marks. A good exercise is to rewrite the code using graph coordinates.

Error checking and adding parameters

We haven't really bothered ourselves with adding error checking to the parameters (what if the first value of the axis coordinate is larger than the second?). We also haven't yet made the code more generic. You can add parameters for the number of marks you want to be shown on the labels.

Graphing a spreadsheet

Graphing functions is nice, but visualizing a spreadsheet is probably the most popular use case for graphs. Having a visual representation of tabular data can result into insights previously hidden behind the numbers.

In this recipe, we will structure the code to use data from a fixed array in the ActionScript program. In the next chapter, we'll go into all kinds of ways to get the data into that array.

Getting ready

Create a new document class called `Recipe5` and have it extend `Sprite`. Also make sure to copy the updated `Graph` class from the provided source package. It has enhanced and more flexible axes methods (if you implemented any of the items mentioned in the *There's more...* section of the *Adding labels and axes* recipe in this chapter, you may have already created a very similar one).

This time we'll focus on only positive numeric data, so we'll put the origin (0,0) of the graph in the bottom-left corner:

```
package
{
  import flash.display.Sprite;

    private const MAX_X:int   = 700;
    private const MAX_Y:int   = 500;
    private const BORDER:int = 50;
    private const TICK:int    = 50;

  public class Recipe5 extends Sprite
  {
    private var graph:Graph;

    public function Recipe5()
    {
      graph = new Graph( -BORDER, MAX_Y + BORDER, MAX_X + BORDER,
-BORDER);
      addChild(graph);
      graph.drawHorizontalAxis(0, 0, MAX_X, TICK, ["0", MAX_X]);
      graph.drawVerticalAxis(0, 0, MAX_Y, TICK, ["0", MAX_Y/2,
MAX_Y]);
      }
    }
  }
```

If you run this program, you should see both axes run from the bottom-left corner and there should be two labels on the horizontal axis and three on the vertical axis.

How to do it...

For now, we'll just show point charts. Feel free to convert this into a line chart (as shown in the *Creating a line graph based on a function* recipe in this chapter) and in later recipes you'll learn how to draw many different types of charts.

If we have the following table:

	A	B	C
1	10	40	
2	20	60	
3			

We want to draw two points: (10,40) and (20,60).

Storing data is easiest in a two dimensional array. In the next chapter, we'll go over many different ways of storing data (such as in files and on the Internet). The array mimics how you represent this data in a program such as MS Excel:

```
private var graph2d:Array = [[0,20],[50,70],[100,0],[150,150],[200,30
0],[250,200],
    [300,400],[350,20],[400,60],[450,250],[500,90],[550,400],
    [600,500],[650,450],[700,320]];
```

All the points are grouped together. Each entry in the array is one (x , y) coordinate on the graph.

The code to draw this dataset is just a simple loop:

```
for (i = 0; i < graph2d.length; i++)
{
    graph.drawPoint(graph2d[i][0], graph2d[i][1], 0x3399ff);
}
```

This structure does have one problem: it's not easy to manipulate the data. You may want to change the data, for instance, if this was connected to live web statistics that are updated every minute (we'll see more on that in the next chapter). Say you want to change the point (150,150) to (150,200). How would you do that? You need to loop over the array and find the correct entry and change it.

However, searching this way in a large array can become slow quite quickly. If the array is always sorted, like in the preceding example, you could implement your own version of a search algorithm to make it quicker. But then you'd need to create your own insertion algorithm to make sure the data remains in order.

No matter how you solve this, if you need to manipulate the data a lot, this is not a good data structure.

See the *There's more...* section of this recipe for other solutions to these problems.

How it works...

The data we want to display is a simple data mapping from one value to the another. Imagine an Excel spreadsheet with two columns. One column holds the *x*-axis values while the other holds the *y*-axis value. Two numbers on the same row present one (x , y) point.

That is why a two-dimensional array is one of the best ways to represent data: it's an easy structure to program and it's easy to read. However, it is hard to manipulate. If you have a fixed data set, this is the structure you want.

There's more...

There are an endless number of possible ways to represent data. Depending on your data source or your specific data set, you may want to look into other options. In the following section, we present the two most popular ones, each with its own advantages and disadvantages. Ultimately, it is possible to combine most advantages into one structure, but it will require additional development.

Two arrays

The easiest solution to store data is in two arrays, one for each column in the spreadsheet:

```
private var graph1x:Array =
[0, 50, 100, 150, 200, 250, 300, 350, 400,
450, 500, 550, 600, 650, 700];
private var graph1y:Array =
[20, 70, 0, 150, 300, 200, 400, 20, 60, 250, 90, 400, 500, 450, 320];
```

And you can draw the graph with a simple loop:

```
for (var i:int = 0; i < graph1x.length; i++)
{
  graph.drawPoint(graph1x[i], graph1y[i], 0xff9933);
}
```

This works effectively and is completely understandable. There is a major drawback to this approach that is already clear in this simple example.

There's no easy way to quickly verify that you have the same number of elements in both arrays. You can write a test in your code, but if you want to edit the data, it's hard to see which value belongs to which.

For instance, the 400 *x*-value maps to 60 on the *y*-axis. That isn't readily apparent from the code. If you forget to add a *y*-value, you run the risk of breaking your entire program.

Associative array

If inserting and updating data is important, you may want to look into a third solution: the object or associative array.

```
private var graphObject:Object = { 0:20,50:70,100:0,150:150,200:300,2
50:200,
300:400,350:20,400:60,450:250,500:90,550:400,
600:500,650:450,700:320 };
```

Although the notation looks similar to the previous one, the data structure that is created internally is quite different. Drawing it is a little more complicated and requires the usage of the *for-in* loop (again we shift the points to demonstrate the difference):

```
for (var s:String in graphObject)
{
   graph.drawPoint(Number(s) + 8, graphObject[s], 0xff3399);
}
```

Because the *x* coordinate is stored as an object property, it is stored as a string. Before we can draw it, we need to convert it back to a number.

This data structure is perfect for manipulation. Instead of having to search through it to find the item we want to change, we just write the following:

```
graphObject[150] = 200;
```

However, there is one very major disadvantage of the associate array and the for-in loop: you should not rely, in any way, on the order in which elements are looped over. So there's no guarantee that the loop will first draw (0,20) and then (50,70), and so on.

Order will become important if you want to draw more complicated charts than the point chart shown. In that case, you need to first convert the object to an array and then sort the array.

Vectors

If you like to work in a more object-oriented manner, and to avoid some of the pitfalls of arrays and increase performance, you may want to look into vectors.

Although the code that you need to write tends to be much more verbose than arrays and objects, they offer a very high level of type safety and have many convenience functions.

For instance, you can store points in the Point objects:

```
var point:Point = new Point(0,20);
```

And store these points in a point vector:

```
var graphVector:Vector.<Point> = new Vector.<Point>();
graphVector.push(point);
```

Associative array to two-dimensional array conversion

If you intend to manipulate your data inside your ActionScript program you will probably want to write at least a conversion function from the associate array to the ordered two-dimensional arrays. Potentially, you'll also need to do this the other way around.

What you need to do is:

▸   Use a for-in loop to construct a two-dimensional array

▸   Use the `Array.sort` method and the custom order function to sort the array

See also

If you're not confident with manipulating (associative) arrays, it's best to look at one of the ActionScript fundamentals books. Both data structures are vital to understanding most of the recipes in this book.

Area charts

In the previous recipes we've learned:

▸   Transforming the data so that it shows up at the right location on the screen

▸   Using the correct data structure so it's easy to display it

In the remaining recipes in this chapter, we will look into ActionScript's drawing methods and show you a few ways to customize the display.

This recipe looks at drawing area charts. They resemble a function chart, but the area between the chart line and the x-axis is filled. They are ideal to represent volumes.

Getting ready

Create a `Recipe6` document class and set up the graph as in the previous recipe. We will use the two-dimensional data set because we will need an ordered data set:

```
package
{
  import flash.display.Sprite;

  public class Recipe6 extends Sprite
  {
    private var graph:Graph;
    private var data:Array = [[0, 20], [50, 70], [100, 0], [150, 150],
[200, 300], [250, 200], [300, 400], [350, 20], [400, 60], [450, 250],
[500, 90], [550, 400], [600, 500], [650, 450], [700, 320]];
```

```
public function Recipe6()
{
  graph = new Graph( -50, 550, 750, -50);
  addChild(graph);
  graph.drawHorizontalAxis(0, 0, 700, 50, ["0", "700"]);
  graph.drawVerticalAxis(0, 0, 500, 50, ["0","250","500"]);
}


}
}
```

How to do it...

1. Add the following code to the `Recipe6` constructor:

    ```
    for (var i:Number = 1; i < data.length; i++)
    {
      graph.drawLine(data[i-1][0], data[i-1][1], data[i][0], data[i]
    [1]);
    }
    ```

    Running the program at this point will yield the data set from the previous recipe, but now connected with a line.

2. In the `Graph` class, we create a copy of the `drawLine` method and name it `drawArea`. In the main program, we now replace the `drawLine` call. The result should still be the same. But now we change the code so that the area is filled:

    ```
    public function drawArea(x1:Number, y1:Number, x2:Number,
    y2:Number):void
    {
      var transformedLocation1:Point = matrix.transformPoint(new
    Point(x1, y1));
      var transformedLocation2:Point = matrix.transformPoint(new
    Point(x2, y2));
      var transformedOrigin:Point    = matrix.transformPoint(new
    Point(0, 0));

      var area:Shape = new Shape();
      area.graphics.beginFill(0xff9933);
      area.graphics.moveTo(transformedLocation1.x,
    transformedLocation1.y);
      area.graphics.lineTo(transformedLocation2.x,
    transformedLocation2.y);
      area.graphics.lineTo(transformedLocation2.x,
    transformedOrigin.y);
      area.graphics.lineTo(transformedLocation1.x,
    transformedOrigin.y);
    ```

```
    area.graphics.endFill();
    addChild(area);
}
```

If you run the program now, you should see an orange area chart. Everything below the line is now nicely filled with the orange color.

How it works...

This recipe is created in two steps: first, display a line chart and next, fill the void beneath the line to obtain an area.

Because drawing a line requires two points, we start counting at 1 instead of 0. In the loop, we draw a line between the previous point and the current one.

There are two other things to note from the code:

▶ We calculate the transformed origin. Actually, we only need the 0 y-coordinate, but it's easier to just use the matrix for this calculation.

▶ Instead of drawing a line between two points, we create a "fill" between four points: the two that were used for the line and the two on the x-axis (with y = 0).

There's more...

As with previous recipes, there's a lot that can be customized. Most of these will be discussed in some of the next recipes, but there's nothing keeping you from starting to experiment.

Having the color as a parameter

Right now, the fill color is fixed. You can make this a variable by using it as an argument to the `drawArea` method.

The fill style

If you check out the ActionScript documentation, you'll find that there are two more ways of creating fills: the `beginGradientFill` and `beginBitmapFill` methods. They are a bit more complicated, but can be used to obtain dramatic effects.

See also

The ActionScript 3.0 reference has a lot more detail on creating and drawing filled shapes. It can be found at the following URL:

```
http://help.adobe.com/en_US/FlashPlatform/reference/actionscript/3/
flash/display/Graphics.html
```

Multiple area charts

In this recipe, we're going to visualize multiple sets of data on one chart.

Getting ready

As usual, create a `Recipe7` document class. We'll start with the code from the previous recipe. Only now, we've slightly changed the data set to demonstrate some of the items covered better. There's also an added set of data. We've chosen to store it in the same array for simplicity, but there are other ways of course.

The following is the starting class:

```
package
{
  import flash.display.Sprite;

  public class Recipe7 extends Sprite
  {
    private var graph:Graph;
    private var data:Array = [[0, 20, 50], [50, 70, 40], [100, 0,
100],
[150, 150, 150], [200, 300, 200], [250, 200, 170],
[300, 170, 160], [350, 20, 120], [400, 60, 80],
[450, 250, 150], [500, 90, 20], [550, 50, 40],
[600, 110, 90], [650, 150, 150], [700, 320, 200]];

    public function Recipe7()
    {
      graph = new Graph( -50, 550, 750, -50);
      addChild(graph);
      graph.drawHorizontalAxis(0, 0, 700, 50, ["0", "700"]);
      graph.drawVerticalAxis(0, 0, 500, 50, ["0", "250", "500"]);

      for (var i:Number = 1; i < data.length; i++)
      {
        graph.drawArea(data[i-1][0], data[i-1][1], data[i][0], data[i]
[1]);
      }

    }

  }

}
```

How to do it...

There are two ways to show multiple area charts. You can stack the charts on top of each other or you can make them transparent and have them overlaid.

We'll cover the transparent overlay first, because it's the easiest.

1. Rewrite the `drawArea` method as follows:

```
public function drawArea(x1:Number, y1:Number, x2:Number,
y2:Number,
colour:uint = 0xff9933, alpha:Number = 1):void
{
  var transformedLocation1:Point = matrix.transformPoint(new
Point(x1, y1));
  var transformedLocation2:Point = matrix.transformPoint(new
Point(x2, y2));
  var transformedOrigin:Point    = matrix.transformPoint(new
Point(0, 0));

  var area:Shape = new Shape();
  area.graphics.beginFill(colour, alpha);
  area.graphics.moveTo(transformedLocation1.x,
transformedLocation1.y);
  area.graphics.lineTo(transformedLocation2.x,
transformedLocation2.y);
  area.graphics.lineTo(transformedLocation2.x,
transformedOrigin.y);
  area.graphics.lineTo(transformedLocation1.x,
transformedOrigin.y);
  area.graphics.endFill();
  addChild(area);
}
```

2. If we now rewrite the main loop, we can draw multiple area charts with transparency:

```
for (var i:Number = 1; i < data.length; i++)
{
  graph.drawArea(data[i - 1][0], data[i - 1][1], data[i][0],
data[i][1],
0xff9933, 0.5);
  graph.drawArea(data[i - 1][0], data[i - 1][2], data[i][0],
data[i][2],
0x3399ff, 0.5);
}
```

Creating stacked charts is a little more complicated. Once again, we start by expanding the `drawArea` method. We add two more parameters that define the bottom *y*-coordinates of the area. In the previous graphs, they've always been zero, so we leave that in as the default:

```
public function drawArea(x1:Number, y1:Number, x2:Number,
y2:Number,
colour:uint = 0xff9933, alpha:Number = 1,
y3:Number = 0, y4:Number = 0):void
{
  var transformedLocation1:Point = matrix.transformPoint(new
Point(x1, y1));
  var transformedLocation2:Point = matrix.transformPoint(new
Point(x2, y2));
  var transformedLocation3:Point = matrix.transformPoint(new
Point(x1, y3));
  var transformedLocation4:Point = matrix.transformPoint(new
Point(x2, y4));

  var area:Shape = new Shape();
  area.graphics.beginFill(colour, alpha);
  area.graphics.moveTo(transformedLocation1.x,
transformedLocation1.y);
  area.graphics.lineTo(transformedLocation2.x,
transformedLocation2.y);
  area.graphics.lineTo(transformedLocation4.x,
transformedLocation4.y);
  area.graphics.lineTo(transformedLocation3.x,
transformedLocation3.y);
  area.graphics.endFill();
  addChild(area);
}
```

Use the following code:

```
for (var i:Number = 1; i < data.length; i++)
{
  graph.drawArea(data[i - 1][0], data[i - 1][1], data[i][0],
data[i][1]);
  graph.drawArea(data[i - 1][0], data[i - 1][1] + data[i - 1][2],
    data[i][0], data[i][1] + data[i][2],
    0x3399ff, 1,
          data[i - 1][1], data[i][1]);
}
```

How it works...

Areas are drawn by moving from one point to the other, either clockwise or counter-clockwise. We rushed over this important point in the previous recipe, but it is important in this one.

Because the areas are a little more complex, you need to be extra careful to get the order right. Otherwise you'll run into some strange phenomena.

When overlaying multiple charts, we use the `alpha` property of the fills. The `alpha` value controls the transparency of the fill. By making the fill translucent, we can see both areas behind each other.

When stacking multiple charts, we need to use the sum of both coordinates to properly place the different data sets. The bottom coordinates of the second data set are given by the first area chart, while the top coordinates are the sum of two data sets.

There's more...

We've seen the basics of drawing multiple data sets on one chart. In later chapters, there will be many more ways of displaying this information. In the meantime, here are a few ways to expand this recipe.

Improving the interface

The `drawArea` method's parameters can be improved upon. In particular if you want to draw a third or fourth set of data points, this is going to become unwieldy.

One option is to accept arrays of *y*-coordinates.

Styling the fill

As with the previous recipe, there are many options to style the fill. We'll look into a few in the next recipe.

Styling a graph

Until now, we've used the most basic way of drawing points, lines, and areas. However, ActionScript's `Graphic` class offers a wealth of different options to make your charts look more attractive.

In this recipe, we will give a short primer of some of the tools at your fingertips. We won't be able to cover them all, but this should help you on your way.

Getting ready

We start by having a graph that shows all three types of charts we've discussed:

```
package
{
  import flash.display.Sprite;

  public class Recipe8 extends Sprite
  {
    private var graph:Graph;
    private var data:Array = [[0, 20], [50, 70], [100, 0], [150, 150],
[200, 300], [250, 200], [300, 400], [350, 20], [400, 60], [450, 250],
[500, 90], [550, 400], [600, 500], [650, 450], [700, 320]];

    public function Recipe8()
    {
      graph = new Graph( -50, 550, 750, -50);
      addChild(graph);
      graph.drawHorizontalAxis(0, 0, 700, 50, ["0", "700"]);
      graph.drawVerticalAxis(0, 0, 500, 50, ["0", "250", "500"]);

      graph.drawPoint(data[0][0], data[0][1] + 50);
      for (var i:Number = 1; i < data.length; i++)
      {
        graph.drawArea(data[i - 1][0], data[i - 1][1], data[i][0],
data[i][1]);
        graph.drawLine(data[i - 1][0], data[i - 1][1] + 25, data[i]
[0], data[i][1] + 25);
        graph.drawPoint(data[i][0], data[i][1] + 50);
      }

    }

  }

}
```

Notice that we have shifted the *y*-coordinate of the different charts, so that it's clear which one is which. If you run this program you should see an area chart, 25 pixels higher a line graph, and the another 25 pixels higher a point chart.

How to do it...

1. Let's look at points first and replace the points with images.

   For this recipe, we will use the freely available SweetiePlus icons, available at `http://sublink.ca/icons/sweetieplus/`. Copy any one of the icons you would like to the `lib` folder of your project. For instance, the heart icon: `heart-16-ns.png`.

   If you open the folder in FlashDevelop, you should see the file appear. Place the cursor in the `Recipe8` class file, just above the graph's `var` definition.

   Now right-click on the image and pick **generate embed code**. This will embed the image into your program and is the easiest and best way to embed small images like this.

> If you use some other software, embedding images might be a little different: In Flash Builder you can use the `[Embed]` metadata tag directly. Refer to: `http://www.adobe.com/devnet/flash/articles/embed_metadata.html`.
>
> In Flash Professional, you can also add the resource to the stage and give it an instance name to address it directly without the need for an `[Embed]` tag.

   Just below the embed code, you now need to connect that embedded image to a class name. It looks like the following code:

```
...
public class Recipe8 extends Sprite
{
  [Embed(source = "../lib/heart-16-ns.png")]
  private var HeartClass:Class;

  private var graph:Graph;
```

   We can now add a new `drawBitmapPoint` method to the `Graph` class:

```
public function drawBitmapPoint(x:Number, y:Number,
BitmapClass:Class):void
{
  var transformedLocation:Point = matrix.transformPoint(new
Point(x, y));

  var bitmapPoint: Bitmap = new BitmapClass();
  bitmapPoint.x = transformedLocation.x - bitmapPoint.width / 2;
```

```
     bitmapPoint.y = transformedLocation.y - bitmapPoint.height / 2;
     addChild(bitmapPoint);
}
```

2. Next we will look at gradients. These allow you to fill an area or a line with a gradually changing color. The complete description of how to apply, position, and create gradients is fairly complicated and beyond the scope of this recipe.

   However, we will explain one example, the drawing of a gradient-filled area:

```
public function drawGradientArea(x1:Number, y1:Number, x2:Number,
y2:Number,
                 y3:Number = 0, y4:Number = 0):void
{
   var transformedLocation1:Point = matrix.transformPoint(new
Point(x1, y1));
   var transformedLocation2:Point = matrix.transformPoint(new
Point(x2, y2));
   var transformedLocation3:Point = matrix.transformPoint(new
Point(x1, y3));
   var transformedLocation4:Point = matrix.transformPoint(new
Point(x2, y4));

   var area:Shape = new Shape();

   var gradType:String = GradientType.LINEAR;
   var colors:Array    = [0xff9933, 0x9933ff];
   var alphas:Array    = [1, 1];
   var ratios:Array    = [100, 255];
   var matrix:Matrix    = new Matrix();
   matrix.createGradientBox(stage.stageWidth, stage.stageHeight,
Math.PI / 2);

   area.graphics.beginGradientFill(gradType, colors, alphas,
ratios, matrix);
   area.graphics.moveTo(transformedLocation1.x,
transformedLocation1.y);
   area.graphics.lineTo(transformedLocation2.x,
transformedLocation2.y);
   area.graphics.lineTo(transformedLocation4.x,
transformedLocation4.y);
   area.graphics.lineTo(transformedLocation3.x,
transformedLocation3.y);
   area.graphics.endFill();
   addChild(area);
}
```

3. You can also apply gradients to lines, but for the final example, we'll look at applying bitmaps to lines:

```
public function drawBitmapLine(x1:Number, y1:Number, x2:Number,
y2:Number,
    BitmapClass:Class):void
{
  var transformedLocation1:Point = matrix.transformPoint(new
Point(x1, y1));
  var transformedLocation2:Point = matrix.transformPoint(new
Point(x2, y2));

  var line:Shape = new Shape();
  line.graphics.lineStyle(16, 0x000000);
  var bitmap:Bitmap = new BitmapClass();
  line.graphics.lineBitmapStyle(bitmap.bitmapData);
  line.graphics.moveTo(transformedLocation1.x,
transformedLocation1.y);
  line.graphics.lineTo(transformedLocation2.x,
transformedLocation2.y);
  addChild(line);
}
```

How it works...

ActionScript's `Graphic` class offers a rich set of drawing primitives. This allows you to create virtually any vector graphic you like. Some of the concepts will feel natural, while others can take a while to properly grasp. It's worth learning the ins and outs of the `Graphics` class because a well-placed gradient or bitmap can really spice up any graph.

As in all other drawing methods we've seen in this chapter, first the coordinates are transformed.

When drawing a bitmap point, the embedded resource class is instantiated into a `Bitmap` class. This is the class that will display the image.

Next we use some simple math to place the bitmap at the center of the coordinates. In ActionScript, the bitmap's (x , y) coordinates reflect the upper-left corner. So if we want to place the center of the bitmap at our coordinates, we need to subtract half of the width and height.

As usual, the final step is adding the bitmap to the graph sprite.

Drawing gradients requires extra work. To draw an area that is filled with a gradient, we use the `beginGradientFill` method. It takes the following parameters:

- The type of gradient, `GradientType.LINEAR` and `GradientType.RADIAL` are supported.

- An array of colors through which the gradient will change. You can have up to 15 colors.

- The alpha values corresponding to the different colors in the previous array.

- The ratios where the full color will apply. The maximum range is [0, 255]. In this case we add a little more of the orange color. See the ActionScript reference for a visual explanation, available at: `http://help.adobe.com/en_US/ FlashPlatform/reference/actionscript/3/flash/display/Graphics. html#beginGradientFill%28%29`.

Optionally, you can also add a matrix that transforms the gradient. This will allow you to correctly place the gradient. In the case of this example, we stretch the gradient over the full screen and rotate it by 90 degrees.

When drawing bitmap fills for lines, there are a few points worth noting:

- Line bitmaps and gradients are applied to the actual drawn line. This means you need both the `lineStyle` and `lineBitmapStyle` methods. You can't take out the first one or you would not see anything drawn.

- The `lineBitmapStyle` method takes a `BitmapData` class as an argument. The difference between this and the `Bitmap` class, is that bitmap is the actual representation on the screen, while `BitmapData` is just the bits that are needed to draw the bitmap. Hence `BitmapData` does not have an *x* or *y* coordinate.

If you want to change the exact placement of the bitmaps, the `lineBitmapStyle` method takes an optional `Matrix` as an argument. This works similar to all the other matrix operations we've seen. Getting this exactly right isn't easy, so you may need to do some experimentation.

There's more...

We've only covered the very tip of the iceberg that is the `Graphics` class.

Transformation

As with most visual elements in ActionScript, bitmaps and gradients can be translated, rotated, made translucent, and much more. It's worth experimenting a little to get to know what's possible.

Gradient lines and points, bitmap areas

We've only shown three examples. However you can combine any style with any type of graph. Feel free to extend the existing `Graph` class with whatever you need for your graphs.

See also

Most ActionScript books have good coverage of the `Graphics` class. But there are also a few that go into much more detail.

Although it can be a bit hard to get into, the live docs also provide a fairly in-depth overview of the features. This is available at: `http://help.adobe.com/en_US/FlashPlatform/reference/actionscript/3/flash/display/Graphics.html`.

Adding legends

Without a little explanation, any graph will quickly become incomprehensible. Especially when showing multiple sets of data, it is important to properly distinguish between the two. A legend can do just that.

Getting ready

For the `Recipe9` class, we start from the overlapping multiple area charts class. So copy that class and rename it to `Recipe9` to follow along.

How to do it...

1. The legend related display methods will receive their own class. We start by creating a new `Legend` class that extends `Sprite`. Optionally, you can add a title:

```
package
{
    import flash.display.Sprite;
    import flash.text.TextField;
    import flash.text.TextFieldAutoSize;

    public class Legend extends Sprite
    {
        private var lineHeight:Number = 20;
        private var lines:int = 0;

        public function Legend(title:String = null)
        {
            if (title != null) {
```

```
                          var titleField:TextField = new TextField();
                          titleField.text = title;
                          titleField.autoSize = TextFieldAutoSize.LEFT;
                          addChild(titleField);
                          lines++;
                      }
                  }
              public function addKey(key:String, color:uint,
          alpha:Number):void
                  {
                      // see further
                  }
          }
      }
```

2. In the main program (`Recipe9`), you can add the legend to the display with the following code:

```
var legend:Legend = new Legend("Legend title");
legend.x = 600;
legend.y = 20;
legend.addKey("First series", 0xff9933, 0.5);
legend.addKey("More data points", 0x3399ff, 0.5);
addChild(legend);
```

3. As you can see, we've already added methods to add the display of actual keys. In typical graph fashion, we want to show a small square containing the color of that data set with some text next to it to name the data set.

   The code isn't overly complicated and uses the `drawRect` method from the `Graphics` class and the plain `TextField` class we've seen before:

```
public function addKey(key:String, color:uint, alpha:Number):void
{
  var keySample:Shape = new Shape();
  keySample.graphics.lineStyle(1);
  keySample.graphics.beginFill(color, alpha);
  keySample.graphics.drawRect(0, lines * lineHeight, 15, 15);
  keySample.graphics.endFill();
  addChild(keySample);

  var keyField:TextField = new TextField();
  keyField.text = key;
  keyField.x = 20;
  keyField.y = lines * lineHeight;
```

```
keyField.autoSize = TextFieldAutoSize.LEFT;
addChild(keyField);

lines++;
}
```

If you run the program now, you'll notice one thing still missing: a nice box around our legend to distinguish it from the actual graph.

4. The only tricky thing is that it needs to be updated dynamically when a key is added. So we store it in an instance variable:

    ```
    private var box:Shape;
    ```

5. Next we create the method to update the box:

    ```
    private function updateBox():void
    {
      if (box != null) {
        removeChild(box);
      }
      box = new Shape();
      box.graphics.lineStyle(1);
      box.graphics.drawRect(-5, -5, width+6, height+6);
      addChild(box);
    }
    ```

6. Now we should execute the `updateBox` method every time the legend changes. So the final step is to add it to the end of the constructor and the `addKey` methods.

How it works...

Just like with the `Graph` class, we use the `Legend` class to hold all of the separate graphical elements of the legend. That way we can just work from the (0,0) origin and not worry about the exact location where the legend will be placed.

Since this would require its own chapter, we won't be going into the details of styling and customizing the `textField` class. The only option that we use the `autoSize` property. It will make sure that the size of the text field fits the text and isn't just left at the default 100x100. This guarantees that the sprite's size will be exactly the size of the text and allows us to easily draw a nice fitting box around the entire legend display.

The line counter is responsible for making sure we can place each individual legend key at the right distance.

You may have noticed that we draw the legend in screen coordinates, not graph coordinates. In many cases, it's easier to place it in the correct location that way. Although if you want to fix the legend in relation to the graph (for instance, always in the bottom, at the center) you may want to think about putting it inside the `Graph` class and use the transformed coordinates. In that case, the `Legend` class would probably be a child of the `Graph` class.

The legend is a sprite, which means you can use the legend like any other one. You can resize it, move it, and even rotate it if you want (you may need to use embedded fonts on the text fields to perform some of those operations).

There's more...

With this recipe, we've only scratched the surface of what you can do with legends.

TextField customization

In this recipe, we've used the very basics of the `textField` class. However, the `textField` class is one of the most versatile ActionScript classes available. It offers so many options that ActionScript reference books need an entire chapter or two to cover it.

So if you want to change the text display, start with the live docs for `textField` and `textFormat` and go from there.

A background

In this recipe, we've kept the legend transparent. It is perfectly possible to add a background color to it. To obtain this, extends the `updateBox` method so it also draws a fill (see the previous recipe). One thing to keep in mind: you need to make sure that the box is drawn behind the keys and title and not on top.

Research the `addChildAt` method to find the solution for this issue: `http://help.adobe.com/en_US/FlashPlatform/reference/actionscript/3/flash/display/DisplayObjectContainer.html#addChildAt%28%29`.

See also

More information on customizing `textField` can be found in the Adobe live docs:

`http://help.adobe.com/en_US/FlashPlatform/reference/actionscript/3/flash/text/TextField.html`.

The `textFormat` class is the main way to change fonts, sizes, and many more options:

`http://help.adobe.com/en_US/FlashPlatform/reference/actionscript/3/flash/text/TextFormat.html`.

Using Flex for charts

No book on ActionScript graphing would be complete without at least mentioning Flex. The Flex software development kit also contains an extensive API for drawing different types of graphs.

The techniques we've discussed in the previous recipes are much more powerful, but depending on the case, a small Flex component might be enough.

Getting ready

Since we need access to the Flex library, we'll need to set up our FlashDevelop workspace differently. The easiest way is to create a new project. When asked for the type of project, pick **Flex 3 project** (instead of **AS3 Project**, which we use throughout the other parts of this book).

If you browse through the files in the `src` directory of your project, you will now find a `Main.mxml` file instead of the previous `Main.as` file. This is the file that describes your user interface. Instead of programmatically adding all the sprites and shapes to your interface, you will add them to this file.

How to do it...

1. Open `Main.mxml`. All the code presented here should be added inside the `mx:Application` tags.

2. First let's start with the data set definition:

```
<mx:Script><![CDATA[
  import mx.collections.ArrayCollection;
  [Bindable]
  public var dataSet:ArrayCollection = new ArrayCollection([
    {x:0,   y1:20,  y2:50},
    {x:50,  y1:70,  y2:40},
    {x:100, y1:0,   y2:100},
    {x:150, y1:150, y2:150},
    {x:200, y1:300, y2:200},
    {x:250, y1:200, y2:170},
    {x:300, y1:170, y2:160},
    {x:350, y1:20,  y2:120},
    {x:400, y1:60,  y2:80},
    {x:450, y1:250, y2:150},
    {x:500, y1:90,  y2:20},
    {x:550, y1:50,  y2:40},
```

```
        {x:600, y1:110, y2:90},
        {x:650, y1:150, y2:150},
        {x:700, y1:320, y2:200}
    ]);
    ]]></mx:Script>
```

3. This is the same set we used in previous recipes. Now we add the actual chart and legend:

```
<mx:Panel title="Our first Flex chart">
    <mx:AreaChart id="areaChart" showDataTips="true"
dataProvider="{dataSet}">
        <mx:horizontalAxis>
            <mx:CategoryAxis
                dataProvider="{dataSet}"
                categoryField="x"
            />
        </mx:horizontalAxis>
        <mx:series>
            <mx:AreaSeries
                yField="y1"
                displayName="First series">
                <mx:areaFill>
                    <mx:SolidColor color="0xff9933" alpha="0.5" />
                </mx:areaFill>
            </mx:AreaSeries>
            <mx:AreaSeries
                yField="y2"
                displayName="More data points">
                <mx:areaFill>
                    <mx:SolidColor color="0x3399ff" alpha="0.5" />
                </mx:areaFill>
            </mx:AreaSeries>
        </mx:series>
    </mx:AreaChart>
    <mx:Legend dataProvider="{areaChart}"/>
</mx:Panel>
```

How it works...

Flex has a few new data structures; in this recipe we use the `ArrayCollection` data structure. This is a specially defined data structure that makes it easy to manage chart data. In fact, if you wanted to include the Flex library in your project, you could use the class for your own graph drawing.

Now let's look at the structure as a display list: the root element is a `Panel` class. This is a simple wrapper class to which you can add a title.

Inside this panel, there are two visual elements: an area chart and a legend. The legend is the easiest of the two explain; we use the default settings and let it read its data from the chart. It's all automatically added and filled.

The area chart is a little more involved:

- The **dataProvider** attribute links this chart to the data we previously defined.
- The **showDataTips** attribute is enabled to show you how quickly you can get some pretty fancy charts with Flex. If this is enabled, you can hover over the data points with your mouse, and you'll see a pop up with more details.
- The horizontal axis is mapped to the x element inside the data set. Note that scaling of the axes happens automatically (but it can be overridden if required).
- Finally we add two data series, both of which we map to the data set we defined previously. We also apply the same fill that was used in the previous recipes.

If you run the program, you will see a graph similar to the one presented in the multiple area charts recipe.

The difference is the way we defined the chart. With Flex you describe how the chart will look and let Flex do the work for you. In plain ActionScript, you have full control, but you have to do all the hard work.

The choice will depend on the application and most likely also on personal preferences.

There's more...

The Flex charting API is immense and with the recipe above, and we haven't even scratched the surface. If you think this style of development is for you, here are a few more things you can do.

Flex without MXML

If you like Flex, but don't like MXML, there's a way to program Flex with virtually no XML. Since Flex wasn't built for this purpose, you'll find fairly little documentation explaining this.

If this is something you want to try out, start with this StackOverflow question:

```
http://stackoverflow.com/questions/141288/possible-to-use-flex-
framework-components-without-using-mxml.
```

ActionScript in Flex

Everything inside the `mx:Script` tags is pure ActionScript code. If you don't like the `ArrayCollection` data structure, you can always write your own bit of ActionScript that maps from any data structure to the one Flex expects.

See also

If you like to get into Flex, there are numerous books. Also, the online documentation is very complete. For charting, your best starting point is available here:

```
http://livedocs.adobe.com/flex/3/html/help.html?content=charts_
intro_7.html.
```

2
Working with Data

In this chapter, we will cover:

- ▶ Preparing your data
- ▶ Embedding CSV files
- ▶ Loading a data file from the Internet
- ▶ Loading a file from the local hard drive
- ▶ Loading data with XML
- ▶ Loading data with Excel files
- ▶ Consuming the REST services
- ▶ Exporting data as CSV to import in Excel
- ▶ Exporting data to a PDF file

Introduction

In the previous chapter we looked at the basics of graph drawing. We investigated the different ActionScript features that allow us to draw graphs of various shapes and sizes. We also looked at how to structure the data to easily create graphical representations.

In this chapter, we are going to investigate how to get that data into your program. Various sources will be discussed. These range from plain files to remote web services.

The final recipes discuss the opposite, extracting the data from your application into a format that other programs can use.

Preparing your data

This first short recipe discusses some general rules that will make your live easier when dealing with graph data.

It also sets you up with a few test files to use throughout the chapter.

Getting ready

Most data in graphs has a tabular form and will usually originate either from a spreadsheet or a database. It's possible to process pretty much any input format with ActionScript 3.0, but some will be easier than others. We will focus on data available in some spreadsheet format. See the *There's more...* section of this recipe for a discussion on databases.

The spreadsheet examples use Microsoft Excel because it is probably the most wide-spread application, but you can use any other spreadsheet application such as the free OpenOffice, or LibreOffice spreadsheet, or even the spreadsheet functionality in Google Docs.

For **CSV** (**comma separated values**) and XML files even a plain text editor, such as Notepad, will suffice.

How to do it...

1. Start by creating a text file, named `data.csv`, in whatever text editor you prefer. Enter the following data:

   ```
   0, 20, 50
   50, 70, 40
   100, 0, 100
   150, 150, 150
   200, 300, 200
   250, 200, 170
   300, 170, 160
   350, 20, 120
   400, 60, 80
   450, 250, 150
   500, 90, 20
   550, 50, 40
   600, 110, 90
   650, 150, 150
   700, 320, 200
   ```

Note that, if you are in a country where the decimal separator is a comma and not a dot, you should start from the following file:

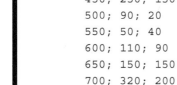

```
0; 20; 50
50; 70; 40
100; 0; 100
150; 150; 150
200; 300; 200
250; 200; 170
300; 170; 160
350; 20; 120
400; 60; 80
450; 250; 150
500; 90; 20
550; 50; 40
600; 110; 90
650; 150; 150
700; 320; 200
```

2. Now open this file in Excel. In the latest version, this should work automatically and you should see the data in three columns. If that doesn't work, use the `import` function to import the CSV file.

3. Save this file as an Excel workbook (`data.xlsx`). This represents a second source of data.

4. While Excel can create XML files, it's a complicated process, so we'll just create one in a text editor. Save the following as `data.xml`:

```
<?xml version="1.0" encoding="UTF-8" ?>
<data>
    <row x="0"   y1="20"  y2="50" />
    <row x="50"  y1="70"  y2="40" />
    <row x="100" y1="0"   y2="100" />
    <row x="150" y1="150" y2="150" />
    <row x="200" y1="300" y2="200" />
    <row x="250" y1="200" y2="170" />
    <row x="300" y1="170" y2="160" />
    <row x="350" y1="20"  y2="120" />
    <row x="400" y1="60"  y2="80" />
    <row x="450" y1="250" y2="150" />
    <row x="500" y1="90"  y2="20" />
    <row x="550" y1="50"  y2="40" />
    <row x="600" y1="110" y2="90" />
    <row x="650" y1="150" y2="150" />
    <row x="700" y1="320" y2="200" />
</data>
```

5. Finally, we will demonstrate how to read files from the Internet. If you have a web server, you can place the `data.csv` file there. Another option is to use Dropbox's public folder: place the `data.csv` file in your `public` folder. Right-click on the file and choose **Dropbox|Copy public link**. This will place a link to the file on the clipboard.

6. We will also show how to use web services for input. For this recipe, we will use the Yahoo! Weather Service, available at `http://developer.yahoo.com/weather/`. An example XML file can be found at `http://weather.yahooapis.com/forecastrss?w=2502265`.

How it works...

As you may have noticed, you will be able to use virtually any input format; although some will be more difficult than others.

Most important is that you keep related variables together. For instance, if an *x* value of 10 corresponds with an *y* value of 20, it is not enough to just have the two numbers in the file; you also need to have a way to indicate that they are related.

In your program, you will need to create what is known as a **parser**, which reads the input file and converts it into a usable ActionScript data structure (as we explained in the first chapter). ActionScript 3.0 comes with parsers for XML and also JSON since Flash Player 11.0. We will see more on JSON when interacting with web services.

The CSV file puts relations on the same line. The file shown in the recipe represents the same data that was used in the previous chapter.

CSV is one of the oldest and easiest data formats. However, on many occasions programs do not follow the RFC 4180 standard and that might create a few interoperability issues. We already saw one such issue: In countries with the comma as decimal separator, you should use the semicolon as data separator for most programs. For instance, a line with decimal data will look like the following format:

```
10; 20,5; 10,95
```

While in the US and many other countries it would look like the following format:

```
10, 20.5, 10.95
```

You may also need to adapt some of the code in the next recipes to adapt to this situation. By default ActionScript assumes the decimal separator is a point, so you will need to do some conversion on those decimals.

XML files hold the data inside tags and attributes. In contrast to the CSV files, you have much more freedom. The recipe shows one possibility.

Although XML does not force you to use a specific decimal number convention, it's usually best to use the point as separator. Most of the related XML technologies do expect a point.

There's more...

There are many more ways to store data. In the end, much of it is down to personal preference and your specific needs, but some of it will also involve ease of use.

Databases

One important data source we have not discussed is databases. The most popular format is the relational database, which stores its data in tables. From a birds-eye view, those tables are somewhat comparable to the spreadsheet worksheets. But there are major differences.

Usually databases are used on servers and are not directly accessed by ActionScript code. This is also the reason why ActionScript has little direct support for databases and why they are not further discussed in this chapter.

The suggested way to deal with databases is to create a REST or SOAP service in a server-side programming language such as PHP, Java, or C# and use that service to read the data from your ActionScript program.

Embedding CSV files

In this recipe, we will demonstrate how to embed the CSV file shown in the previous recipe, how to read and parse the data in that file, and ultimately how to display the data in the file.

Getting ready

Create a new project for this chapter and place the three datafiles from the previous recipe in the `lib` folder of the project (`data.csv`, `data.xlsx` and `data.xml`). Copy the `Graph` and `Legend` classes from the previous chapter into the `src` folder. We will be using those again.

If you didn't complete the chapter, you can just start from the example project supplied with the book.

To avoid excessive code, we will also use the `StringHelper` class from the Adobe ActionScript live docs that can be found at `http://help.adobe.com/en_US/FlashPlatform/reference/actionscript/3/String.html#includeExamplesSummary`. Create a class called `StringHelper` in the `src` folder and copy the code into it.

Now create a new `Recipe1` class in the `src` folder of your project:

```
package
{
    import flash.display.Sprite;
    public class Recipe1 extends Sprite
    {
        private var graph:Graph;

        public function Recipe1()
        {
            graph = new Graph( -50, 550, 750, -50);
            addChild(graph);
            graph.drawHorizontalAxis(0, 0, 700, 50, ["0", "700"]);
            graph.drawVerticalAxis(0, 0, 500, 50, ["0", "250", "500"]);
        }


    }


}
```

This is the starting point of this recipe.

How to do it...

Follow these steps to load the CSV file and display its data:

1. Create an empty line just before the declaration of the `graph` variable and place the cursor there.

2. Open the `lib` folder in the project view. Right-click on the `data.csv` file and select **Generate Embed Code**. This will add the following line to the program:

    ```
    [Embed(source="../lib/data.csv", mimeType="application/octet-stream")]
    ```

3. Under that line, add the class name to bind the embedded resource to:

    ```
    private var DataClass:Class;
    ```

4. Now add a private function to the class that will parse the CSV file:

    ```
    private function parseCSV(text:String):Array
    {
        var data:Array = [];
        var lines:Array = text.split('\n');
        for (var i:int = 0; i < lines.length; i++)
        {
    ```

```
    if (stringHelper.trim(lines[i], '') == '')
    {
      continue;
    }

    var dataLine:Array = []
    var numbers:Array = lines[i].split(',');
    for (var j:int = 0; j < numbers.length; j++)
    {
dataLine.push(Number(stringHelper.trim(numbers[j], '')));
    }
    data.push(dataLine);
  }
  return data;
}
```

5. This function takes a string as an argument and creates a multi-dimensional number array and can be used in the constructor with all the methods we created in *Chapter 1, Getting Started with Graph Drawing*. For instance:

```
var data:Array = parseCSV(new DataClass());
for (var i:int = 0; i < data.length; i++)
{
    graph.drawPoint(data[i][0], data[i][1]);
    graph.drawPoint(data[i][0], data[i][2], 0x9933ff);
}
```

How it works...

Embedding resources is the easiest way to add items to your ActionScript program. You may remember we have used a similar approach to adding images when styling the graph. This time however, we embed a text document instead of an image.

Converting a file into its useable bits and pieces is called **parsing**. As you can see from the code, parsing a CSV is fairly straightforward, as mentioned in the following steps:

1. Split the file in lines.
2. Split every line at the comma (if your CSV file uses semicolons, you should adapt the code right here).
3. Remove all the unnecessary whitespace around the number.
4. These pieces are still strings, so we convert them to a number.
5. Finally they are added to the data array.

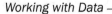

Before trying to process a line, we check if the line is empty. In that case we skip the line (this is a precaution since many text editors add an empty line at the end of the file).

There's more...

Parsing text files can be a tricky thing. There are a few ways to make this more robust.

CSV parsing

Although CSV parsing is fairly easy, there are a few intricacies. If you want to follow the official standard, you are probably better off using an existing open source library instead of creating your own.

For instance, "csvlib" supports the RFC 4180 standard and can be found at `http://code.google.com/p/csvlib/`.

See also

If you are interested in text processing and want to try out a different approach of parsing CSV files, you can also use regular expressions (or regex) to split the file into its components.

For instance, Taytay (`http://taytay.com/?p=106`) uses the following regex to parse CSV lines, and it complies with most of the official spec:

```
lines[i].split(/,(?=(?:[^\"]*\"[^\"]*\")*(?![^\"]*\"))/g)
```

More information on ActionScript's regular expression handling and the `RegExp` class can be found here: `http://help.adobe.com/en_US/FlashPlatform/reference/actionscript/3/RegExp.html`.

Loading a data file from the Internet

This recipe looks at using the `URLLoader` class to load a CSV data file from the Internet. It's very similar to the previous recipe, but it gives you the ability to dynamically load files from the Internet. Thus you can update the files without needing to change the ActionScript program.

Getting ready

Make sure you have a copy of the `data.csv` file somewhere on the Internet. If you don't have a site, you can use DropBox as described in the first recipe of this chapter. This recipe will use a link to my own DropBox folder, but it's much more instructive if you can use your own and change the data to see the effect.

Start by creating a copy of the previous `Recipe1` class and name it `Recipe2`. This will be our basis.

How to do it...

In the following steps, we'll replace the embed code with code that will load the file from the Internet:

1. Remove the embed code and the `DataClass` property. We won't need these anymore.

2. Now move the parsing and function drawing code into its own function (don't forget to remove the original code in the constructor):

```
private function onComplete(event:Event):void {
    var data:Array = parseCSV(event.target.data);
    for (var i:int = 0; i < data.length; i++)
    {
      graph.drawPoint(data[i][0], data[i][1]);
      graph.drawPoint(data[i][0], data[i][2], 0x9933ff);
    }
}
```

3. And finally replace the code you removed with the `URLLoader` class:

```
var loader:URLLoader = new URLLoader();
loader.load(new URLRequest("http://dl.dropbox.com/u/2497061/data.csv"));
loader.addEventListener(Event.COMPLETE, onComplete);
```

4. Run the program and you should see the same graph as in the previous chapter. Only now, it might take a few seconds before the file is downloaded and it appears.

How it works...

This recipe relies completely on the `URLLoader` class in ActionScript. This class makes it possible to load files from the Internet. Because loading files across a network might take some time, the class uses events to tell us what's happening.

In the example program we only listen to the `Event.COMPLETE` event. The URL loader will fire this event when loading of the resource is completed.

Notice that when moving the parsing code, we also changed the source of text data. Instead of using the embedded class, we use the data that is supplied by the `COMPLETE` event. This data property holds the raw data that was loaded from the URL.

There's more...

The code in this recipe only scratches the surface of the `URLLoader` class. Before you use it in a real program, it is best to enhance the application a little.

Other events

The URLoader class will fire many more events, some of which might be important for the correct functioning of your program:

- ▸ IOErrorEvent.IO_ERROR: This event is triggered when something happens during transfer. If this event occurs, no COMPLETE event will follow, so it's best to listen to this one so you can show the user a friendly error message.

- ▸ HTTPStatusEvent.HTTP_STATUS: This event allows you to react intelligently to a few problems that may occur at the server side. For instance, a 404 HTTP status means the file was not found.

- ▸ ProgressEvent.PROGRESS: This event can be used to track the progress of the download. This is useful for big files.

Relative URL

In this recipe, we have used an absolute URL pointing to a DropBox folder. It is also possible to use a relative URL, for instance, new UrlRequest("../lib/data.csv"). In that case, the application will try to locate the file in the folder where it is running.

Security and cross-domain policies

If you try to put the application as it is on a random server, you will notice that it cannot load the data file. This is due to security restrictions inside Flash. By default, an ActionScript application can only access resources on exactly the same domain. If you want to read a file on another domain, that domain needs to have a cross-domain policy that allows access. Because we can't access nor change the DropBox cross-domain policy, we cannot make this recipe work in the current configuration. You will need to move the file to your own servers.

See also

- ▸ More information on the cross-domain policy file can be found online at http://kb2.adobe.com/cps/142/tn_14213.html.

- ▸ More information on the URLLoader class and its related classes and events is also freely available on the Adobe livedocs: http://help.adobe.com/en_US/FlashPlatform/reference/actionscript/3/flash/net/URLLoader.html.

Loading a file from the local hard drive

In the previous recipe, we've already seen one way of loading a file from the hard drive through relative URLs. There are a few shortcomings to that approach though, as follows:

- ▸ If the Flash application is on a website, you cannot use the URLLoader class to load a file from the user's hard drive

> ▸ Even if this was possible, we'd need to implement something so that the user can choose which file to load

In this recipe, we will demonstrate how to use a file dialog to let the user select which file to show.

Getting ready

Again, copy and paste the previous recipe's code into a new class called `Recipe3`. Rename the class name and the constructor and remove the three lines that create and start the URL loader. Leave the `onComplete` method as we will re-use it in this recipe.

```
package
{
    import flash.display.Sprite;
    import flash.events.Event;
    import flash.events.HTTPStatusEvent;
    import flash.events.MouseEvent;
    import flash.net.FileFilter;
    import flash.net.FileReference;
    import flash.text.TextField;
    import flash.text.TextFieldAutoSize;
    public class Recipe3 extends Sprite
    {
        private var graph:Graph;
        private var stringHelper:StringHelper = new StringHelper();

        public function Recipe3()
        {
            graph = new Graph( -50, 550, 750, -50);
            addChild(graph);
            graph.drawHorizontalAxis(0, 0, 700, 50, ["0", "700"]);
            graph.drawVerticalAxis(0, 0, 500, 50, ["0", "250",
"500"]);
        }

        private function onComplete(event:Event):void {
          var data:Array = parseCSV(event.target.data);
          for (var i:int = 0; i < data.length; i++)
        {
          graph.drawPoint(data[i][0], data[i][1]);
          graph.drawPoint(data[i][0], data[i][2], 0x9933ff);
        }
        }
    }
```

```
    private function parseCSV(text:String):Array
    {
      var data:Array = [];
      var lines:Array = text.split('\n');
      for (var i:int = 0; i < lines.length; i++)
      {
        // skip empty and comment lines
        if (stringHelper.trim(lines[i], '') == '')
        {
            continue;
        }

        var dataLine:Array = []
        var numbers:Array = lines[i].split(',');
        for (var j:int = 0; j < numbers.length; j++)
        {
          dataLine.push(Number(stringHelper.trim(numbers[j], '')));
        }
        data.push(dataLine);
      }
      return data;
    }
  }

}
```

How to do it...

1. We will use the `FileReference` class to let the user browse and select a file. So start by adding a private field to the `Recipe3` class:

   ```
   private var loadFile:FileReference;
   ```

2. The file dialog box will be triggered by clicking on a text field. Place the following code in the `Recipe3` constructor:

   ```
   var loadText:TextField = new TextField();
   loadText.text = "click here to load a file";
   loadText.autoSize = TextFieldAutoSize.LEFT;
   loadText.addEventListener(MouseEvent.CLICK, onClick);
   addChild(loadText);
   ```

3. The `onClick` method will open the file dialog and indicate what files can be selected. Add the following method:

```
private function onClick(event:MouseEvent):void {
    loadFile = new FileReference();
    loadFile.addEventListener(Event.SELECT, onSelect);
    var fileFilter:FileFilter = new FileFilter("CSV files",
"*.csv");
    loadFile.browse([fileFilter]);
}
```

4. Once a file is selected, the `onSelect` method is the one that will actually open the file:

```
private function onSelect(event:Event):void {
    loadFile.removeEventListener(Event.SELECT, onSelect);
    loadFile.addEventListener(Event.COMPLETE, onComplete);
    loadFile.load();
}
```

5. The `onComplete` method is responsible for actually parsing and displaying the file. It is exactly the same as the one used in the previous recipe.

6. Now run the program, click on the **click here** text, and select `data.csv`. Once again you should see the same graph, but now it was loaded from the local hard drive after you selected it.

How it works...

As a security restriction, the `FileReference.browse` method can only be used in response to a keyboard or mouse event. That is why we used a text field with click listener. In a real program, you may probably want to add some graphical touches to the text field so it resembles a button.

As we've seen in this recipe and the previous one, Flash has many security restrictions. All are there to protect the user, but they can cause trouble for the programmer. Therefore you should not rely on the default FlashViewer that is used when you are developing an application. Make sure that you also regularly test the application in the environment where it will eventually run (usually this will be on a website, inside an HTML page).

We will see the `FileReference` class back in later recipes, as it is responsible for many file related operations that involve a dialogue box. Right here, we use the browse method to bring up a selection dialogue. The optional parameter specifies what files can be selected.

Once a selection has been made (the SELECT even fires), it is possible to call the load method to actually load the file in memory. The events it provides are similar to the ones of the `URLLoader` event, only now the chance of errors actually occurring is a lot lower (there are no servers or networks involved; the file is loaded in the local memory and never sent to the server).

There's more...

In the previous recipe, we already summarized the most important events, but `FileReference` has one more that's interesting to look at.

Cancel file browsing

When the user is browsing and he clicks on the **Cancel** button or closes the dialog in any other way, a `Event.CANCEL` event is fired. This can be used to act on closing the dialog.

See also

The recipes on exporting data will use the other half of the `FileReference` class. Namely the one for saving files to the local hard drive.

The full `FileReference` documentation can be found in the Adobe livedocs: `http://help.adobe.com/en_US/FlashPlatform/reference/actionscript/3/ flash/net/FileReference.html`.

Loading data with XML

In this recipe, we'll rewrite the embedded recipe so it can read XML files. ActionScript 3.0 has very thorough support for the XML format, so you may notice that this recipe is the easiest one of the entire chapter.

Because so much data, these days, is transmitted in XML or variants such as RSS, it may also prove to be the most useful.

Getting ready

Create a `Recipe4` document class and have it extend `Sprite`. Set up the `Graph` class as in the previous recipes:

```
package
{
    import flash.display.Sprite;
    public class Recipe4 extends Sprite
```

```
{
    private var graph:Graph;

    public function Recipe4()
    {
        graph = new Graph( -50, 550, 750, -50);
        addChild(graph);
        graph.drawHorizontalAxis(0, 0, 700, 50, ["0", "700"]);
        graph.drawVerticalAxis(0, 0, 500, 50, ["0", "250", "500"]);


    }


}


}
```

How to do it...

1. Embed the XML file and associate a class with it. If you use FlashDevelop's **Generate Embed Code** option from the context menu, it will not add the correct mime type, so make sure you add it:

   ```
   [Embed(source="../lib/data.xml", mimeType="application/octet-
   stream")]
   private var DataClass:Class;
   ```

2. Inside the constructor, load and parse the XML file:

   ```
   var data:XML = new XML(new DataClass());
   ```

3. Now draw the graph:

   ```
   for (var i:int = 0; i < data.row.length(); i++)
   {
   graph.drawPoint(data.row[i].@x, data.row[i].@y1);
   graph.drawPoint(data.row[i].@x, data.row[i].@y2, 0x9933ff);
   }
   ```

4. That's all there is to it. The resulting application shows, once again, the same graph, but now loads the data from the XML file.

How it works...

We don't need to write any code to parse the XML file. That's because ActionScript 3.0 has this built in by default. In this regard, processing an XML file is a lot easier than parsing a CSV file.

The XML file is not parsed into an array, but into an object that holds all the XML data. So using the object is a little more complicated, but very intuitive.

We can access the nodes inside the XML file as if they were simple properties. So `data.row` represents the collection of XML nodes that are named **row**. If you look back at the first recipe, you'll see that all individual points are stored in **row** nodes. So `data.row` returns a list of all the points in the graph.

Attributes can be read similarly, only now we need to add the `@` (at) sign before the name. In this example, `data.row[0].@x` represents the x attribute of the first row node in the XML document.

In some cases, the `@`-syntax won't work. For instance, if the attribute name is identical to a reserved keyword such as *if*. For such cases, you can use the following syntax:

```
data.row[0].attribute("x");
```

There's more...

Now that you've seen the basics of loading and using XML files, you can use that knowledge in many different ways and places.

Loading from other sources

The techniques for using XML files presented in this recipe can be combined without issue with any of the loading techniques. For instance, you can use the recipe on loading files from the Internet or harddrive just as well.

Different XML structures

The ActionScript XML parser will load any file that is valid XML. So if the format you are using is slightly different, you simply need to adapt the loop so it reads the correct nodes and properties.

See also

The entire XML API is explained with examples on the live docs:

```
http://help.adobe.com/en_US/FlashPlatform/reference/actionscript/3/
XML.html.
```

Loading data from Excel files

Lots of chart data originates in Excel, so it is only natural to want to directly read Excel files. In general, reading Excel files can be complicated and error prone. Many of the tools available for ActionScript are also fairly experimental. So for most applications, you will probably want to use CSV or XML files as mentioned in the previous recipes, or JSON as we'll discuss in the next recipe.

However, in circumstances where you have good control over the version(s) of Excel used and the layout of the Excel spreadsheet, reading them directly could be a huge time-saver for your users.

Getting ready

For this recipe, we will use the freely available ActionScript 3 XLSX reader by *Ben Morrow*. It can be downloaded from the GitHub page, `https://github.com/childoftv/as3-xlsx-reader`. If you are comfortable using Git and GitHub, it is easiest to clone the repository on your local drive. If you don't have the Git software installed, it is best to use the **Downloads** link on the page. This will enable you to download a file with the latest release.

No matter how you obtain the code, you should make sure the `com` source folder is available to your application. The quickest and most reliable way is to copy it into the `src` folder of your project (you can also add it to the classpath). Once copied, your project should look like the following screenshot:

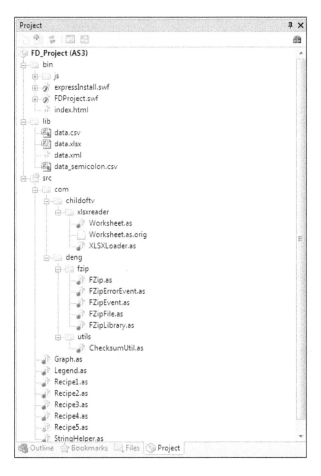

Now create a new `Recipe5` class as before:

  ▶ Have the class extend `Sprite`

  ▶ Set up the `Graph` as before

How to do it...

1. First embed the Excel file and give it a class name:

```
[Embed(source="../lib/data.xlsx", mimeType="application/octet-
stream")]
private var DataClass:Class;
```

2. The Excel loader class works similar to the `URLLoader` class. It uses events and callbacks, so we create a private field to hold it:

```
private var xlsLoader:XLSXLoader;
```

3. Inside the `Recipe5` constructor, after we have set up the graph, we start the loading of the Excel file:

```
xlsLoader = new XLSXLoader();
xlsLoader.addEventListener(Event.COMPLETE, onComplete);
xlsLoader.loadFromByteArray(new DataClass());
```

4. Now it's a matter of adding the `onComplete` method, which will do the actual graph drawing:

```
private function onComplete(event:Event):void
{
    var sheet:Worksheet = xlsLoader.worksheet("data");
    var rowX:XMLList   = sheet.getRowsAsValues("A");
    var rowY1:XMLList  = sheet.getRowsAsValues("B");
    var rowY2:XMLList  = sheet.getRowsAsValues("C");
    for (var i:int = 0; i < rowX.length(); i++)
    {
        graph.drawPoint(rowX[i], rowY1[i]);
        graph.drawPoint(rowX[i], rowY2[i], 0x9933ff);
    }
}
```

5. That's all there is to it. Running this program should, once again, yield the same result. Only now are we reading the data from an Excel file.

How it works...

The bulk of the work is done by the `XLSXLoader` class. It will make sure the Excel file is converted into a data structure that we can use. It has a similar interface to the `URLLoader` class, so its usage should feel familiar.

You may notice a lot of trace output if you run the program. This alone should make clear that this code is experimental and you should think twice before using it in an actual product. There are other libraries available, but they have similar restrictions.

The `onComplete` method only uses a small part of the `Worksheet` interface. If you investigate that code a little, you'll notice that the Excel file is actually an XML file. So you can use ActionScript's XML handling shortcuts, such as accessing attributes with the @ symbol and tags through the property of the same name.

There's more...

Reading Excel files can be a major challenge. If you run into issues, you can try a different library, or you may want to find ways to remove Excel from the program altogether.

as3xls

There is one other library for reading Excel files in ActionScript that deservers your attention, and that is **as3xls**. It can be found at `http://code.google.com/p/as3xls/` and is a little more mature then the one used in the recipe. It hasn't been updated since 2008 and therefore will give you issues with the latest Excel versions.

See also

▶ The *Preparing your data* recipe

Consuming the REST services

Many websites expose their data through web services. These services usually fall into two categories, SOAP or REST. Many data APIs now tend to prefer the more lightweight REST, which is what we will use in this recipe.

A **REST** service will usually provide its data in the XML or JSON format. **JSON** is actually a way of representing data in a piece of JavaScript code. This makes it easy for JavaScript applications to use the data.

For instance, the data we've previously used could look like the following code snippet:

```
{
  "data" : {
    "0":    [20, 50],
    "50":   [70, 40],
    "100":  [0, 100],
    "150":  [150, 150],
    "200":  [300, 200],
    "250":  [200, 170],
    "300":  [170, 160],
    "350":  [20, 120],
    "400":  [60, 80],
    "450":  [250, 150],
    "500":  [90, 20],
    "550":  [50, 40],
    "600":  [110, 90],
    "650":  [150, 150],
    "700":  [320, 200]
  }
}
```

You'll notice many similarities with ActionScript. More information on the JSON format can be found at `http://www.json.org/`.

Since version 11 of the Flash Player, ActionScript also has a JSON parser out of the box, so you'll see this is just as easy to use as XML. If you have to target older Flash players, it's probably easiest to work with XML if you have the choice.

In this recipe we use the free World Weather Online API to show a five-day forecast.

Getting ready

First of all, to enable the JSON support, right-click on the project and open the properties. Choose a Flash Player version of 11.0 or higher.

Create a new `Recipe6` class that extends `Sprite`. We will set up the graph a little differently than in previous recipes:

```
package
{
    import flash.display.Sprite;
    import flash.events.Event;
    import flash.geom.Point;
    import flash.net.URLLoader;
    import flash.net.URLRequest;
    public class Recipe6 extends Sprite
```

```
    {
        private var graph:Graph;

        private var request:String = "";

        public function Recipe6()
        {
            graph = new Graph( -1, 40, 7, -10);
            addChild(graph);
            graph.drawHorizontalAxis(0, 0, 4, 100, ["0", "1", "2",
"3", "4"]);
            graph.drawVerticalAxis(0, 0, 40, 60, ["0", "20", "40"]);

        }
    }

}
```

In order to access the API service of World Weather Online, you need to have an account. So head over to `http://www.worldweatheronline.com/` and click on the **FREE signup** button.

After you have validated your e-mail address, you will automatically get an option to use the request builder at `http://www.worldweatheronline.com/feed-generater.aspx`.

On this screen, enter the following information:

▸ The API key that you received through mail

▸ Choose JSON as format

▸ Enter your town in the **Search by** fields

▸ Choose a five-day forecast

Now click on the **generate** button. Copy this URL and place it in the `request` field of the `Recipe5` class.

If you like, you can take a look at the output and investigate how the JSON format is structured and what data is supplied by the API.

How to do it...

With all preparation out of the way, the actual recipe is pretty straightforward:

1. In the constructor of the `Recipe6` class, we use the `URLLoader` class that we looked at in the *Loading a data file from the Internet* recipe, to load the JSON file:

    ```
    var loader:URLLoader = new URLLoader();
    loader.load(new URLRequest(request));
    loader.addEventListener(Event.COMPLETE, onComplete);
    ```

2. In the private `onComplete` method we parse the JSON and display a linegraph:

```
private function onComplete(event:Event):void {
    var data:Object = JSON.parse(event.target.data);
    var forecasts:Array = data.data.weather;

    var previousPoint:Point = new Point(0, forecasts[0].tempMaxC);
    for (var i:int = 1; i < forecasts.length; i++)
    {
    var point:Point = new Point(i, forecasts[i].tempMaxC);
    graph.drawLine(previousPoint.x, previousPoint.y, point.x,
point.y);
    previousPoint = point;
    }
}
```

How it works...

If you followed the previous recipes, you'll find fairly little new code in this one. The `URLLoader` class was already described in the recipe on loading files from the Internet. It works exactly the same, only now it will load a JSON formatted file instead of a CSV file. It will also throw the same progress, error, and many other events that you can listen for.

The only real new thing is the `JSON.parse()` call. This class was introduced in the latest ActionScript update. It will take a JSON formatted file and construct an object with the same structure exactly as you would expect in a JavaScript program.

Once the JSON file is parsed, we can walk the structure as we would do with any object or XML file. `data.data.weather` will look inside the `data` object for a nested object, also called `data`. It will then look for the array named `weather`.

There's more...

Web services and web APIs are all around us when surfing the Internet. Once you know they are there, you'll notice them in many places.

More web APIs

There's a virtually endless amount of websites offering data through APIs. If you are looking for something specific, the *programmableweb* API directory at `http://www.programmableweb.com/apis` is a great starting point.

Using SOAP services

If you want to consume data from a SOAP service, you're going to have to do a lot of additional work. SOAP services usually require multiple calls to obtain results. They also require that you abide by stricter rules, whereas REST services tend to be pretty lenient in the input they accept.

The easiest way to integrate SOAP is to use the existing Flex components that are explained here: `http://livedocs.adobe.com/flex/3/html/help.html?content=data_access_3.html`.

Since SOAP calls are plain XML, you can always use that directly.

Exporting data as CSV to import in Excel

Until now, we've always read files and displayed them. In the final recipes of the chapter, we will show how to export the data that we have available inside the program. This can be useful if you want to allow further processing of the data in other programs.

For instance, imagine that you import and process data from a REST service. Users may want to take that data out of the application and use it in Excel to perform their own calculations or create a custom graph.

This recipe looks at exporting to the CSV format that can be used to load the data in Excel and other spreadsheet programs.

Getting ready

For this recipe, we will start from a simple data array, but of course the data could be coming from anywhere.

Start by creating a `Recipe7` document class:

```
package
{
    import flash.display.Sprite;
    import flash.events.Event;
    import flash.events.MouseEvent;
    import flash.net.FileReference;
    import flash.text.TextField;
    import flash.text.TextFieldAutoSize;

    public class Recipe7 extends Sprite
    {
```

```
        private var graph:Graph;
        private var data:Array = [[0,20],[50,70],[100,0],[150,150],[20
0,300],[250,200],[300,400],[350,20],[400,60],[450,250],[500,90],[550,4
00],[600,500],[650,450],[700,320]];


        public function Recipe7()
        {
            graph = new Graph( -50, 550, 750, -50);
            addChild(graph);
            graph.drawHorizontalAxis(0, 0, 700, 50, ["0", "700"]);
            graph.drawVerticalAxis(0, 0, 500, 50, ["0","250","500"]);

            for (var i:int = 0; i < data.length; i++)
            {
                graph.drawPoint(data[i][0] + 4, data[i][1]);
            }
        }


    }

}
```

This should display a familiar point graph.

How to do it...

Follow the next steps to create a CSV file that can be used in Excel:

1. We are going to trigger the file saving through a mouse click. Therefore, in the Recipe7 constructor add the following code:

   ```
   var loadText:TextField = new TextField();
   loadText.text = "click here to save to file";
   loadText.autoSize = TextFieldAutoSize.LEFT;
   loadText.addEventListener(MouseEvent.CLICK, onClick);
   addChild(loadText);
   ```

2. The FileReference class will once again be our gateway to the user's filesystem. So we add a private variable to the class:

   ```
   private var saveFile:FileReference;
   ```

3. The onClick method is where the bulk of the action is. Add it to the Recipe7 class:

   ```
   private function onClick(event:MouseEvent):void
   {
       saveFile = new FileReference();
       saveFile.addEventListener(Event.COMPLETE, onComplete);
   ```

```
        var csv:String = "";
        for (var i:int = 0; i < data.length; i++)
        {
            var line:String = "";
            for (var j:int = 0; j < data[i].length; j++)
            {
                line += data[i][j];
                if (j != data[i].length - 1)
                {
                line += ","; // international users: replace with ;
                }
            }
        }
        csv += line + "\n";
    }

    saveFile.save(csv, "data.csv");
}
```

4. Finally, for demonstration purposes, we also add an `onComplete` method that fires when the file is saved:

```
private function onComplete(event:Event):void
{
    trace("file was saved");
}
```

5. If you run the program, you can click on the **save file** text. This will show a popup with a default filename proposed. You can change it if you like. After clicking on the **Save** button the file will be created.

6. This file should open without issues in Excel.

How it works...

The `FileReference` class is a class you will be using in almost any case, when you want to interact with the user's files. It allows you to create a popup file chooser for various purposes. We've already seen the load method. In this recipe, we use it to save a file.

The `onClick` method in the recipe is a mirror of the `parseCSV` method that was used in the previous recipes. It combines the elements of the data structure into the text format. It creates lines for every datapoint and puts the individual elements in the file, separated by commas (or semicolons if that's what your version of Excel accepts).

The `onComplete` method can be used to give visual feedback that the file was saved successfully. Keep in mind that most of the users will not see the output that `trace` generates. So for a real application, you will probably want to show a text field or something similar in the interface.

There's more...

When using CSV files, there are a few things to take into consideration.

Semicolon or comma

The same CSV issue that we've experienced before pops up here too. If you expect to serve international customers, you should make sure they have an option to switch the CSV separator.

CSV header

If you want to indicate what the data actually is, you may want to insert a first line in the CSV file with comma-separated names for each of the columns. This can make it easier to understand and process the file in other applications.

Exporting data to a PDF file

Except for extracting the data for further processing, it is also typical that you would want to create reports of the data. In this case, PDF is one of the most popular formats, because it looks virtually identical on every system.

Generating PDF files is a huge topic, so we can't show everything, but this recipe should get you started.

Getting ready

We will use the purePDF library to create the PDF file. It can be found at `http://code.google.com/p/purepdf/`. Download the library through the download link. At the time of this writing, `purePDF_0.77.20110116.zip` was the current version.

The library comes packaged as an SWC class library. To use these in FlashDevelop, move both files into the `lib` folder of your project. Inside FlashDevelop, right-click on the files and choose **Add to Library**. Their filenames should turn blue in the project view.

Now create a `Recipe8` document class and copy the same starting code from the previous recipe.

How to do it...

Add the export functionality as follows:

1. As in the previous recipe, we will also trigger the saving of the file from a textfield, so add the following code to the `Recipe8` constructor:

```
var loadText:TextField = new TextField();
loadText.text = "click here to save to file";
loadText.autoSize = TextFieldAutoSize.LEFT;
loadText.addEventListener(MouseEvent.CLICK, onClick);
addChild(loadText);
```

2. There's one more thing we need to do in the constructor and that is registering the font we'll use for PDF writing:

```
FontsResourceFactory.getInstance().registerFont( BaseFont.
HELVETICA, new BuiltinFonts.HELVETICA() );
```

3. Next we implement the `onClick` method, where the bulk of the work is done:

```
private function onClick(event:MouseEvent):void
{
    saveFile = new FileReference();
    saveFile.addEventListener(Event.COMPLETE, onComplete);

    var pdf:ByteArray = new ByteArray();
    var writer:PdfWriter = PdfWriter.create(pdf, PageSize.A4);
    var document:PdfDocument = writer.pdfDocument;

    document.addTitle("Data file");
    document.open();

    var table:PdfPTable = new PdfPTable(2);
    table.addStringCell("x");
    table.addStringCell("y");

    for (var i:int = 0; i < data.length; i++)
    {
        for (var j:int = 0; j < data[i].length; j++)
        {
```

```
                           table.addStringCell(data[i][j]);
                    }
             }

             document.add(table);
             document.close();
             saveFile.save(pdf, "data.pdf");
       }
```

4. And as in the previous recipe, we can also add an `onComplete` method to signal the user that the file was stored:

```
private function onComplete(event:Event):void
{
      trace("file was saved");
}
```

How it works...

The `save` method, from the `FileReference` class, has the same limitations as the `load` method we saw in a previous recipe. You can only call it after an action from a user, which is why we connect it to clicking on a text field.

Using fonts in PDF files is fairly complicated, although if you know how they are dealt with in Flash, you've already got a good basis. In general, you can use a built-in font (which we do in this recipe) or you can embed your own font. In any case, these fonts must first be registered before they can be used.

More information on using fonts can be found on the purePDF wiki at `http://code.google.com/p/purepdf/wiki/FontsHowTo`.

The PDF writing we did in this recipe was close to the minimal possible to generate a well-formed PDF. Creating a PDF consists of two parts:

- ▶ Setting all the header fields and file properties (such as page size). This has to be done before opening the document.
- ▶ Adding the actual content to the PDF. In this recipe we add a table containing our data. This has to happen between opening and closing the document.

The main difference between this recipe and the previous one is that we don't need to bother ourselves with the details of the PDF format. In the CSV recipe, we needed to worry about placing commas or semicolons and new lines at the right places. In this recipe, the **purePDF** library takes care of all of that for us and we can describe the PDF through the usage of the classes in the library.

There's more...

Generating PDF files is a huge topic and can easily cover an entire book. Therefore this recipe was only a minimal primer. Now we'll look at a few more things you can do.

Headers and footers

Once you get to understand how PDF works, it is surprisingly easy to create nicely formatted headers and footers. It's also possible to add page numbers should you have multiple pages in your document.

See for instance this example to get started:

```
http://code.google.com/p/purepdf/source/browse/examples/src/
HeaderFooter1.as.
```

Adding images

You can add several types of images to spice up your PDF. In fact, you could extract the bitmap data from the graph we drew with the ActionScript application and put that next to the data points.

This example is a good start: `http://code.google.com/p/purepdf/source/browse/examples/src/ImageBitmapData.as`.

To obtain the bitmap data, you can draw the graph to a `BitmapData` object:

```
http://help.adobe.com/en_US/FlashPlatform/reference/actionscript/3/
flash/display/BitmapData.html#draw%28%29.
```

See also

PurePDF is a port of the popular iText PDF library (see `http://itextpdf.com/`). This open source library is available for Java and C#. And while some things have been changed to fit ActionScript, almost all of the documentation for iText will also be applicable to purePDF.

The book *iText in Action* printed by *Manning* and written by *Bruno Lowagie*, the iText creator, is a very thorough guide to the iText library and is the perfect companion if you want to continue creating PDF files.

3
Creating Bar Charts

In this chapter, we will cover:

- ▸ Drawing a bar chart with Flex
- ▸ Building vertical bar charts
- ▸ Creating comparison bar charts
- ▸ Drawing histograms
- ▸ Creating sparklines to enrich text content
- ▸ Making 3D bar charts

Introduction

This chapter will give us all the tools to create multiple bar charts. Be it vertical, horizontal, comparison, or histograms, this chapter will provide solid bases to improve those charts even more. We will use the same methodology for every chart and re-use the axes from previous recipes.

Drawing a bar chart with Flex

The Flex framework offers some charting components that are fairly easy to use. It is not ActionScript per say, but it still compiles to the SWF format. Because the resulting charts look good and are pretty customizable, we decided to cover it in one recipe. There is a downside though to using this: the Flex framework will be included in your SWF, which will increase its size. Future recipes will explain how to do the same thing using just ActionScript.

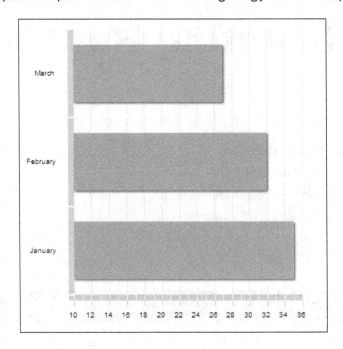

Getting ready

Open FlashDevelop and create a new Flex Project.

How to do it...

The following are the steps required to build a bar chart using the Flex framework.

Copy and paste the following code in the `Main.mxml` file. When you run it, it will show you a bar chart.

```
<?xml version="1.0" encoding="utf-8"?>
<s:Application xmlns:fx="http://ns.adobe.com/mxml/2009"
        xmlns:s="library://ns.adobe.com/flex/spark"
```

```
          xmlns:mx="library://ns.adobe.com/flex/mx" minWidth="955"
minHeight="600">
  <fx:Script>
    <![CDATA[
      import mx.collections.ArrayCollection;

      [Bindable]
      private var monthsAmount:ArrayCollection = new ArrayCollection(
[
        { Month: "January", Amount: 35},
        { Month: "February", Amount: 32 },
        { Month: "March", Amount: 27 } ]);
    ]]>
  </fx:Script>
  <mx:BarChart id="barchart" x="30" y="30"
dataProvider="{monthsAmount}">
    <mx:verticalAxis>
      <mx:CategoryAxis categoryField="Month"/>
    </mx:verticalAxis>
    <mx:horizontalAxis>
      <mx:LinearAxis minimum="10"/>
    </mx:horizontalAxis>
    <mx:series>
      <mx:BarSeries
        yField="Month"
        xField="Amount"
        />
    </mx:series>
  </mx:BarChart>
</s:Application>
```

How it works...

When you create a new Flex project, Flash Builder will generate for you the XML file and the `Application` tag. After that, in the `script` tag we created the data we will need to show in the chart. We do so by creating an `ArrayCollection` data structure, which is an array encapsulated to be used as `DataProvider` for multiple components of the Flex framework, in this case `mx:BarChart`.

Once we have the data part done, we can start creating the chart. Everything is done in the `BarChart` tag. Inside that tag you can see we linked it with `ArrayCollection`, which we previously created using this code: `dataProvider = "{monthsAmount}"`.

Inside the `BarChart` tag we added the `verticalAxis` tag. This tag is used to associate values in the `ArrayCollection` to an axis. In this case we say that the values of the month will be displayed on the vertical axis.

Next comes the `horizontalAxis` tag, we added it to tell the chart to use 10 as a minimum value for the horizontal axis. It's optional, but if you were to remove the tag it would use the smallest value in `ArrayCollection` as the minimum for the axis, so one month, in this case, March, would have no bar and the bar chart wouldn't look as good.

Finally, the series tag will tell for a column, what data to use in `ArrayCollection`. You can basically think of the series as representing the bars in the chart.

There's more...

As we mentioned earlier, this component of the Flex framework is pretty customizable and you can use it to display multiple kinds of bar charts.

Showing data tips

Multiple options are available using this component; if you want to display the numbers that the bar represents in the chart while the user moves the mouse over the bar, simply add `showDataTips = "true"` inside the `BarChart` tag and it is done.

Displaying vertical bars

If you would like to use vertical bars instead of horizontal bars in the graph, Flex provides the `ColumnChart` charts to do so. In the previous code, change the `BarChart` tag to `ColumnChart`, and change `BarSeries` to `ColumnSeries`. Also, since the vertical axis and horizontal axis will be inverted, you will need `verticalAxis` by `horizontalAxis` and `horizontalAxis` by `verticalAxis` (switch them, but keep their internal tags) and in the `ColumnSeries` tag, `xField` should be `Month` and `yField` should be `Amount`. When you run that code it will show vertical bars.

Adding more bars

By adding more data in the `ArrayCollection` data structure and by adding another `BarSeries` tag, you can display multiple bars for each month. See the Adobe documentation at the following link to learn how to do it: `http://help.adobe.com/en_US/FlashPlatform/reference/actionscript/3/mx/charts/BarChart.html`.

See also

▶ The *Creating pie charts with Flex* recipe in *Chapter 4, Drawing Different Types of Graphs*.

Building vertical bar charts

Now that we have built a bar chart using Flex, we are ready to do the same in pure
ActionScript. This bar chart version will allow you to expand it in multiple ways and will remove
the weight that the Flex framework adds to the file size. Now a bit about bar charts; Bar charts
are good when you don't have too much data (more than 20 bars starts to make a big chart),
or when you've averaged it. It is a quick way to compare data visually.

Getting ready

All we will need for this is to start a new project in FlashDevelop. Also, it would help to read
about preparing data and about axes in the *Adding labels and axes* recipe in *Chapter 1,
Getting Started with Graph Drawing*.

How to do it...

This section will refer a lot to the code provided with the book; check the Bar Chart folder
within code files for *Chapter 3*. You will notice that we divided all the elements in the charts
into their own classes.

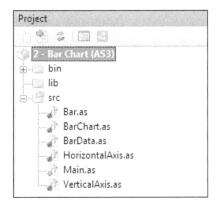

1. It all starts in the `Main.as` file, where we create the data that we will use to display in
   the chart after that we just create the chart and add it to the display list.

```
var data:Vector.<BarData> = new Vector.<BarData>();
data.push(new BarData("January", 60));
data.push(new BarData("February", 100));
data.push(new BarData("March", 30));

var chart:BarChart = new BarChart(data, 400, 410);
chart.x = 30;
chart.y = 30;
addChild(chart);
```

2. From here you can look into the `BarData` class, which it is just two variables, a string and a number that represents the data that we are going to show.

3. We now need to create a class for all the elements that comprise a bar chart. They are: the bars, the vertical axis, and the horizontal axis. Now this recipe is building a vertical bar chart so the vertical axis is the one that will have numerical marks and the horizontal axis will have labels on the marks.

4. First the `Bar` class: This class will only draw a rectangle with the height representing the data for a certain label. The following is its constructor:

```
public function Bar(width:int, height:int) {
   graphics.beginFill(0xfca25a);
   graphics.drawRect(-width/2, 0, width, -height);
   graphics.endFill();
}
```

5. The horizontal axis will take the x coordinate of the created bars and will place a label under it. Notice how it uses functions created in *Chapter 1, Getting Started with Graph Drawing*:

```
public function HorizontalAxis(listOfMark:Vector.<Number>,
data:Vector.<BarData>, width:Number) {
   drawAxisLine(new Point(0, 0), new Point(width, 0));

   for (var i:int = 0; i < listOfMark.length; i++) {
      drawAxisLine(new Point(listOfMark[i], -3), new
Point(listOfMark[i], 3));

      var textField:TextField = new TextField();
      textField.text = data[i].label;
      textField.width = textField.textWidth + 5;
      textField.height = textField.textHeight + 3;
      textField.x = listOfMark[i] - textField.width / 2;
      textField.y = 5;
      addChild(textField);
   }
}
```

6. Now the vertical axis will make 10 marks at regular interval and will add a label with the associated value in it:

```
for (var i:int = 0; i < _numberOfMarks; i++) {
   drawAxisLine(new Point( -3, (i + 1) * -heightOfAxis / _
numberOfMarks ), new Point(3, (i + 1) * -heightOfAxis / _
numberOfMarks));
   var textField:TextField = new TextField();
   textField.text = String(((i + 1) / (_numberOfMarks)) *
maximumValue );
```

```
    textField.width = textField.textWidth + 5;
    textField.height = textField.textHeight + 3;
    textField.x = -textField.width - 3;
    textField.y = (i + 1) * -heightOfAxis / _numberOfMarks -
textField.height / 2;
    addChild(textField);
}
```

7. Finally, the `BarChart` class will take the three classes we just created and put it all together. By iterating through all the data, it will find the maximum value, so that we know what range of values to put on the vertical axis.

```
var i:int;
var maximumValue:Number = data[0].data;
for (i = 1; i < data.length; i++) {
  if (data[i].data > maximumValue) {
    maximumValue = data[i].data;
  }
}
```

8. After that we create each bar, notice that we also keep the position of each bar to give it to the horizontal axis thereafter:

```
var listOfMarks:Vector.<Number> = new Vector.<Number>();
var bar:Bar;
for (i = 0; i < data.length; i++) {
  bar = new Bar(_barWidth, data[i].data * scaleHeight);
  bar.x = MARGIN + _barSpacing + _barWidth / 2 + i * (_barWidth +
_barSpacing);
  listOfMarks.push(bar.x - MARGIN);
  bar.y = height - MARGIN;
  addChild(bar);
}
```

9. Now all we have left to do is create the axes and then we are done; this is done really easily as shown in the following code:

```
_horizontalAxis = new HorizontalAxis(listOfMarks, data, width -
MARGIN);
_horizontalAxis.x = MARGIN;
_horizontalAxis.y = height - MARGIN;
addChild(_horizontalAxis);

_verticalAxis = new VerticalAxis(height - MARGIN, maximumValue);
_verticalAxis.x = MARGIN;
_verticalAxis.y = height -MARGIN;
addChild(_verticalAxis);
```

How it works...

So we divided all the elements into their own classes because this will permit us to extend and modify them more easily in the future.

So let's begin where it all starts, the data. Well, our `BarChart` class accepts a vector of `BarData` as an argument. We did this so that you could add as many bars as you want and the chart would still work. Be aware that if you add many bars, you might have to give more width to the chart so that it can accommodate them.

You can see in the code, that the width of the bar of determined by the width of the graph divided by the number bars. We decided that 85 percent of that value would be given to the bars and 15 percent would be given to the space between the bars. Those values are arbitrary and you can play with them to give different styles to the chart.

Also the other important step is to determine what our data range is. We do so by finding what the maximum value is. For simplicity, we assume that the values will start at 0, but the validity of a chart is always relative to the data, so if there are negative values it wouldn't work, but you could always fix this. So when we found our maximum value, we can decide for a scale for the rest of the values. You can use the following formula for it:

```
var scaleHeight:Number = (height - 10) / maximumValue;
```

Here, `height` is the height of the chart and `10` is just a margin we leave to the graph to place the labels. After that, if we multiply that scale by the value of the data, it will give us the height of each bar and there you have it, a completed bar chart.

There's more...

We created a very simple version of a bar chart but there are numerous things we could do to improve it. Styling, interactivity, and the possibility of accommodating a wider range of data are just some examples.

Styling

This basic chart could use a little bit of styling. By modifying the color of the bars, the font of the labels, and by adding a drop shadow to the bars, it could be greatly enhanced. You could also make all of them dynamic so that you could specify them when you create a new chart.

Interactivity

It would be really good to show the values for the bars when you move the mouse over them. Right now you can kind of get an idea of which one is the biggest bar but that is all. If this feature is implemented, you can get the exact value.

Accommodating a wider data range

As we explained earlier, we didn't account for all the data range. Values could be very different; some could be negative, some could be very small (between 0 and 1), or you would want to set the minimum and maximum value of the vertical axes. The good thing here is that you can modify the code to better fit your data.

See also

The next recipe will iterate on this one giving you a more complex chart. Also, you could check the previous recipe to learn how to do this using the Flex framework.

Creating comparison bar charts

In the previous recipe, we learned how to make a simple bar chart. The relation of the data was one-to-one; one label, one value. Now we will make this a bit more complex by adding one more dimension. We will create a bar chart in which the bars are replaced by bar charts. It can be hard to understand it like this, but it gets clearer if you look at the data. For this recipe we will compare the medals (bronze, silver, and gold) won by three different countries at a sporting event.

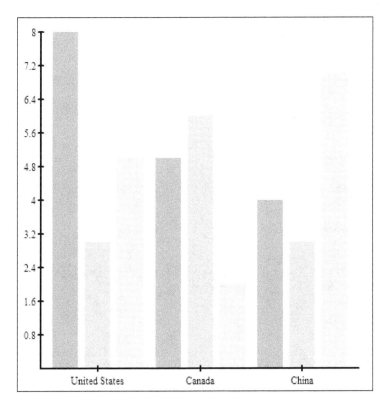

Getting ready

A good starting point is to copy over the project from the previous recipe (see the *Building vertical bar charts* recipe). We will modify it a lot, but the core of it will be similar.

How to do it...

The following are the steps required to build a comparison bar chart:

1. As usual, when we create a new chart, we always start with the data. So we create a new class for it called `ComparisonChartData`. Check the file out; it is basically a label and a vector of `BarData` from the previous project.

2. After that, in the main class we will generate the data. This example will use the number of medals won for countries as data. After that we create the chart quite similarly as in the *Drawing a bar chart with Flex* recipe in this chapter.

3. Now if you look at the classes `VerticalAxis.as`, `HorizontalAxis.as`, and `Bar.as`, you will notice that they have been only slightly modified. The `HorizontalAxis` class has been made a bit more data agnostic and requires a list of labels instead of being passed the data, that way we will be able to use the same class for bar chart and the comparison bar chart. The `Bar` class is now passed a color so that we can specify the color of the bar.

4. Most of the changes happen in the `ComparisonBarChart` class. First we must determine the size of the bars:

```
_categoryWidth = (chartWidth - MARGIN) * (1 - CATEGORY_PERCENT) /
data.length;
_categorySpacing = (chartWidth - MARGIN) * CATEGORY_PERCENT /
(data.length + 1);

_barWidth = _categoryWidth * (1 - BAR_PERCENT) / data[0].bars.
length;
_barSpacing = _categoryWidth * BAR_PERCENT / (data[0].bars.length
- 1);
```

5. After that we loop over the data and create all the bars:

```
for (i = 0; i < data.length; i++) {
  var markX:Number = _categorySpacing + _categoryWidth / 2 + i *
(_categoryWidth + _categorySpacing);
   listOfMarks.push(markX);
   listOfLabels.push (data[i].label);
   for (j = 0; j < data[i].bars.length; j++) {
     bar = new Bar(_barWidth, data[i].bars[j].data * scaleHeight,
data[i].bars[j].color);
```

```
        bar.x = MARGIN + markX - _categoryWidth / 2 + j * (_barWidth +
    _barSpacing) + _barWidth / 2;
        bar.y = chartHeight - MARGIN;
        addChild(bar);
      }
    }
}
```

How it works...

As we mentioned in the *Introduction*, we added a dimension to the chart so the data must reflect it. In this case we reuse the `BarData` class we had in the previous class, which is still very relevant (our chart will still have bars) but we create another class (`ComparisonChartData`) to hold a list of `BarData`.

After that the only hard part is determining the space allowed for each category (in this example: each country). We use the same formula as for determining the size of the bars in the `BarChart` recipe. Each category will be subdivided into multiple bars. So from the category width we can now find the width of the bars. We also took the liberty of assigning 15 percent for the space between the bars.

Finally we loop over all the data. Since our data is more complex now, we must do a loop inside of another loop to create all the bars. We find the position of the marks inside the first loop much like we found the position of the bars in the `BarChart` class. And from that position, we find the position of each of the bars for each of the categories.

There's more...

We added complexity to the `BarChart` code and created the `ComparisonBarChart`. In the following section we will look at how to improve it.

Adding a legend

Not having a legend for the previous chart was fine because you could have understood what it was depicting just by looking at it. But in the case of more complex data, a legend could really help explaining what we are trying to show with the chart. Fortunately, creating a legend is really easy. You should create a class for it, which you could re-use in other charts or graph.

See also

Definitely have a look at the recipe *Building vertical bar charts* in this chapter, creating bar charts from which this one was made. Also, you can easily tweak the recipe *Drawing a bar chart in Flex* in the chapter, creating bar charts to replicate what was shown in this recipe but using Flex.

Drawing histograms

Well truth be told, we won't really be making histograms with this recipe but mostly bar charts in the style of histograms. Histograms are very rigid in their nature and follow really specific mathematical functions to represent frequency and density. You can read more on histograms on Wikipedia: `http://en.wikipedia.org/wiki/Histogram`. What we are going to do here is build a histogram styled bar chart (no space between the bars) that uses a function as input. You can think of this as a different way to do an area chart or a line chart.

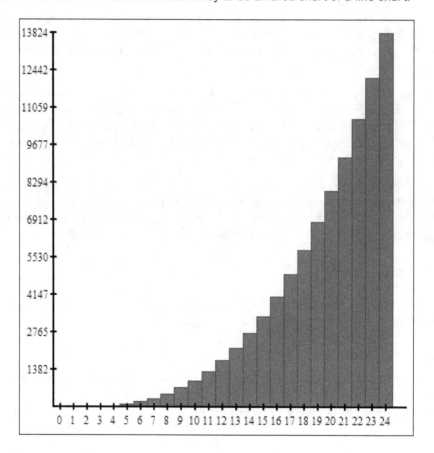

Getting ready

The data for this recipe is a bit different as it uses a mathematical function instead of a data set. You can get a mathematical function using interpolation or by having a program such as Microsoft Excel do it for you.

How to do it...

The following are the steps required to build a histogram using ActionScript 3:

1. Now if you look at our `Main.as` class, you will notice that it is quite small compared to the previous recipe. For this recipe, we don't need to create data; we will use a function to get our data. The function used in this case is the one as follows:

```
public function dataFormula(xValue:Number):Number {
    return (xValue * xValue * xValue);
}
```

2. Once we have this function we can create the chart:

```
var chart:Histogram = new Histogram(dataFormula, 400, 410, 25);
```

3. Next, in the `Bar.as` file we will add a style to the line because the bars will be really close in this chart and this will help differentiate them.

4. Finally, the `Histogram.as` file is different than `BarChart.as` and takes a function as a parameter in the constructor. From that function, we will determine the maximum value and we will create the bars.

```
var maximumValue:Number = data(0);
for (i = 1; i < numberOfBars; i++) {
    if (data(i) > maximumValue) {
        maximumValue = data(i);
    }
}

var scaleHeight:Number = (chartHeight - 10) / maximumValue;

var listOfMarks:Vector.<Number> = new Vector.<Number>();
var listOfLabels:Vector.<String> = new Vector.<String>();
var bar:Bar;
for (i = 0; i < numberOfBars; i++) {
    bar = new Bar(_barWidth, data(i) * scaleHeight);
    bar.x = 10 + _barWidth / 2 + i * (_barWidth);
    listOfMarks.push(bar.x - 10);
    listOfLabels.push(String(i));
    bar.y = chartHeight - 10;
    addChild(bar);
}
```

How it works...

Contrary to the other recipe, this one won't use a list of numbers as data but a function in the code called `dataFunction`. This example will use the function $y = x3$. The value on the vertical axis is equal to the value on the horizontal axis multiplied by itself two times (to the power of three). But you could use any function that takes a number and returns one.

Since we want the graph to be in the style of a true histogram, we don't need to compute any space between the bars. To get the width of the bars, we take the width of the graph divided by the number of bars plus one. We add one to the number of bars so that the last bar doesn't come too close to the end of the graph on the right-hand side.

We are now ready to use our function to get our data. Since we know it takes a number and returns a number, by giving it our value of the horizontal axis it will return the value of the vertical axis. The only code we have to write to do so is `data (horizontalAxisValue)`. In our case that value is the index of our loop. Note that we could have modified the `HorizontalAxis` class to be like the `VerticalAxis` class, but it still worked (the labels weren't too big) so we left it as it is.

There's more...

Accepting a wider data range would improve the `Histogram` class, but also, you could use it in a different way by making it draw a lot of bars.

Data range

Here again the data range is very important. It would be good to modify the code for this recipe so that it could accept a minimum value and a step value. In this example, our minimum was 0 and our step value was 1. But that may not fit for every function or data.

So many bars

One interesting thing to note here is that if you set the number of bars to be very high, you will end up creating an area chart since the bars will be really thin. If you want to use this chart in this way, I would suggest modifying the `HorizontalAxis` class because we used it as it is from the `BarChart` recipe and it would create way too many labels.

See also

▸ The *Building vertical bar charts* recipe

Creating sparklines to enrich text content

Sparklines are small line charts that are used to augment the value of some other content by giving a visual trend of a specific metric. One of the easy examples of applications that use sparklines is Google Analytics.

As you can see in the previous screenshot, the sparklines on the left give you a clearer background about the numbers on the right. So as of today, you had 13,935 visits but those varied in a specific pattern in the previous month.

Getting ready

Just start a new project in FlashDevelop. This will be a really simple recipe.

How to do it...

The following are the steps required to build sparklines:

1. Since sparklines are a pretty simple graph, we only have two classes for this recipe. In the main class, we generate the data and instantiate the `Sparkline` class. All of the drawing is done inside `Sparkline.as`.

2. We will only use the `graphics` function of the `Sprite` class to draw the line and the axes:

```
graphics.lineStyle(1, 0x0000ff);
graphics.moveTo(0, chartHeight-data[0] * scaleHeight);
for (i = 1; i < data.length; i++) {
  graphics.lineTo(i * _stepSize, chartHeight-data[i] *
scaleHeight);
}

graphics.lineStyle (1, 0);
graphics.moveTo(0, chartHeight);
graphics.lineTo(0, 0);

graphics.moveTo(0, chartHeight);
graphics.lineTo(chartWidth, chartHeight);
```

How it works...

Using the Flash Drawing API, the previous code will draw the two axes and draw a line that will represent our data.

We based the data on visits to a website for a day. We randomly assigned values ranging from 9000 to 15500. This graph will give us an idea of how the traffic varied during the previous month.

The thing to notice here is that since this line graph is so small, there are no labels anywhere. The goal here is not to check a precise data point, but more to derive a trend from the graph.

We still need, like in the other graph, to determine the highest value in the data set to convert values to pixels. In this case, since we didn't provide x and y coordinates, we use the index of the vector as the horizontal coordinate; that is why we need to find the `stepSize` value. After that, we can just iterate over the data and draw a succession by using the `lineTo` calls.

```
for (i = 1; i < data.length; i++) {
graphics.lineTo(i * _stepSize, chartHeight-data[i] * scaleHeight);
}
```

From there the job is mostly done; we only need to draw the axes. This is done easily by the `lineTo` calls since we don't need to add labels.

There's more...

By coloring the area under the line and averaging the data we could improve on the sparkline recipe.

Adding the area under the line

The graphs from Google Analytics also have the area under the line drawn, so if we wanted to replicate that it wouldn't be too hard. We would have to make a second `for loop` before the one we already have and add a `beginFill` call before it. After that we have to make sure we close the shape so that the fill is complete. We draw the fill before so that is doesn't hide the line. You could also do it all in one `loop` if you started `lineStyle` just before drawing the top side of the area and if you remove it just after.

Averaging the data

As you can see, the line is a bit jerky in the graph. Since we are more interested in the trend with sparklines, you could average the data for every two or three values. This would give you fewer data points and you would lose some precision, but it would, in return, give you a smoother line and it might be easier to see the trends.

Making 3D bar charts

In the recipe *Building vertical bar charts* in this chapter, we showed how to make a simple bar chart in ActionScript. For this recipe, we wanted to spice it up a bit and make it 3D.

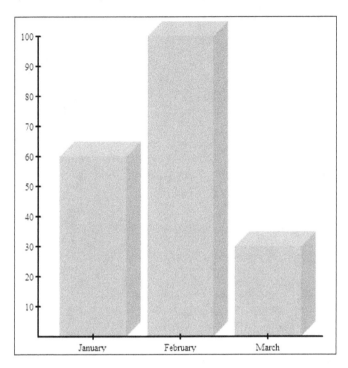

Getting ready

Get the code from the *Building vertical bar charts* recipe.

How to do it...

The following steps will show you how to convert a 2D bar chart to 3D:

1. Take `BarData.as`, `HorizontalAxis.as`, `VerticalAxis.as`, and `Main.as` from the *Building vertical bar charts* recipe from this chapter; these files are not going to change.

2. Now in `BarChart.as`, increase the space between the bars. These are the lines that change:

```
_barWidth = (width - 10) * 70 / 100 / data.length;
_barSpacing = (width - 10) * 30 / 100 / (data.length + 1);
```

3. The big changes will be in the `Bar.as` file. First we will add two helper functions to go back and forth between the color model, as shown in the following code snippet:

```
private function _hexToRGB(hex:uint):Object {
var rgbObj:Object = {
red: ((hex & 0xFF0000) >> 16),
green: ((hex & 0x00FF00) >> 8),
blue: ((hex & 0x0000FF))
};
return rgbObj;
}
private function _RGBtoHEX(red:int, green:int, blue:int):uint {
return red << 16 | green << 8 | blue;
}
```

4. We will need to compute a new color for the top and right part. The following code will show us how we get the color for the top part:

```
var baseColor:Object = _hexToRGB(color);

baseColor.red += baseColor.red * 0.1;
if (baseColor.red > 255) {
baseColor.red = 255;
}
baseColor.green += baseColor.green * 0.1;
if (baseColor.green > 255) {
baseColor.green = 255;
}
baseColor.blue += baseColor.blue * 0.1;
if (baseColor.blue > 255) {
baseColor.blue = 255;
}


var topColor:uint = _RGBtoHEX(baseColor.red, baseColor.green,
baseColor.blue);
```

5. All that is left to do, is draw two parallelograms that will make our bar look 3D:

```
graphics.beginFill(topColor);
graphics.moveTo(-width / 2, -height);
graphics.lineTo(-width / 2 + xOffset, -height - yOffset);
graphics.lineTo(width / 2 + xOffset, -height - yOffset);
graphics.lineTo(width / 2, - height);
graphics.lineTo( -width / 2, -height);

graphics.beginFill(rightColor);
```

```
graphics.moveTo(width / 2, 0);
graphics.lineTo(width / 2 + xOffset, 0 - yOffset);
graphics.lineTo(width / 2 + xOffset, -height - yOffset);
graphics.lineTo(width / 2, - height);
graphics.lineTo(width / 2, 0);
```

How it works...

We are basically taking every class from the *Building vertical bar charts* recipe, unchanged, except for `Bar.as` and `BarChart.as`.

In `BarChart.as`, we made a small modification to leave more space between our bars. Indeed, we will need space to have our 3D representing shapes. Before, we had 15 percent of space between bars; we will up that to 30 percent (in step 2).

The meaty part is in `Bar.as`. We will add two parallelograms to simulate the 3D effect, one for the top and the other for the side to give a sense of depth. Those are pretty simple to draw; we find the *x* and *y* of the off-setted top part of our parallelogram (once you have this point you can use it to find all the other points of the shape) and using the `lineTo` function, we can draw lines until we are back to the starting position (that is, step 6).

That already gives us a 3D looking shape, but there is a small problem. Since every piece is the same color, it reduces the 3D effect. That is why we are going to change the color of the top and right parallelograms. The top one is going to be of a lighter color and the right part is going to be of a darker color than the color specified in the parameters.

To compute those colors, we will need to decompose the hex colors provided into red, green, and blue. For each of those components, we are going to add or remove 10 percent of their value (add for lighter, remove for darker) thus keeping a similar color. That is exactly what we do in step 5.

Finally we convert it back to hexadecimal, as it is the format that the `beginFill` function expects.

Now our 3D bar chart looks great!

There's more...

By using gradients and a real 3D engine you could improve on this recipe.

Using gradient

Another option to using different color tones and to accentuate the 3D effect, would be to use a gradient on the top and right parts. It would make your bar chart look a bit more refined.

Using a real 3D engine

Here we faked the 3D, but to get really good results that are easier to animate or to interact with, you should use a real 3D engine such as Away3D, which you can find here: `http://away3d.com/`.

See also

▸ The *Building vertical bar charts* recipe

4
Drawing Different Types of Graphs

In this chapter, we will cover:

- ▶ Drawing a pie chart with Flex
- ▶ Creating donut charts
- ▶ Drawing meters and gauges
- ▶ Making Venn diagrams
- ▶ Building pyramid charts
- ▶ Drawing bubble charts
- ▶ Creating tag clouds
- ▶ Creating a treemap

Introduction

This chapter will go through an array of different charts, each presented in different recipes; some are common such as the **Venn diagram**, and some are less common, such as the **Treemap**. Interestingly enough, four charts from this chapter can be used to represent the exact same data. Those are the pie chart, the donut chart, the pyramid chart, and the treemap. They all give an idea of proportion, but each with its own little twist or visual differences. After this chapter, you will have a good tool kit of different graphs that you can use for multiple data sets.

Drawing a pie chart with Flex

In the previous chapter we covered creating a bar chart with Flex. This recipe will expand on that topic and will show you how to create a pie chart using Flex. Pie charts are great for visualizing data that adds up to 100 percent (think about who voted for whom in an election) or to show proportion between different numbers.

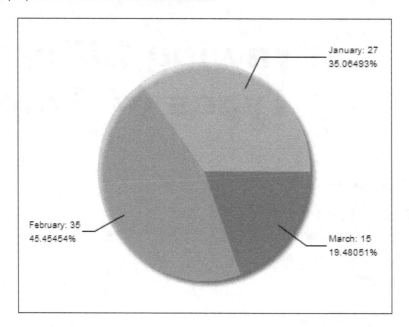

Getting ready

As in the *Drawing a bar chart with Flex* recipe in *Chapter 3, Creating Bar Charts*, you will need to have either Flash Builder installed or Flash Develop with the Flex SDK downloaded.

How to do it...

The following is the code to draw a pie chart:

```
<?xml version="1.0" encoding="utf-8"?>
<s:Application xmlns:fx="http://ns.adobe.com/mxml/2009"
        xmlns:s="library://ns.adobe.com/flex/spark"
        xmlns:mx="library://ns.adobe.com/flex/mx" minWidth="955"
minHeight="600">
  <fx:Script>
    <![CDATA[
      import mx.collections.ArrayCollection;
```

```
        [Bindable]
        private var monthsAmount:ArrayCollection = new ArrayCollection(
  [
            { month: "January", value: 27},
            { month: "February", value: 35 },
            { month: "March", value: 15} ]);
        private function displayLabel(data:Object, field:String,
  index:Number, percentValue:Number):String {
            var temp:String= String(percentValue).substr(0,8);
            return data.month + ": " + data.value + '\n' + temp + "%";
        }
     ]]>
   </fx:Script>
   <fx:Declarations>
     <!-- Define custom colors for use as pie wedge fills. -->
     <mx:SolidColor id="color1" color="0x70ddff" alpha="0.6"/>
     <mx:SolidColor id="color2" color="0x56baec" alpha="0.6"/>
     <mx:SolidColor id="color3" color="0x2b78d2" alpha="0.6"/>
   </fx:Declarations>
   <mx:PieChart id="piechart1" x="30" y="30"
  dataProvider="{monthsAmount}" showDataTips="true">
     <mx:series>
        <mx:PieSeries field="Amount" labelPosition="callout"
  fills="{[color1, color2, color3]}" labelFunction="{displayLabel}" />
     </mx:series>
   </mx:PieChart>
</s:Application>
```

How it works...

If you read the recipe about drawing a bar chart using Flex, you will notice that the code is fairly similar. When you create a Flex project it will generate for you the .xml file and the `Application` tag. Right after those tags, you get the `Script` tag, where you can put the ActionScript code inside a .mxml file. This is where we created the `ArrayCollection` data structure used as data to be visualized in the pie chart.

We will skip the `Declarations` tag for now and go right to the `PieChart` tag. This tag is pretty simple; it gives an ID to the chart so we can reference it later and position it on the screen using *x* and *y* coordinates. Finally it associates this chart with the data created in the ActionScript code using the argument `dataProvider = "{monthsAmount}"`. You can also see that we added `showDataTips` discussed in *Chapter 3, Creating Bar Charts*, which also works for displaying data tips on a mouse over.

Now `PieSeries` is the tag where we added the new code. First we need to tell the chart which values to consider inside the `ArrayCollection` data structure; we do this in the argument field. We set `field = "Amount"`, where amount is a value name inside `monthsAmount ArrayCollection`. After that, we tell the chart how to display the labels. The `labelPosition` argument can take multiple values such as `none`, `inside`, `outside`, `callout`, and `insideWithCallout`. `none` will not put any labels on the pie chart. `inside` and `outside` are pretty obvious and will put the labels respectively inside and outside the chart. `callout` will put the label outside the chart but also add a line from the associated wedge to the label. `insideWithCallout` will draw the label inside the chart, but if the wedge is too small to contain the label, it will use the `callout` positioning instead.

In this use of the `Pie Chart` component, we decided to go a bit further and style it by changing the default colors. We did so in the declaration tag. We created three colors that we passed in the `PieSeries` tag by their ID, as shown in the following code snippet:

```
fills="{[color1, color2, color3]}"
```

Finally, in order to make the chart easier to understand we formatted the labels so that there would be the name of the value beside the number. We do so inside the function `displayLabel`, which we also pass to the `PieSeries` tag.

There's more...

The `PieChart` component has a lot of options and customizations you can do. The following is a small one.

Bevel or not

By adjusting the alpha on the custom colors we defined, the `PieChart` component will be beveled or not. Any value below one will have a bevel, a full alpha of one won't. We would advise to use the same alpha for each color as it will look better.

See also

The *Creating donut charts* recipe uses pure ActionScript to create a pie chart with a little twist.

Creating donut charts

Very similar to pie charts, donut charts allow you to vary the visual if you have been using pie charts a lot. And since we used Flex to build the pie chart in the previous recipe, we thought it would be good to show how to build a pie chart/donut chart using pure ActionScript 3.

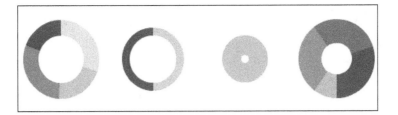

Getting ready

This recipe bases some of its code on the wedge class by Adobe's evangelist Lee Brimelow; you can check it here: `http://www.leebrimelow.com/?p=430`. Apart from that you can look up the code you will get from `http://www.packtpub.com`.

How to do it...

The following are the steps required to build a donut chart:

1. We will start by creating the data class in this case `DonutChartData.as`.

   ```
   public var color : uint;
   public var percent : Number;
   public function DonutChartData(newPercent:Number, newColor:uint){
     percent = newPercent;
     color = newColor;


   }
   ```

2. From there we will create the visual building block of this chart: `DonutChartWedge.as`. This class could also be used in a pie chart. The following is the part where we draw the wedge using the Flash drawing API:

   ```
   startPointX = Math.cos(angle) * radius;
   startPointY = Math.sin(-angle) * radius;

   graphics.lineTo(startPointX, startPointY);

   for (var i:int=0; i < numOfSegs; i++) {
     angle += segAngle;
     angleMid = angle - (segAngle / 2);
     midPoint = radius / Math.cos(segAngle / 2);
     anchorX = Math.cos(angle) * radius;
   ```

```
    anchorY = Math.sin(angle) * radius;
    controlX = Math.cos(angleMid) * midPoint;
    controlY = Math.sin(angleMid) * midPoint;
    graphics.curveTo(controlX, controlY, anchorX, anchorY);
}
// Close the wedge
graphics.lineTo(0, 0);
graphics.endFill();
```

3. Next, we create the mask in the shape of a circle with a hole in the middle. It will transform a pie chart into a donut chart. This is done inside `DonutChart.as`.

```
_donutMask.graphics.lineTo(outerRadius, 0);
midPoint = outerRadius / Math.cos(segAngle / 2);
for (i = 0; i < numOfSegs; i++) {
    angle += segAngle;
    angleMid = angle - (segAngle / 2);
    anchorPointX = outerRadius*Math.cos(angle);
    anchorPointY = outerRadius*Math.sin(angle);
    controlPointX = Math.cos(angleMid) * midPoint;
    controlPointY = Math.sin(angleMid) * midPoint;
    _donutMask.graphics.curveTo(controlPointX, controlPointY,
anchorPointX, anchorPointY);
}
_donutMask.graphics.moveTo(0, 0);
_donutMask.graphics.lineTo(innerRadius, 0);
midPoint = innerRadius / Math.cos(segAngle / 2);
for (i = numOfSegs; i > 0; i--) {
    angle -= segAngle;
    angleMid = angle + (segAngle / 2);
    anchorPointX = innerRadius * Math.cos(angle);
    anchorPointY = innerRadius * Math.sin(angle);
    controlPointX = Math.cos(angleMid) * midPoint;
    controlPointY = Math.sin(angleMid) * midPoint;
    _donutMask.graphics.curveTo(controlPointX, controlPointY,
anchorPointX, anchorPointY);
}
addChild(_donutMask);
```

4. Still inside `DonutChart.as`, from the data we will create all the wedges:

```
var wedge:DonutChartWedge;
_chartWedgeVector = new Vector.<DonutChartWedge>();
if (data != null){
    for (i=0; i < data.length; i++){
```

```
        wedge = new DonutChartWedge(radius, data[i].percent * 360,
    data[i].color);
        _wedgeHolder.addChild(wedge);
        _chartWedgeVector.push(wedge);
         if (i != 0){
         wedge.rotation = _chartWedgeVector[i - 1].rotation + _
    chartWedgeVector[i - 1].arc;
         }
      }
    }
```

How it works...

The data for a donut chart is simple; it is a percentage (value between 0 and 1) and a color. Usually you would want all of your percentage to add up to one, but this implementation of the donut chart will work even if it doesn't.

As for the `DonutChartWedge.as` file, it is a slight modification to Lee Brimelow's `Wegde` code. In his version, you would pass it to `Shape` or `Sprite` and it would draw the wedge on it. We preferred to make the wedge itself a `Sprite` class as it could be used in the future to make the chart animated or interactive.

The code uses basic trigonometry to find points on the circle and draw a succession of arcs in order to simulate a bigger arc of a circle. You see, Flash graphics API uses quadratic Beziers in its `curveTo` function and because of this if we want to draw an arc of a circle we must do this in little chunks.

If we were to leave it like this, our class would be creating pie charts. The part that makes it a donut chart is the mask we create in `DonutChart.as`. To create the donut shape of the mask we draw two concentric circles filling the area between those circles. We do this in a very similar fashion as when we create the wedges. Note that a big part of the code is converting angles from degrees to radians in order to use trigonometry.

There's more...

We would need to add labels to make this chart more complete. Also, there is a little trick to use the `DonutChart.as` as a pie chart.

Labels

Labels would have added a large amount of code so we omitted them. But if you wanted to add them it wouldn't be too hard. You would basically make a `switch` statement and depending of the middle angle of a wedge, position and align the labels. You could also add the labels inside the wedges, but you have to make sure the chart is big enough.

Donut chart as a pie chart

If you wanted to use the `DonutChart.as` file as a pie chart , it would be possible to do so. The difference between the donut chart and the pie chart is that the donut chart has a mask on it hiding the middle part of the chart. If you made the mask show the full chart, then you would have a pie chart. To do so, make the `strokeWidth` property on `donutChart` equal to the `radius` property and there you have it, a pie chart.

See also

The donut chart fills similar needs as the pie chart so you could check out the previous recipe. Also, this recipe is using calls to the `curveTo` function to draw parts of circles, and the next recipe (drawing meters and gauges) will also use the `curveTo` functions.

Drawing meters and gauges

Meters and gauges are really good to convey some information really rapidly, and that is why they are used often in dashboards. They actually give more than just one piece of information; they also give an idea of the range the value can take and also if animated, it can give an idea of how much the value fluctuates.

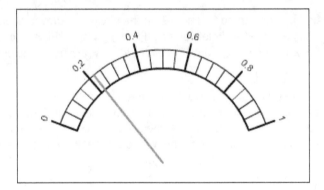

Getting ready

Having some notion about trigonometry and the unit circle (refer to `http://en.wikipedia.org/wiki/Unit_circle`) can be useful for this recipe. Also, some of the code will be based on Adobe evangelist Lee Brimelow's wedge class available at `http://www.leebrimelow.com/?p=430`, so it might be worth a look.

How to do it...

The following are the steps required to build a meter:

1. In this case the data is only one value so we don't need to create a data structure for it. We can start right away by creating a function in `Meter.as` to create arcs of circles. We call it `_drawArc`. It takes a shape and a radius as parameters and will draw an arc in the shape:

```
numberOfSegments = Math.ceil(METER_TOTAL_ARC / 45);
segAngle = METER_TOTAL_ARC / numberOfSegments;
 segAngle = segAngle / 180 * Math.PI;
angle = 0;
startingPointX = Math.cos(angle) * radius;
startingPointY = Math.sin(-angle) * radius;
shape.graphics.moveTo(startingPointX, startingPointY);
for (var i:int=0; i< numberOfSegments; i++) {
  angle += segAngle;
  angleMid = angle - (segAngle / 2);
  midPoint = radius / Math.cos(segAngle / 2);
  anchorX = Math.cos(angle) * radius;
  anchorY = Math.sin(angle) * radius;
  controlX = Math.cos(angleMid) * midPoint;
  controlY = Math.sin(angleMid) * midPoint;
  shape.graphics.curveTo(controlX, controlY, anchorX, anchorY);
}
```

2. We can then use this function to create the two arcs that compose our meter.

3. After that we will create the lines that will form the gradation of our meter. We will do it this in two steps. First we will create the small ones that are more numerous and then the bigger ones. All of this is done in the function `_drawLines`.

4. We can now move on to adding labels. We do so in the `_addLabels` function. The code is mostly similar to the one for drawing the lines, but with labels we have to rotate them so they are a tangent to the circle.

5. Finally we draw the arrow that will show the value of the data:

```
private function _drawArrow():void {
  var arrow:Shape = new Shape();
  arrow.x = innerRadius * 2;
  arrow.y = innerRadius * 2;
  arrow.rotation = -90 - METER_TOTAL_ARC / 2;
  addChild(arrow);
  arrow.graphics.lineStyle(2, 0xff0000);
  arrow.graphics.lineTo(outerRadius * Math.cos(METER_TOTAL_ARC *
percent * Math.PI / 180), outerRadius * Math.sin(METER_TOTAL_ARC *
percent * Math.PI / 180));
}
```

How it works...

In step 1, we showed the code to draw an arc. That code relies on calls to the function `curveTo` from the `Graphics` class. Since that class uses quadratic Beziers to draw curves, we can't draw our arc in one single call to `curveTo`. That is why we must make multiple successive calls in a `for` loop. We divided our main arc into multiple segments and drew those instead.

Now our meter needs two arcs of the same angle but of different radii; that is why we put the code to draw an arc in a function, so that we could reuse it for the both of them. You will also notice that the code is really similar to the `DonutChartWedge.as` class from the previous recipe. The only difference is that here we do not need to create a shape; we are just drawing a curve.

Apart from the labels, the rest of the code (gradation marks and arrow) is just about drawing lines along the radius of a circle. Here we use trigonometry to find the *x* and *y* of the starting position and ending position of our lines. The *x* position is radius times the cosine of the angle in radians. The *y* position is the same except we use the sine of the angle instead of the cosine.

Finally we need to position the labels. Here we had no choice but to embed the font. We used the `swc` approach to do so, but anyway embedding a font would have worked. We needed to do this because you can't rotate `TextField` with a font that hasn't been embedded. In that case the text will just disappear. To find the *x* and *y* of where we should put the labels, we use the previous sine and cosine formula. Now we want the labels to be a tangent to the circle, so we will add 90 degrees to the angle they represent and they will be properly oriented.

There's more...

Animation and using the Flash IDE could really make your gauges and meters stand out.

Animation

It is easy to animate a meter or a gauge. Since it only has one value, you `Tween` that value to make the visualization more dynamic.

Using the Flash IDE

We drew the entire meter just by using the graphic API in ActionScript, but by using the Flash authoring tool, we could add a bit more even faster. We could add a color gradient behind the line and we could give the arrow a shape instead of just being a line.

See also

The *Creating donut charts* recipe in this chapter also uses the `curveTo` function from the `Graphics` class. Also you could check out the *Creating sparklines to enrich text content* recipe from *Chapter 3, Creating Bar Charts*. They are also very good to put in a dashboard.

Making Venn diagrams

Venn diagrams are well known for data visualization. They are used to show the intersection between sets of data. As an example, you could have two groups of objects: one object could belong to both groups, while another could only belong to the first group. Venn diagrams help show that relationship. In this recipe, we will demonstrate how to create Venn diagrams that use two, three, and four sets of data.

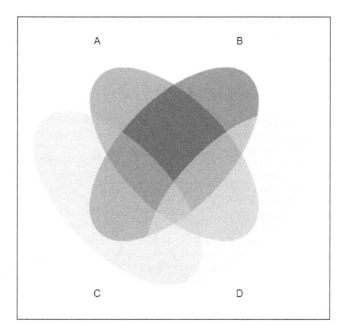

Getting ready

Reading the Wikipedia page on Venn diagrams could help you to understand the background behind those diagrams: `http://en.wikipedia.org/wiki/Venn_diagram`.

How to do it...

The following are the steps required to make a Venn diagram:

1. First we will need to create the building blocks for our Venn diagrams: the circles and ellipse. The following is the code for the ellipses:

```
public class VennEllipse extends Sprite {
    public function VennEllipse(circleWidth:Number, color:uint) {
        graphics.beginFill(color, 0.5);
        graphics.drawEllipse(-circleWidth/2, -circleWidth/4,
circleWidth, circleWidth / 2);
        graphics.endFill();
    }
}
```

2. After that we will create a class for each possible number of sets of data, in our case two, three, and four. We start with two sets and we draw the circles and labels as required.

```
public function createGraph():void {
    var circle1:VennCircle = new VennCircle(_graphWidth * 0.6,
0xff0000);
    addChild(circle1);

    var circle2:VennCircle = new VennCircle(_graphWidth * 0.6,
0x0000ff);
    circle2.x = _graphWidth * 0.4;
    addChild(circle2);

    var textFormat:TextFormat = new TextFormat("Arial", 14);

    var label1:TextField = new TextField();
    label1.defaultTextFormat = textFormat;
    label1.text = _labels[0];
    label1.width = label1.textWidth + 5;
    label1.height = label1.textHeight + 3;
    label1.x = _graphWidth * 0.6 / 2 - label1.width / 2;
    label1.y = _graphWidth * 0.6 + 10;
    addChild(label1);

    var label2:TextField = new TextField();
    label2.defaultTextFormat = textFormat;
    label2.text = _labels[1];
    label2.width = label2.textWidth + 5;
    label2.height = label2.textHeight + 3;
```

```
     label2.x = _graphWidth * 0.6 / 2 - label2.width / 2 + _
graphWidth*0.4;
     label2.y = _graphWidth * 0.6 + 10;
     addChild(label2);
  }
```

3. For three sets, it is quite similar to two sets, for which we just had a circle and a label.

4. Four sets are a bit more complex and require that we use ellipses instead of circles. The following is the code for creating those ellipses:

```
var ellipse1:VennEllipse = new VennEllipse(_graphWidth * 0.75,
0xff0000);
     ellipse1.y = _graphWidth * 0.45;
     ellipse1.x = _graphWidth * 0.52;
     ellipse1.rotation = 45;
     addChild(ellipse1);

     var ellipse2:VennEllipse = new VennEllipse(_graphWidth *
0.75, 0x0000ff);
     ellipse2.y = _graphWidth * 0.45;
     ellipse2.x = _graphWidth * 0.52;
     ellipse2.rotation = -45;
     addChild(ellipse2);

     var ellipse3:VennEllipse = new VennEllipse(_graphWidth *
0.75, 0xffff00);
     ellipse3.y = _graphWidth * 0.40 + _graphWidth * 0.2;
     ellipse3.x = _graphWidth * 0.52 + _graphWidth * 0.2;
     ellipse3.rotation = -45;
     addChild(ellipse3);

     var ellipse4:VennEllipse = new VennEllipse(_graphWidth *
0.75, 0x00ff00);
     ellipse4.y = _graphWidth * 0.40 + _graphWidth * 0.2;
     ellipse4.x = _graphWidth * 0.52 - _graphWidth * 0.2;
     ellipse4.rotation = 45;
     addChild(ellipse4);
```

5. After that we will need an interface to abstract those classes, but it is very simple:

```
public interface IVennDiagram {
    function createGraph():void;
    function setLabels(labels:Vector.<String>):void;
    function setGraphWidth(graphWidth:Number):void;
  }
```

6.   Once that is done we create the `VennDiagram.as` file, which is basically a `switch` statement depending on how many labels are present.

7.   Finally the `Main.as` class shows the created Venn diagram and the data.

How it works...

The thing with Venn diagrams is that depending on how many sets (groups) they illustrate, they are very different. To palliate to that, we will create a different class for each number of sets that our data will represent: `Venn2Circles.as`, `Venn3Circles.as`, and `Venn4Ellipses.as`.

`Venn2Circles.as` and `Venn3Circles.as` are simple. We just need to position the circles and the labels correctly and we are done. Note that the fill color of the circles is semitransparent so that the intersecting region gets its own color (a mix of the other circle's color).

When we use four sets it gets a bit more complicated. We need to use ellipses instead of circles if we want a diagram that has all the possible intersecting regions and is still easy to understand. Ellipses are different than circles; you draw them from their top-left corner instead of their center. Since we are going to rotate them, we will offset them so that the rotation point is at the center of the ellipse. After that it is only a matter of positioning the ellipses.

Once we have those three classes done, we will create an interface for them so that the `VennDiagram.as` class that we will create thereafter can use any of them interchangeably and it will also keep the code very clean. The `VennDiagram.as` class is only a `switch` statement that looks at how many labels were given to the graph and decides which of the classes, `Venn2Circles.as`, `Venn3Circles.as`, or `Venn4Ellipses.as`, can be used.

The `Main.as` class shows how to create the labels (in this case, the labels are the data) and uses the similar syntax we have been using to create the graph.

There's more...

By making it interactive and adding the possibilities to use more sets we could improve on this recipe.

Interactivity

One very good feature that could be implemented would be the one where if you mouse over one region of the diagram, then a label would open up and indicate which intersection of sets it is. This could be done using `hitTestPoint` and testing against all the circles or ellipses.

More sets

As we introduce more sets, the diagram gets more complex and harder to understand. If we wanted our `VennDiagram.as` class to support five or six sets, we would need to use different shapes other than circles and ellipses. I would advise going with Edwards' Venn diagrams, available at `http://en.wikipedia.org/wiki/Venn_diagram`, because they are much clearer and could be done using the `curveTo` calls (a lot of them could use the `curveTo` calls, but it could still be done).

Building pyramid charts

Pyramid charts are very similar to pie charts and can be mostly used for the same purpose. But there is one more piece of information that can be given by using pyramid charts, a sense of hierarchy. The pyramid has a top and bottom layer and there are layers in between too, usually the top layer being the most important.

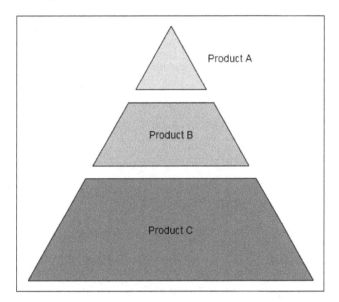

Getting ready

Look at the project files in the code folder. Also, having a good grasp on the Pythagorean theorem, available at `http://en.wikipedia.org/wiki/Pythagorean_theorem`, is important.

How to do it...

The following are the steps required to create a pyramid chart:

1. First we will create the data structure to represent a layer in our pyramid chart. The following is `PyramidData.as`:

```
public class PyramidData {
    public var startingPercent:Number;
    public var endingPercent:Number;
    public var label:String;
    public var color:uint;
    public var labelOustideOfChart:Boolean;

    public function PyramidData(newStartingPercent:Numb
er, newEndingPercent:Number, newLabel:String, newColor:uint,
newLabelOutsideOfChart:Boolean = false ) {
        startingPercent = newStartingPercent;
        endingPercent = newEndingPercent;
        label = newLabel;
        color = newColor;
        labelOustideOfChart = newLabelOutsideOfChart;
    }
}
```

2. After that we can create the `PyramidChart.as` file. It uses the Flash graphics API to draw each layer.

```
var lenghtOfTop:Number = data[i].startingPercent * graphWidth *
Math.sin(30 * Math.PI / 180);
var lenghtOfBottom:Number = data[i].endingPercent * graphWidth *
Math.sin(30 * Math.PI / 180);

point1 = new Point (graphWidth / 2 - lenghtOfTop, data[i].
startingPercent * graphHeight);
point2 = new Point (graphWidth / 2 - lenghtOfBottom, data[i].
endingPercent * graphHeight);
point3 = new Point (graphWidth / 2 + lenghtOfBottom, data[i].
endingPercent * graphHeight);
point4 = new Point (graphWidth / 2 + lenghtOfTop, data[i].
startingPercent * graphHeight);

graphics.beginFill(data[i].color);
graphics.lineStyle(1, 0);
graphics.moveTo(Math.round(point1.x), Math.round(point1.y));
graphics.lineTo(Math.round(point2.x), Math.round(point2.y));
graphics.lineTo(Math.round(point3.x), Math.round(point3.y));
graphics.lineTo(Math.round(point4.x), Math.round(point4.y));
graphics.lineTo(Math.round(point1.x), Math.round(point1.y));
```

3. Finally in `Main.as` we generate the data and we create the pyramid chart.

How it works...

As you can see our data here is a bit more complicated. It has five properties to represent a layer in the pyramid chart. The most important properties are `startingPercent` and `endingPercent`. These will tell you where to start and end a layer. It is a value between 0 and 1; 0 being the top of the pyramid and 1 being the bottom. As you can see in the example, the values don't have to be continuous for it to work. Having a gap in between layers gives it a different style. The caveat to this is that if layers overlap it won't look as good.

The `PyramidChart.as` class refers to a bit of math to draw every piece of the graph. We decided to draw an equilateral triangle (where the three sides of the triangle are of the same length) for our pyramid because it is more pleasing to the eyes, but we could also have used an isosceles triangle (where two sides of the triangle are of the same length). Each side of the triangle will be the equal to the width of the graph. Once we know this we can figure out the height of the triangle by using the Pythagorean theorem.

```
graphHeight = Math.sqrt(graphWidth * graphWidth - (graphWidth / 2 *
graphWidth / 2));
```

From there we need to draw each layer based on the data given. Each layer will be a trapezoid and we will need to find the coordinates of each of its four corners. These corners are located along the sides of our equilateral triangle. So by using the `startingPercent` and `endingPercent` properties and a bit of trigonometry, we will end up with our points. The following code snippet shows how we can find our first point:

```
var lenghtOfTop:Number = data[i].startingPercent * graphWidth * Math.
sin(30 * Math.PI / 180);
point1 = new Point (graphWidth / 2 - lenghtOfTop, data[i].
startingPercent * graphHeight);
```

You can see in the `Math.sin` function that we use 30 degrees as an angle. Since we have an equilateral triangle, all the angles in it are 60 degrees. Our calculations use half of the triangle to get a right triangle; the top angle will be half of 60 degrees and therefore, 30 degrees. The sine formula uses radians and not degrees so we must convert it; that's why we multiply it by PI and divide it by 180 degrees.

Once we have our four points, it is just a matter of using the Flash drawing API and tracing lines between them.

The last part is to add the labels. Now we can either put the labels inside the graph or outside, but sometimes the labels will be too wide and won't fit inside the graph so there will be no choice but to put them outside. We added a Boolean value in the `PyramidData` class so that we can indicate where we want the labels to be.

If the label is outside the graph, it should start at the same *x* coordinate as the bottom-right corner of its layer (that is, the trapezoid). If it is inside the layer, its width should be the smallest width (the top part) of the layer. That way we can be sure that the labels will never intersect with the sides of the graph.

There's more...

Users should consider using getters and setters, and 3D to make this chart better.

Getters and setters

In this recipe and the previous ones, we used public variables in our data for the sake of simplicity. But in this case the `startingPercent` and `endingPercent` property values must be between 0 and 1, so it might be good to check for that and give an error message if they are not. This would make the code sturdier.

3D!

Pyramid charts are good, but this recipe uses a triangle as the base shape of the chart. Now by going with a real 3D pyramid, it would make it look even better. There's no need to use a 3D engine. Just emulating it with the graphics API would be enough to enhance the look.

See also

▸ The *Drawing a pie chart with Flex* recipe

Drawing bubble charts

Bubble charts are an evolution of the point chart. By being able to modify the size of the point (bubble in this case) we can visualize one more dimension for our data. Actually, by adding colors to the bubble and a legend (a **legend** contains a list of the variables appearing in the chart and an example of their appearance) you could even visualize four dimensions. An example of using the bubble chart would be to plot the impact of education on the salary over the years between United States, China, and Russia. The *x* axis would represent the years, the *y* axis would be the salaries, the size of the bubbles would be degree of education (bigger being having more education), and the colors would represent the countries. This is depicted in the following figure:

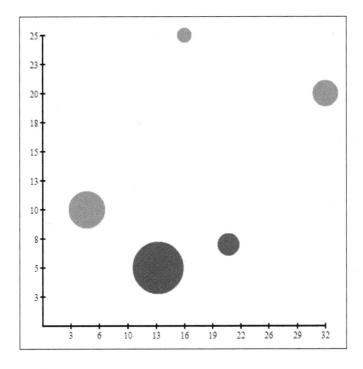

Getting ready

Take a look at the files in the `Bubble Chart` folder in the code files downloadable from `www.packtpub.com`. This chart will also use horizontal and vertical axes so it might be good to read *Chapter 1, Getting Started with Graph Drawing* and *Chapter 3, Creating Bar Charts*.

How to do it...

The following are the steps required to build a bubble chart:

1. We start by creating our data holder: `BubbleChartData.as`.

```
public var x:Number;
public var y:Number;
public var amount:Number;
public var color:uint;
public function BubbleChartData(newX:Number, newY:Number,
newAmount:Number, newColor:uint) {
  x = newX;
  y = newY;
  amount = newAmount;
  color = newColor;
}
```

2. This chart has three building blocks: `Bubbles.as`, `VerticalAxis.as`, and `HorizontalAxis.as`. The `Bubble.as` class draws a circle using the drawing API. `VerticalAxis.as` is exactly the same as in the *Drawing histograms* recipe from *Chapter 3, Creating Bar Charts*. Now to create the `HorizontalAxis.as` class, we have to modify `VerticalAxis.as` to switch the `height` and `y` values with the `width` and `x` values.

3. Once the building blocks are created, we can move on to the `BubbleChart` class. We first loop over the data once to find the maximum value on the *x* axis and on the *y* axis.

4. After that we loop over the data a second time to create all the different bubbles.

5. The last step is to instantiate the two axes.

6. The `Main.as` class then puts everything together.

How it works...

There is not much in the `BubbleChart` class that we haven't covered in previous recipes. The only tricky part is finding the right scale for each axis and for the size of the bubbles. In this example, we didn't need to scale the values for the size of the bubbles, but the user could provide a minimum size and a maximum size for them. If so, we can then map the range of the data over the range of size; that will give us our scaling ratio.

For the rest, the data portion is a bit more complex because it has one or two properties, but nothing extravagant.

There's more...

Since the bubble chart has more data, it becomes fundamental to have ways to get the precise data.

Interactivity

The easiest way to do this is to have rollovers when the mouse goes over the bubbles. Since this chart already has a lot of information on it, having the precise data on rollover doesn't clutter it.

Legends

We mentioned that the color of the bubble could also bear meaning; the easiest way to convey that meaning is by using a legend.

See also

▶ The *Building point charts* recipe in *Chapter 1, Getting Started with Graph Drawing*

Creating tag clouds

Tag clouds are good tools to analyze text. They quickly give a good idea of which topics are being approached by an article or a post.

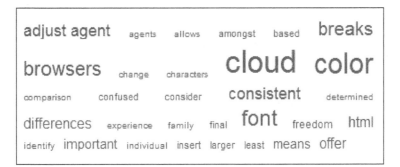

Getting ready

Open the folder containing the code for this recipe.

How to do it...

The following are the steps required to build a tag cloud:

1. The first step, which we won't be explaining in this recipe, is to parse a text and get data of how frequently each word occurs. You will probably want to only use the top 50 words and remove propositions and only use nouns.

2. Create the data structure for this visualization. In this case it is simply a pairing of a label and occurrences (a count of how many times a word appears in the text).

3. Once we get this, we can start creating the `TagCloud.as` class.

4. We first have to determine the number that represents the lowest and the highest occurrences by looping through all the data.

5. With that in hand, we can find the value for `fontRatio` that will be used to assign a font size for each word. The formula is quite simple:

```
var fontRatio:Number = (maxTextSize - minTextSize) / (maxOccurence
- minOccurence);
```

6. Now we can loop the data again and create a text field for each word. We will keep track of the width of each new text field.

```
for (i = 0; i < data.length; i++) {

  textfield = new TextField();

  textFormat.size = (data[i].occurences - minOccurence) *
fontRatio + minTextSize;

  textfield.defaultTextFormat = textFormat;

  textfield.text = data[i].label;

  textfield.width = textfield.textWidth + 5;

  textfield.height = textfield.textHeight+ 3;

  _currentLineWidth += textfield.width;

  if (_currentLineWidth >= graphWidth) {

  _createCurrentLine();

    _currentLineWidth += textfield.width + minSpace;

  } else {

    _currentLineWidth += minSpace;

  }

  _currentLine.push (textfield);

}
```

7. When we have a full line we call the function _createCurrentLine, which will position and add to the stage each word of the line.

8. Finally, when we are done looping, we create the last line with the words that are left.

9. The class Main.as shows the format of the data and how to instantiate a TagCloud.

How it works...

In this case the data is very simple, a label and a word count (occurrences). Getting this data might be a bit more complicated since you have to parse some text. Once that part is done, generating a TagCloud is pretty easy.

Finding the minimum occurrence and the maximum one is trivial; you loop over the data and compare each occurrence value with the current one. We need to find those in order to map the occurrence range to the font size range. That is what we do when we compute the `fontRatio` value. We use that ratio when we loop over the data the second time, and we assign each `TextField` its corresponding text size.

```
textFormat.size = (data[i].occurences - minOccurence) * fontRatio +
minTextSize;
```

After this is done we can get the size of each `TextField` in order to create the lines of `TagCloud`. We can keep track of the length of the current line; if the current line is smaller than the specified graph's width, we can add the current `TextField` in a `Vector`. If it isn't, that is we have a full line, we can call the function to create a new line.

That function (`_createCurrentLine`) loops over the `_currentLine` `Vector` and finds the maximum height of all `TextFields` in it as well as the width of all added `TextFields`. We will use the width of all `TextFields` to compute the space in between `TextFields` so that our `TagCloud` can look justified. Once we have those two values it is just a matter of positioning the text fields.

When we are done looping over the data and creating full lines, we will call `_createCurrentLine` one more time with the remaining words. The only difference this time is that we won't justify those `TextFields`, but align them to the left.

There's more...

By also modifying the alpha and using embedded fonts we could make our `TagCloud` class better.

Modifying the alpha

A bit like what we did for the font size, we could also map our occurrence range on an alpha range that goes from 0.5 to 1. That way, the bigger a word is, ithe more filled with color it is. The less important words would be dimmer, conveying the meaning of the tag cloud in a better way.

Using embedded fonts

For the sake of simplicity, we didn't use embedded fonts in this recipe, but if you want to improve the positioning of the text fields, you would need to use them. Flash has some trouble determining the size of the text when it is not using embedded fonts, which is why in this recipe we adjust it a bit by using the following assignment:

```
textfield.width = textfield.textWidth + 5;
```

If you used embedded fonts, you wouldn't need to do this, thus making your tag cloud look better.

Creating a treemap

In this recipe we are going to build a treemap. **Treemaps** are used to represent the data structure of a tree (nodes that have nodes as children). In this example, we are going to use it more as a rectangular pie chart. Wherever you can use a pie chart, you will be able to use this treemap, but it will give you the ability to use something a bit different.

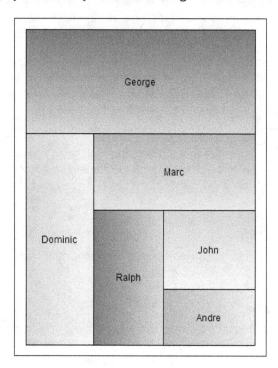

Getting ready

Open the files in the `Treemap` folder in the downloadable code files from www.packtpub.com.

How to do it...

1. Let's start by creating the data structure that is `TreemapData.as`:

```
public var color : uint;
public var percent : Number;
public var label:String;
```

```
public function TreemapData(newPercent:Number, newColor:uint,
newLabel:String) {
   percent = newPercent;
   color = newColor;
   label = newLabel;
}
```

2. From there we can jump to `Treemap.as`. We will need to inversely sort the data as our first step. To do so we will create a sorting function and pass it to the `sort` function of `Array`. The following is what the sorting function looks like:

```
private function _sortData(a:TreemapData, b:TreemapData):int {

   if (a.percent > b.percent) {

      return -1;

   } else if (a.percent < b.percent) {

      return 1;

   } else {

      return 0;

   }

}
```

3. Once our data is sorted we will draw a rectangle for each of our objects in the data.

```
matrix.createGradientBox(currentWidth, dataHeight,Math.PI /
2,currentPoint.x, currentPoint.y);
graphics.beginGradientFill(GradientType.LINEAR, [data[i].color,
data[i].color], [1, 0.3], [0, 255], matrix);
graphics.drawRect(currentPoint.x, currentPoint.y, currentWidth,
dataHeight);
```

4. After that we update our values so that our next rectangle can be drawn in the right place.

5. The file `Main.as` generates the data and instantiates an instance of the `Treemap` class.

How it works...

By using the treemap chart as a pie chart, we follow this principle: the first rectangle will be the size of its percent times the total area. It will take the full width of the graph and as much height as needed to be of the correct size.

The second rectangle will start after the previous rectangle (*y* equal to the height of the previous rectangle), and will take the full height of the remaining space and as much width as needed to be of the correct size.

We repeat those principles by dividing the remaining space first in width and afterwards in height. We do so until we have no more sections in our data. For this graph to look good, it is important that it adds up to 1.

Until now the code was pretty easy. It's just drawing rectangles, but we also added a little stylistic element. Instead of using a simple fill for our rectangles, we went with a gradient fill. Using gradient fills is a bit more complex because you need to use the `createGradientBox` function of the `Matrix` class. But all this function does is define the bounding area, the rotation, and the starting point of the gradient. Note that we are creating a gradient over the alpha of the color for each section of the graph, so it would work for any color.

Until now in the book, mostly every recipe has been using vectors to store the data, but this recipe uses an array. We did so because a vector is a much more rigid (but it is faster in general) structure than an array so it doesn't have a sort functionality which we need in this case.

There's more...

You will need a strategy to show small values and also there is another way you can use a treemap to represent the tree data structure.

Representing small values

You have to use the right chart for the right data, so using the treemap when you have many fields, with very small percentages, it might not be the best. But if you really want to use a treemap then you would need to improve on the labeling. By having labels that are outside the graph and point to their respective rectangles, you could have a way to convey information to the reader.

Using a tree as data

A tree is represented with nodes that can have children. In turn these children can have children. Each child represents a branch and a branch in a treemap is a rectangle. The root (the first node) is represented as the entire graph. We divide the graph into rectangles for each child the root bears. We repeat this process for every rectangle until we find a leaf (a node that doesn't have children). Recursion is a good way to code this.

See also

- ▶ The *Drawing a pie chart with Flex* recipe
- ▶ The *Creating donut chart* recipe
- ▶ The *Building pyramid charts* recipe

5
Adding Interaction

In this chapter, we will cover:

- ▸ Zooming and panning around a graph
- ▸ Sending data updates to the graph
- ▸ Making the points interactive: Hovering
- ▸ Selecting data points in the graph
- ▸ A dynamic graph based on an editable table
- ▸ Dragging data points to new values
- ▸ Linking graphs

Introduction

Now that we know how to draw graphs, it's time to look at one of ActionScript's strengths: interacting with the user. In this chapter, we'll see many ways you can give the user control over the graph.

You will notice that this is only a starting point. There are so many options and so many ways to interact with a graph, it would be impossible to describe them all. An application such as Google Maps demonstrates many of the different ways:

- ▸ Drag the graph to show parts that are not displayed
- ▸ Zoom in and out to show details or the overview
- ▸ Hover over markers to show more information
- ▸ Click and select markers to perform actions
- ▸ Display different versions of the same data (also called overlays in many applications)

With the recipes in this chapter, we want to give you a great start and encourage you to experiment.

Zooming and panning around a graph

Complicated graphs can sometimes offer too much data to fit on one screen. One option to make this manageable is to offer a zoom function, so users can zoom in on the data they would like to investigate closely.

When zoomed in, you also want to enable the user to move the graph so he can investigate different areas of the graph. This is called **panning**.

Getting ready

We will once again build on the code used in the previous chapters. If you skipped any of the recipes, you can download the code files and start from there.

To start from scratch, create a new workspace and copy the Graph and PointGraph classes from the previous chapters into your source folder (you can find them in the provided code files).

We'll start the recipe from an existing point graph with some random data:

```
package com.graphing.zoompan
{
    import com.graphing.PointGraph;

    public class Recipe1 extends Sprite
    {
        private var _graph:PointGraph;
        private var _data:Array = [[0,20],[50,70],[100,0],[150,150],[2
00,300],[250,200],[300,400],[350,20],[400,60],[450,250],[500,90],[550,
400],[600,500],[650,450],[700,320]];

    public function Recipe1()
        {
            _graph = new PointGraph();
            _graph.data = _data;
            _graph.graphWidth = 800;
            _graph.graphHeight = 600;
            _graph.graphLeft = -50;
            _graph.graphRight = 750;
            _graph.graphTop = 550;
            _graph.graphBottom = -50;
            _graph.createGraph();
```

```
        addChild(_graph);

        _graph.drawHorizontalAxis(0, 0, 700, 50, ["0", "700"]);
        _graph.drawVerticalAxis(0, 0, 500, 50, ["0", "250", "500"]);
        }
    }
}
```

How to do it...

First we will add a layer between the graph and the stage. This will be the layer that's responsible for the zooming and panning:

1. Add a private `Sprite` variable to the `Recipe1` class:

    ```
    private var _zoomPanLayer:Sprite;
    ```

2. Add this as a background to the stage (feel free to change the color to get a better idea of what's happening in the next steps):

    ```
    _zoomPanLayer = new Sprite();
    _zoomPanLayer.graphics.beginFill(0xffffff);
    _zoomPanLayer.graphics.drawRect(0, 0, 800, 600);
    _zoomPanLayer.graphics.endFill();
    addChild(_zoomPanLayer);
    ```

3. And finally we will add the graph to this layer and not to the stage. Replace `addChild(_graph)` with the following piece of code:

    ```
    _zoomPanLayer.addChild(_graph);
    ```

    Now we are ready to add buttons to zoom in and out of the graph. For the buttons, we create a helper class that will allow us to use bitmaps as buttons.

4. Create the a new class `BitmapButton`:

    ```
    package com.graphing {
        import flash.display.Bitmap;
        import flash.display.Sprite;
        public class BitmapButton extends Sprite {
            public function BitmapButton(bitmap:Bitmap) {
                addChild(bitmap);
            }
        }
    }
    ```

5. We embed two button images in the `Recipe1` class:

```
[Embed(source = "../../../../lib/zoom-in-16.png")]
private var ZoomInBitmap:Class;
[Embed(source = "../../../../lib/zoom-out-16.png")]
private var ZoomOutBitmap:Class;
```

6. And we add the following code to the stage:

```
var zoomInButton:BitmapButton = new BitmapButton(new
ZoomInBitmap());
zoomInButton.x = 800 - 2 * 16 - 8;
zoomInButton.y = 8;
zoomInButton.addEventListener(MouseEvent.CLICK, zoomIn);
addChild(zoomInButton);

var zoomOutButton:BitmapButton = new BitmapButton(new
ZoomOutBitmap());
zoomOutButton.x = 800 - 16 - 8;
zoomOutButton.y = 8;
zoomOutButton.addEventListener(MouseEvent.CLICK, zoomOut);
addChild(zoomOutButton);
```

7. All that is left is adding the actual zooming functions. These are deceptively simple:

```
private function zoomIn(event:MouseEvent):void {
    _zoomPanLayer.scaleX += 0.1;
    _zoomPanLayer.scaleY += 0.1;
}

private function zoomOut(event:MouseEvent):void {
    _zoomPanLayer.scaleX -= 0.1;
    _zoomPanLayer.scaleY -= 0.1;
}
```

Run the program and you should be able to zoom in and out by clicking on the buttons.

It's also possible to use the mousewheel to zoom:

1. In the constructor of the `Recipe1` class, start listening for mouse wheel events:

```
_zoomPanLayer.addEventListener(MouseEvent.MOUSE_WHEEL, zoomWheel);
```

2. Use the delta property of the event to calculate the new zoom level:

```
private function zoomWheel(event:MouseEvent):void {
    var direction:int = event.delta > 0 ? 1 : -1;
    _zoomPanLayer.scaleX += direction * 0.1;
    _zoomPanLayer.scaleY += direction * 0.1;
}
```

Run the program again and you should now be able to use the mouse wheel to zoom in and out.

To pan the image, we will let the user drag his mouse: move the mouse while holding the left button down.

1. To capture this action, we need to listen to the mouse up and down events. In the constructor add the following code snippet:

```
_zoomPanLayer.addEventListener(MouseEvent.MOUSE_DOWN, startPan);
_zoomPanLayer.addEventListener(MouseEvent.MOUSE_UP, endPan);
```

2. And now it's only a matter of implementing those methods:

```
private function startPan(event:MouseEvent):void {
    _zoomPanLayer.startDrag();
}

private function endPan(event:MouseEvent):void {
    _zoomPanLayer.stopDrag();
}
```

This will enable the user to pan the image by dragging the mouse.

How it works...

In this recipe, we once again exploited the power of the ActionScript display list. We never touched the actual graph; all zooming and panning was handled by the intermittent layer.

When we added the layer responsible for zooming and panning, you may have noticed we drew a rectangle. This can be used for showing a nice background, but it is also important for the panning function.

If we didn't draw the background, the mouse down and up events would only fire when the mouse was over the actual graph elements, such as the text, axes, and points. So if you'd click between the points, no event would be fired and no panning would occur.

The `BitmapButton` helper class looks superfluous, but it is needed to properly capture click events. A normal bitmap is not an interactive object in ActionScript, so it does not capture mouse and other events. Therefore we wrap it in a sprite, which is an interactive element and can capture mouse clicks.

If you'd like to change the zoom speed, this can be easily achieved by changing the `0.1` value, we add or subtract, from the current scale.

To perform panning, we use ActionScript's built-in support for dragging elements. This is the easiest way to implement generic dragging of elements. In later recipes, we'll see a few other ways of implementing similar actions.

There's more...

Let's look at a few ways to change or improve on what we've done in this recipe.

Cleaning up the code

There are a few parts in the code that you may want to clean up a little if you want to use it in larger projects and/or make it more reusable. For instance, it's probably a good idea to replace many of the variables with constants:

- The size of the screen and the location of the graph (shown in the very first listing of the recipe). If these are extracted into constants, it will be easier to change the size and resolution of your application.

- The scroll speed constant that we used (0.1 in this recipe). It's a good idea to store this in one location, especially if you want to experiment with different speeds, or have the user control the speed.

Using the mousewheel

If you embed the ActionScript program in a website, you may run into issues when using the mouse wheel. There is a workaround using a little piece of JavaScript available at `http://cookbooks.adobe.com/post_Workaround_to_support_mouse_wheel_ for_FireFox_with-13086.html`.

Centering on zoom

When you zoom in and out of the graph, you may have noticed that whatever is at the center of the screen, does not remain in the center. Or in the case of using the mouse wheel, whatever is under the cursor will move away.

This can be solved by adding a slight translation to the graph after zooming. Although the idea is simple, it's an interesting math puzzle to get it right.

This blog post explains the different transformations that are required to get this right: `http://www.gasi.ch/blog/zooming-in-flash-flex/`.

Fix axes

Right now, the axes are part of the graph and will move together with the graph points. It's an interesting, but not straightforward job to fix the axes to the stage and change the scale and labels when moving and zooming. To obtain this effect, you need to draw the axes separate from the graph (so they are not inside the layer) and you will need to manage their look inside the different handlers we wrote.

Sending data updates to the graph

Dynamic graphs can update their display whenever the underlying data changes. For instance, you may interrogate a REST service every minute for stock prices and may want the display to reflect the latest data.

There are many ways you may want to update the graph:

> ▸ Update the entire graph with a new data set
>
> ▸ Add data to the graph and possibly remove the oldest data
>
> ▸ Update random values

This recipe will demonstrate the first problem, since it can be used to solve all three. However, depending on your situation, you may want to add custom manipulation routines to the graph (see the *There's more...* section towards the end of this recipe).

Getting ready

This recipe starts from the following document class:

```
package com.graphing.dataupdate
{
    import flash.display.Sprite;
    import com.graphing.PointGraph;

    public class Recipe2 extends Sprite
    {

        private var _graph:PointGraph;
        private var _data:Array  = [[0,20],[50,70],[100,0],[150,150],[
200,300],[250,200],[300,400],[350,20],[400,60],[450,250],[500,90],[550
,400],[600,500],[650,450],[700,320]];
        private var _data2:Array = [[0,30],[50,80],[100,10],[150,160],
[200,310],[250,210],[300,410],[350,30],[400,70],[450,260],[500,100],[5
50,410],[600,510],[650,460],[700,330]];

        public function Recipe2()
        {
            _graph = new PointGraph();
            _graph.data = _data;
            _graph.graphWidth = 800;
            _graph.graphHeight = 600;
            _graph.graphLeft = -50;
            _graph.graphRight = 750;
```

```
            _graph.graphTop = 550;
            _graph.graphBottom = -50;
            _graph.createGraph();
            addChild(_graph);

            _graph.drawHorizontalAxis(0, 0, 700, 50, ["0", "700"]);
            _graph.drawVerticalAxis(0, 0, 500, 50, ["0", "250",
    "500"]);
        }
    }
}
```

As you can see it is identical to the previous recipes. We have added a second data set, which is what we want to replace the first one with.

How to do it...

First let's add a button that will trigger the update:

1. Embed a bitmap in the `Recipe2` class:

```
[Embed(source = "../../../../lib/badge-circle-direction-right-24-
ns.png")]
private var UpdateButtonBitmap:Class;
```

2. And add it to the stage with a click listener:

```
var button:BitmapButton = new BitmapButton(new
UpdateButtonBitmap());
button.addEventListener(MouseEvent.CLICK, onClick);
addChild(button);
```

3. Finally we need to implement the listener:

```
private function onClick(event:MouseEvent):void {
_graph.updateData(_data2);
}
```

Those are the only changes necessary for the `main` class. The real work will be done in the `PointGraph` class.

1. First we modify the `drawPoint` method so it returns the `point` shape:

```
public function drawPoint(x:Number, y:Number, color:uint =
0xff9933):Shape
{
    var transformedLocation:Point = _matrix.transformPoint(new
Point(x, y));
    var point:Shape = new Shape();
    point.graphics.beginFill( color , 1 );
```

```
point.graphics.drawCircle( 0 , 0 , 3 );
point.x = transformedLocation.x;
point.y = transformedLocation.y;
addChild(point);
return point;
}
```

2. Next we add a private array that will store all the updateable shapes in the graph, as shown in the following code snippet:

```
private var _shapes:Array = [];
```

3. Now we can update the method that draws the points so that it also stores them in the _shapes array:

```
private function drawDataPoints():void {
    for (var i:int = 0; i < _data.length; i++)
    {
        var point:PointGraphPoint = drawPoint(_data[i][0], _
data[i][1]);
        if (_draggable) {
        point.makeDraggable();
        }
        _shapes.push(point);
    }
}
```

This is all the infrastructure we need to create the updateData method that we used in the onClick method:

```
public function updateData(newData:Array):void {
    _data = newData;

    for (var i:int = 0; i < _shapes.length; i++ ) {
        removeChild(_shapes[i]);
    }
    _shapes = [];

    drawDataPoints();
}
```

How it works...

The changes to the main Recipe2 class are only made to trigger the update. They could be replaced with virtually anything. You could add a timer and other events, based on remote data that is received, and so on.

Most of the code changes that we needed to make were related to keeping track of everything that can change. Basically we need access to it when an update needs to be performed.

We choose to use an array because it is an easy datastructure to manipulate, but you could just as well separate the graph elements that are static and those that are dynamic in two separate sprites.

The options are limitless and should be adapted to your specific problem.

There's more...

The following are a few ways in which you may want to change the recipe to suit your specific situation.

Scrolling data

If you have a historical display and you want to add new data. It's probably interesting to implement a push/pop API to the graph so that only the most recent data is shown. The push method adds a new data point, while the pop method removes the oldest one. Or you could combine both in one function.

You may also want to have the time axis update whenever the data is scrolled through so that it shows the correct time.

Random access

Another extension is to have the possibility to update a single point. For instance, if you have a bar chart of different stock prices, you may only want to update the stock for which the price has changed.

In that case, you may want to use an associative array to store the shapes instead of the simple array that was used here. You can also update the updateData function to take two parameters: the x-coordinate (stock name) that changed and the y-coordinate representing the new value.

Undo

For several reasons, you may want to go back to the state before the graph was changed. For instance, you want to have an undo function or you want to look back through the historical data.

In our current recipe, this can be implemented by creating a two dimensional _shapes array and adding a private "revision" variable. Instead of deleting the old data, we simply add one to the revision and add it do the array.

That way, it is possible to rollback to any revision at any time.

Keep in mind that, if you have many updates, you may want to limit the number of revisions you store, to not run out of memory.

Dispatching and listening for events

If updates come from many different sources in your program, you can organize the change/ update infrastructure as an event listener pattern. Your graph listens for a new data-change event that you create. And the various parts dispatch this event.

Creating and dispatching custom events is explained in these blog posts:

```
http://www.learningactionscript3.com/2007/11/20/dispatching-custom-
events/
```

```
http://www.learningactionscript3.com/2008/11/11/passing-arguments-
with-events/
```

```
http://www.adobe.com/devnet/actionscript/articles/event_handling_as3.
html
```

Setting this up will take a little work, but it is a very elegant solution that integrates perfectly with the philosophy of the display list. All objects that are put on the display list already offer many events that one can listen for (keyboard, mouse, and screen changes). Events allow you to program in an asynchronous way, where you don't need to wait for something to happen. Instead, the program will tell you something has happened and execute the relevant code for you. This way of programming will create a responsive user interface that does not freeze when it is waiting for something to happen.

Making the points interactive: Hovering

In this recipe we focus on enriching the data display itself. When the user puts the mouse cursor over one of the points, we want to emphasize that point and show a small popup that displays more information about that point.

For example, we display the exact coordinates, but in a real-life application, you may want to show many other types of information. For instance, in a map display, you can show more information on the location that's beneath the cursor. In a results display, you might only show the average results, but when hovering over a point, you can also show the highest and lowest values.

Getting ready

We will start from the class that we have seen many times before:

```
package com.graphing.hover
{
    import flash.display.Sprite;
    import com.graphing.PointGraph;

    public class Recipe3 extends Sprite
    {
```

```
        private var _graph:PointGraph;
        private var _data:Array = [[0, 20], [50, 70], [100, 0], [150,
150], [200, 300], [250, 200], [300, 400], [350, 20], [400, 60], [450,
250], [500, 90], [550, 400], [600, 500], [650, 450], [700, 320]];

        public function Recipe3()
        {
            _graph = new PointGraph();
            _graph.data = _data;
            _graph.graphWidth = 800;
            _graph.graphHeight = 600;
            _graph.graphLeft = -50;
            _graph.graphRight = 750;
            _graph.graphTop = 550;
            _graph.graphBottom = -50;
            _graph.createGraph();
            addChild(_graph);

            _graph.drawHorizontalAxis(0, 0, 700, 50, ["0", "700"]);
            _graph.drawVerticalAxis(0, 0, 500, 50, ["0", "250",
"500"]);
        }
    }
}
```

How to do it...

First we will restructure the `PointGraph` code a bit, so that it's a little more modular and we can add some of the functionality more easily.

Let's extract the actual point shape into a new class, called `PointGraphPoint` (our first idea was to call this class simply `point` but that would have caused a lot of confusion with ActionScript's built-in `point` class):

1. Start by adding a `PointGraphPoint` class:

```
package com.graphing
{
    import flash.display.Sprite;
    import flash.events.Event;
    import flash.events.MouseEvent;
    import flash.geom.Point;

    public class PointGraphPoint extends Sprite
    {
        public function PointGraphPoint(point:Point, color:uint)
```

```
        {
            graphics.beginFill( color , 1 );
            graphics.drawCircle( 0 , 0 , 5 );
            x = point.x;
            y = point.y;
        }
    }
}
```

2. And now use that code in the `drawPoint` method of the `PointGraph` class:

```
public function drawPoint(x:Number, y:Number, color:uint =
0xff9933):PointGraphPoint
{
    var transformedLocation:Point = _matrix.transformPoint(new
Point(x, y));
    var point:PointGraphPoint = new PointGraphPoint(transformedLoc
ation, color);
    addChild(point);
    return point;
}
```

Now let's add a little zoom animation. When the user hovers the mouse over the point, it should become slightly bigger to emphasize it. This effect can be obtained fairly easily.

1. In the `PointGraphPoint` class's constructor start listening for the mouse over and out events:

```
addEventListener(MouseEvent.MOUSE_OVER, onMouseOver);
addEventListener(MouseEvent.MOUSE_OUT, onMouseOut);
```

2. And the implementation of the event handlers:

```
private function onMouseOver(event:MouseEvent):void {
    scaleX = 1.5;
    scaleY = 1.5;
}

private function onMouseOut(event:MouseEvent):void {
    scaleX = 1;
    scaleY = 1;
}
```

Now let's show a message when the mouse is over a point in the graph. For this recipe, we want to show the coordinates of the point, so the user doesn't have to use the axes to find out.

To display the information, we create a separate class.

3. Create a new class called `HoverInfo` with the following code:

```
package com.graphing.hover
{
    import flash.display.Sprite;
    import flash.text.TextField;

    public class HoverInfo extends Sprite {
        private var _text:TextField;

        public function HoverInfo() {
            _text = new TextField();
            _text.text = "info";
            _text.x = 5;
            _text.y = -20;
            addChild(_text);
        }

        public function set text(value:String):void {
            _text.text = value;
        }
    }

}
```

4. Add the following instance to the `Recipe3` class:

```
private var _hoverInfo:HoverInfo = new HoverInfo();
```

5. To display it when the user hovers over a point, we first add the event listeners in the `Recipe3` constructor:

```
_graph.addEventListener(MouseEvent.MOUSE_OVER, onMouseOver);
_graph.addEventListener(MouseEvent.MOUSE_OUT, onMouseOut);
```

6. And implement those:

```
private function onMouseOver(event:MouseEvent):void {
    if (event.target is PointGraphPoint) {
        addChild(_hoverInfo);
        _hoverInfo.text = event.target.message;
        _hoverInfo.x = event.target.x;
        _hoverInfo.y = event.target.y;
    }
}

private function onMouseOut(event:MouseEvent):void {
    if (_hoverInfo.parent != null) {
        removeChild(_hoverInfo);
    }
}
```

You may have noticed that the actual text we display is taken from `event.target.message`. The `event.target` event is the `PointGraphPoint` class in this case, so we still need to add this field to it:

```
public var message:String;
```

Now it's a matter of filling up the point's message field with the message you'd like to show. In this case, we do this in the `drawPoint` method of the `PointGraph` class:

```
point.message = "(" + x + "," + y + ")";
```

How it works...

In this recipe, we've attached the event listeners in two ways. It's a good idea to know the two options and apply them as you see fit:

- ▶ For emphasis on the points, we attached the listener to a single point. As we've seen, this results in very compact code that's very easy to read, because the code is present right in the `PointGraphPoint` class.

- ▶ To show the message, we used a different approach: A listener is added to the entire graph, so the mouse over event will trigger every time the user hovers over a point or any element of the axes. In the listener method, we distinguished between the specific graph element from which the event came. This works because events are "bubbled" through the `DisplayList` hierarchy. In this case, only two listeners are needed, which can service the entire graph.

The second approach results in a more complicated and potentially a more confusing code. So in general, the first way is preferable, but it's good to know the options.

We also showed a slight performance optimization in how the `HoverInfo` class is used. We only instantiate it once and re-use it when information is displayed. Since the user's mouse pointer can only be over one point, this technique works. If you want to create something similar, where multiple information boxes will be displayed (for instance on a multi-touch display), you will need to adapt the approach.

There's more...

This recipe can be extended in many ways.

Attaching data to points

In the case of this recipe, we decided to attach the message directly to the data point. In many cases, this may not be possible, but you will need at least a way to identify the individual point, otherwise there's no way to know what message to show (unless it's always the same).

In general, you will probably replace the message field by an object that can hold any kind of data. For instance, if you are showing a time based graph, you could put the time in there and show a message based on that. Or you could put a database ID in the field and use it to look up information from the database when the user hovers over the point.

Better display

To keep the recipe simple and concise, little attention was given to the actual display. Given that the `HoverInfo` class is a standalone entity within the display list, you can put anything in there. You may add bitmaps or use the `graphics` class to draw something.

Selecting data points in the graph

In this recipe, we will look at selecting data points in the graph. You can have a system to select one point at a time, or multiple points. In this recipe we will look at the more difficult, latter option.

We'll show how to implement a dragging action, where you drag the mouse, forming a rectangle around the points you want to select. Selecting multiple points can be used in several ways: if you are editing a graph and want to remove or changed multiple points at once or if you want to zoom in on a specific area.

Getting ready

The starting point is exactly the same as the previous recipe. To keep your workspace tidy, copy it into a new `Recipe4` document class.

How to do it...

Implementing a select action involves two steps:

1. Let the user define the area in which we will have to select the items.
2. Calculate which items are in the selection area.

In order to manage everything we'll need a few variables. Add the following fields to the `Recipe4` class:

```
private var _selection:Shape = new Shape();
private var _selectionArea:Shape;
private var _selectionStart:Point;
```

In the constructor we attach the selection area and event listeners:

```
addChild(_selection);
stage.addEventListener(MouseEvent.MOUSE_DOWN, mouseDown);
stage.addEventListener(MouseEvent.MOUSE_UP, mouseUp);
```

The bulk of the work is done inside those listeners:

```
private function mouseDown(event:MouseEvent):void {
    if (_selectionArea != null) {
        removeChild(_selectionArea);
    }
    _selection.graphics.clear();

    _selectionArea = new Shape();
    addChild(_selectionArea);
    _selectionStart = new Point(mouseX, mouseY);
    addEventListener(Event.ENTER_FRAME, enterFrame);
}

private function mouseUp(event:MouseEvent):void {
    for (var i:int = 0; i < _graph.points.length; i++) {
        if (_selectionArea.hitTestObject(_graph.points[i])) {
            addSelection(_graph.points[i]);
        }
    }

    removeChild(_selectionArea);
    removeEventListener(Event.ENTER_FRAME, enterFrame);
    _selectionArea = null;
}
```

The listener attached to the "enter frame" event needs to be implemented:

```
private function enterFrame(event:Event):void {
    var g:Graphics = _selectionArea.graphics;
    g.clear();
    g.lineStyle(1, 0x555555);
    g.moveTo(_selectionStart.x, _selectionStart.y);
    g.lineTo(mouseX, _selectionStart.y);
    g.lineTo(mouseX, mouseY);
    g.lineTo(_selectionStart.x, mouseY);
    g.lineTo(_selectionStart.x, _selectionStart.y);        }
```

And last but not least, we use a small helper method to show which elements were selected:

```
private function addSelection(pgp:PointGraphPoint):void {
    _selection.graphics.beginFill(0x888888, .5);
    _selection.graphics.drawCircle(pgp.x, pgp.y, 7);
    _selection.graphics.endFill();

    trace("Selected " + pgp.message);
}
```

How it works...

To completely understand everything that is happening, it's important to know what the variables we introduced are for:

- ▸ `_selection`: This variable contains the circles we draw to mark that the items are selected. This is an overlay that we use to indicate the selection. It's also the first thing that gets cleared and removed when the selection is cleared.

- ▸ `_selectionArea`: This is the shape that will display the box around the area during the selection process. It is only visible while the user is dragging the mouse.

- ▸ `_selectionStart`: This is the starting point of the selection. We keep this to be able to draw the area.

In this recipe, we use a technique that is commonly used when implementing drag gestures:

- ▸ In the mouse down listener, a new event listener is attached to the "enter frame" event.

- ▸ In the mouse up listener, this event listener is removed.

- ▸ The "enter frame" listener is called every time Flash refreshes the image. This listener is responsible for continuously updating the rectangle that shows the selection the user is making.

In the mouse up listener, we check all the graph points and verify whether or not they lie inside the selection. We use the ActionScript `hitTestObject` method for this, but we could just as well have compared the coordinates of both objects (although the code would have been a bit longer).

The `addSelection` function shown here is just an example of what you can do with the selection. In this case, it just draws a gray transparent circle over the points to show the selection. And it prints the message associated with that data point.

There's more...

Depending on how you are going to use the selection, you may want to consider a few alternatives and extensions.

Selection by clicking

If you only want to select individual points, it's a lot easier to just use the mouse click listener. There's no need for the mouse down or mouse up code that was shown here.

Drawing selected items

In the previous recipe, the highlight to indicate the selection is drawn on top of the image, completely separate from the points in the chart. This has the advantage of being the most flexible solution.

However, if you have different shapes of points you may run into a few issues. A possibility is to extend the `PointGraphPoint` class and add a `setSelected` method that controls how the point is drawn when selected.

Adding to and removing from a selection

Many applications that allow for selecting multiple items, also allow you to add and remove items from the selection by pressing *Ctrl* or *Shift* while making a selection.

Implementing this can be done fairly and easily by using the `controlKey` and `shiftKey` properties of the mouse event. You can check these properties in the mouse up or down listeners and change your actions accordingly.

A dynamic graph based on an editable table

In this chapter, we are going to combine a few of the previous recipes and make a graph editable by showing a table to the user in which he can change the values at will.

We'll use the infrastructure that was created in the *Sending data updates to the graph* recipe in this chapter, to send new data to the graph.

Getting ready

This recipe starts from virtually the same class, only now we've freed up some screen space underneath the graph where we will put the editable table:

```
package com.graphing.dynamictable
{
    import flash.display.Sprite;
    import com.graphing.PointGraph;
```

```
public class Recipe5 extends Sprite
{
    private var _graph:PointGraph;
    private var _data:Array = [[0, 20], [50, 70], [100, 0], [150,
150], [200, 300], [250, 200], [300, 400], [350, 20], [400, 60], [450,
250], [500, 90], [550, 400], [600, 500], [650, 450], [700, 320]];

    public function Recipe5()
    {
        _graph = new PointGraph();
        _graph.data = _data;
        _graph.graphWidth = 800;
        _graph.graphHeight = 480;
        _graph.graphLeft = -50;
        _graph.graphRight = 750;
        _graph.graphTop = 550;
        _graph.graphBottom = -50;
        _graph.createGraph();
        addChild(_graph);

        _graph.drawHorizontalAxis(0, 0, 700, 50, ["0", "700"]);
        _graph.drawVerticalAxis(0, 0, 500, 40, ["0", "250",
"500"]);
    }
}
}
```

How to do it...

To keep things tidy, we're going to put all code related to a new class called `EditTable`.
Let's first add it to the display:

1. Add a private property that will hold the display:

   ```
   private var _edit:EditTable;
   ```

2. And initialize it in the constructor:

   ```
   _edit = new EditTable(_data, _graph);
   _edit.y = 500;
   _edit.x = 25;
   addChild(_edit);
   ```

3. Now create a new class called `EditTable` and have it implement `Sprite`.
   We will also store the references to the data and graph in private fields so we
   can use them later:

   ```
   package com.graphing.dynamictable {
       import com.graphing.PointGraph;
   ```

```
import flash.display.Sprite;
import flash.events.Event;
import flash.text.TextField;
import flash.text.TextFieldAutoSize;
public class EditTable extends Sprite {
    private var _data:Array;
    private var _graph:PointGraph;

    public function EditTable(data:Array, graph:PointGraph) {
        _data = data;
        _graph = graph;
    }
}
}
```

4. Now we add the display of the values in a grid underneath the graph. In the `EditTable` constructor add this loop:

```
for (var i:int = 0; i < data.length; i++)
{
    var tf:TextField = new TextField();
    tf.text = data[i][1];
    tf.width = 48;
    tf.height = 20;
    tf.border = true;
    tf.type = "input";
    tf.x = i * 50;
    tf.addEventListener(Event.CHANGE, onChange);
    addChild(tf);
}
```

5. You may have noticed that we added a change listener. So we need to implement it:

```
private function onChange(event:Event):void {
    var field:TextField = event.target as TextField;
    var index:int       = getChildIndex(field);
    var value:Number    = Number(field.text);

    _data[index] = [index * 50, value];

    _graph.updateData(_data);
}
```

Run the program and you should see a grid that you can change at will. The changes will be reflected as you type in the graph.

How it works...

The recipe's main functionality is split into two parts: drawing the editable table and executing the updates.

The table is drawn in the constructor and uses `TextField` objects. To keep the code compact we use mostly standard fields, but all the customizations that we've seen can be done here too.

Setting the field's type to `input` will turn it into a field that can be edited. In the case of editable fields, it's usually a good idea to show the border. When the user deletes all the data in the field, the field would no longer be visible without a border.

The change listener is fired every time the text inside the field changes.

The listener finds the position of the field in the display list. This position is the same as the position of the data point in the data set. This is because we used a `for` loop in the constructor to go from one point to the next. If you use other techniques to draw the table or add more elements, keep that in mind.

Finally we cast the input to a number, update the data set, and send it to the graph. You may want to do some data validation here in a real program.

There's more...

We've just described the basic components of an interactive graph. There are of course many things that you'll want to customize.

Data validation

Though mentioned at the end of the previous section, data validation should not be underestimated. It is very valuable for a user to get feedback on why something isn't working.

So you may want to change the border of the field to red and add some popup text when a user enters invalid data.

Zoom/pan on entry

In the recipe, if you enter data that is outside of the current view, you won't be able to see it. You can add the zooming and panning code from the *Zooming and panning around the graph* recipe. You can also automatically recalculate the zoom level based on the user's input data so everything is visible at all times.

Dragging data points to new values

In this chapter, we'll use a few ideas from the previous recipes to make that actual graph data draggable. When the recipe is implemented, the user can click-and-drag data points to new locations.

Getting ready

We will start from the familiar point graph:

```
package com.graphing.drag
{
    import flash.display.Sprite;
    import com.graphing.PointGraph;

    public class Recipe6 extends Sprite
    {
        private var _graph:PointGraph;
        private var _data:Array = [[0,20],[50,70],[100,0],[150,150],[2
00,300],[250,200],[300,400],[350,20],[400,60],[450,250],[500,90],[550,
400],[600,500],[650,450],[700,320]];

        public function Recipe6()
        {
            _graph = new PointGraph();
            _graph.data = _data;
            _graph.graphWidth = 800;
            _graph.graphHeight = 600;
            _graph.graphLeft = -50;
            _graph.graphRight = 750;
            _graph.graphTop = 550;
            _graph.graphBottom = -50;
            _graph.createGraph();
            addChild(_graph);

            _graph.drawHorizontalAxis(0, 0, 700, 50, ["0", "700"]);
            _graph.drawVerticalAxis(0, 0, 500, 50, ["0", "250",
"500"]);
        }
    }
}
```

How to do it...

Since we want to drag individual points, we will add all the functionality in the `PointGraphPoint` class. However, we want to enable and disable this functionality from within our main program.

1. In the `Recipe6` constructor, just before the `createGraph` call, enable dragging:

   ```
   _graph.draggable = true;
   ```

2. Now in the `PointGraph` class, we need to add the following property:

   ```
   private var _draggable:Boolean = false;
   public function set draggable(value:Boolean):void {
       _draggable = value;
   }
   ```

3. And finally, we need to forward this setting to the actual points. This happens in the `drawDataPoints` method.

   ```
   private function drawDataPoints():void {
       for (var i:int = 0; i < _data.length; i++)
       {
           var point:PointGraphPoint = drawPoint(_data[i][0], _
   data[i][1]);
           if (_draggable) {
               point.makeDraggable();
           }
           _shapes.push(point);
       }
   }
   ```

Now that we've made sure we can control the behavior from the main application, it's time to actually implement the dragging methods. In `PointGraphPoint` add the following:

```
public function makeDraggable():void {
    addEventListener(MouseEvent.MOUSE_DOWN, mouseDown);
}

private function mouseDown(event:MouseEvent):void {
    stage.addEventListener(MouseEvent.MOUSE_UP, mouseUp);
    stage.addEventListener(Event.ENTER_FRAME, enterFrame);
}

private function mouseUp(event:MouseEvent):void {
    stage.removeEventListener(Event.ENTER_FRAME, enterFrame);
    stage.removeEventListener(MouseEvent.MOUSE_UP, mouseUp);
}
```

```
private function enterFrame(event:Event):void {
    y = stage.mouseY;
}
```

That's all there is to it. If you re-run the program and click-and-drag on a point, you will be able to move it up and down.

How it works...

As we've seen in the recipe on selecting data, the dragging gesture contains the following three steps:

1. Start dragging when the mouse button is pressed on the point. At this point, we attach the two event listeners for the next two stages.

2. Draw updates during the dragging motion. Implemented by the `enterframe` listener, this gets called every time Flash refreshes the screen. In this recipe, we have limited the motion of the point to the y-axis. The point can only be moved up or down. If you like, you can enable motion in both directions.

3. End the dragging when the mouse button is released. All event listeners are removed and here you can process the new value (not shown in this recipe).

There's more...

There are quite a few things you can do to extend this recipe and make it even more useful.

Processing the new location

To keep the recipe short, we haven't done anything with the new value, after the dragging is completed. To do this, you need to program a flow of information from the point through the graph and back to the main program.

One extension you will certainly want to add is updating the `_data` array in the `PointGraph` class. If you don't, it contains different information than what is drawn on the screen. To do this, you can use events and listeners, or you can use the `parent` property of the point to obtain a reference to the graph.

Once you got hold of the parent you can call an update location method that updates the data set. Don't forget that you need to convert the point's coordinates back to graph coordinates, but this can be done with the matrix.

More freedom

In the `enterFrame` method, you can restrict the motion to whatever you like. Or not restrict it at all. For instance, you can make sure the dragging remains inside the graph bounds.

Adding and removing points

Another typical manipulation of the graph could be adding and removing data points. You can add buttons to create and remove points, or you could add a context menu. Both can work equally well.

Linking graphs

If zooming and panning is not enough to give a clear insight into the data, another option is to link graphs. When a user selects a data point he wants to inspect, a new graph opens, giving a detailed look at the information.

This recipe will work with two datasets and show the basics of interacting in graphs. You can adapt this to suit your specific situation.

Getting ready

This recipe will start, once again, from the initial graph. Although the end result is the same, we have restructured the code a little to help us keep everything organized when we start adding the recipe's code. We've also added a second graph and dataset that will represent our *zoomed in* data.

```
package com.graphing.link
{
    import com.graphing.PointGraphPoint;
    import flash.display.Sprite;
    import com.graphing.PointGraph;
    import flash.events.MouseEvent;

    public class Recipe7 extends Sprite
    {
        private var _graph:PointGraph;
        private var _data:Array = [[0, 20], [50, 70], [100, 0], [150,
150], [200, 300], [250, 200], [300, 400], [350, 20], [400, 60], [450,
250], [500, 90], [550, 400], [600, 500], [650, 450], [700, 320]];

        private var _graph2:PointGraph;
        private var _data2:Array = [[0,30],[50,80],[100,10],[150,160],
[200,310],[250,210],[300,410],[350,30],[400,70],[450,260],[500,100],[5
50,410],[600,510],[650,460],[700,330]];

        public function Recipe7()
        {
            initGraph();
```

```
        addChild(_graph);
    }

    private function initGraph():void {
        _graph = new PointGraph();
        _graph.data = _data;
        _graph.graphWidth = 800;
        _graph.graphHeight = 600;
        _graph.graphLeft = -50;
        _graph.graphRight = 750;
        _graph.graphTop = 550;
        _graph.graphBottom = -50;
        _graph.createGraph();

        _graph.drawHorizontalAxis(0, 0, 700, 50, ["0", "700"]);
        _graph.drawVerticalAxis(0, 0, 500, 50, ["0", "250",
"500"]);
    }
  }

}
```

How to do it...

We first create the graph that will be shown when the user clicks on a point:

1. Add a function inside the `Recipe7` class that creates the second graph, half the size of the original one, positioned in the middle of the screen.

```
private function initGraph2():void {
    _graph2 = new PointGraph();
    _graph2.data = _data2;
    _graph2.graphWidth = 400;
    _graph2.graphHeight = 300;
    _graph2.graphLeft = -50;
    _graph2.graphRight = 750;
    _graph2.graphTop = 550;
    _graph2.graphBottom = -50;
    _graph2.createGraph();

    _graph2.x = 200;
    _graph2.y = 150;

    _graph2.drawHorizontalAxis(0, 0, 700, 50, ["0", "700"]);
    _graph2.drawVerticalAxis(0, 0, 500, 50, ["0", "250", "500"]);
}
```

2. In the `Recipe7` constructor, call this method so the second graph is initialized correctly. Add the following line underneath `initGraph()`:

```
initGraph2();
```

The next step is actually showing the graph when the user clicks on a data point.

3. In the constructor, start listening for clicks.

```
_graph.addEventListener(MouseEvent.CLICK, onClickDetail);
```

4. In the click listener, show the second graph and hide the first one:

```
private function onClickDetail(event:MouseEvent):void {
    if (event.target is PointGraphPoint) {
        _graph.alpha = .2;
        addChild(_graph2);
        event.stopPropagation();
        stage.addEventListener(MouseEvent.CLICK,
onClickHideDetail);
    }
}
```

5. And finally we need to hide the second graph and display the first one again when the user clicks another time.

```
private function onClickHideDetail(event:MouseEvent):void {
    stage.removeEventListener(MouseEvent.CLICK,
onClickHideDetail);
    _graph.alpha = 1;
    removeChild(_graph2);
}
```

If you run the program now and click on any data point, it will fade out the original graph and show a half-size second graph in the middle of the screen. If you click anywhere, the second graph will hide.

How it works...

This recipe is a combination of all the techniques we've seen in this chapter.

First we use the properties of the `graph` object to create one in the middle of the screen and only half the size of the original one. Obviously, you can create any graph you like inside the `initGraph2` method. You can even add a parameter and make it dependent upon the point selected. Although in that case you may need to run the method inside the click listener, so it generates the correct graph each time (see the *There's more...* section for more details on this extension).

Notice that we don't add the second graph to the stage, so it will remain invisible. When the user clicks on the first graph, we filter out only the clicks on actual points.

To show the second graph, we simply fade out the first one by adjusting the alpha value and attaching the second graph to the stage. Since we add it after the first graph, it will show up on top of it.

Calling the event's `stopPropagation` method will make sure that the event is not sent to other event handlers. In this case, if we didn't stop the propagation of the event, it would also fire the new click handler we attached to hide the second graph. Try to comment out this line and see what happens.

Hiding the second graph is almost the reverse of showing it. We remove the `hide` handler, remove the second graph from the stage, and change back the alpha value of the first graph.

There's more...

Now let's talk about some other options, or possibly some pieces of general information that are relevant to this task.

Multiple data sets

In a real example, you will probably want to show a different data set depending on what point the user clicked on. This can be achieved by analyzing the `event.target` event in the `onClickDetail` method.

The `event.target` event can be cast to a `PointGraphPoint` class. This can be used to obtain data on the selected point, which in turn can be used to select the correct data set, or even the correct graph, if you want to show completely different graph types.

Animation

*Chapter 7, Animating a Graph,*will give you some techniques to animate your graphs. This can be used to create a smooth transition between the two graphs. For instance, you could fade in the new graph while fading out the old one. Or you can create a zooming animation to give the impression of zooming into the selected data.

6

Mapping Geographical and Spatial Data

In this chapter we will cover:

- ▶ Showing a map using the openscales.org API
- ▶ Adding points of interest to a map
- ▶ Parsing data to use as region fill
- ▶ Coloring a map
- ▶ Adding multiple layers to a map
- ▶ Overlaying a heat map

Introduction

This chapter will show how to bring data and maps together to derive further meaning. We will start with simple recipes just showing a map and points of interest, and end up generating heat maps. All the maps will use the **OpenScales** API, sometimes in a dynamic manner where you can move and explore the map, and sometimes in a more static way to show just one area.

Showing a map using the openscales.org API

This recipe will show how to display a map using the API found at
`http://www.openscales.org`.

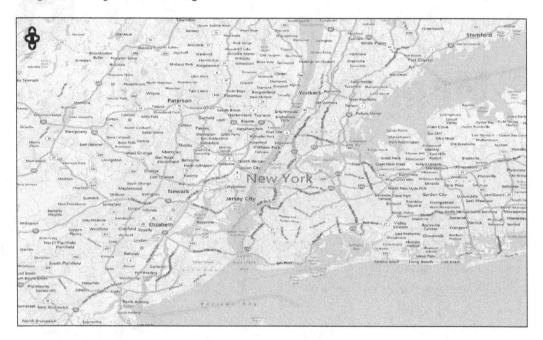

Getting ready

Download the latest library code for OpenScales from their website. It is better to download it directly from their repository: `https://bitbucket.org/gis/openscales/downloads`, as the download link on their homepage isn't always up-to-date.

How to do it...

The following are the steps needed to show an OpenScales map:

1. Instantiate the map:

```
_map = new Map();
_map.size = new Size(1200, 700);
//this is the area in pixel that will be shown on the screen

_map.center = new Location(-73.98,40.77, "EPSG:4326");
//these are longitudes and latitudes coordinates
```

```
_map.resolution = new Resolution(100, "EPSG:900913");
_map.maxResolution = new Resolution(10000, "EPSG:900913");
_map.minResolution = new Resolution(2, "EPSG:900913");
```

2. Create the layers that will be inside this map:

```
var mapnik:Mapnik=new Mapnik("Mapnik");
//_map.addLayer(mapnik);

var bing:Bing = new Bing("Ar3-LKk-acyISMevsF2bqH70h21mzr_
FN9AhHfi7pS26F5hMH1DmpI7PBK1VCLBk");
_map.addLayer(bing);

bing = new Bing("Ar3-LKk-acyISMevsF2bqH70h21mzr_FN9AhHfi7pS26F5hMH
1DmpI7PBK1VCLBk","Aerial");
//_map.addLayer(bing);
```

3. Add some controls to interact with the map:

```
_map.addControl(new WheelHandler());
_map.addControl(new DragHandler());
_map.addControl(new Pan(new Pixel(10,10)));
```

4. Add the map to the stage:

```
addChild(_map);
```

How it works...

For this recipe and all recipes using 2D maps, we decided to use OpenScales, available at http://www.openscales.org. Google Maps are probably the most used online maps but they decided to deprecate their ActionScript 3 API. **OpenScales** is an abstraction over multiple online mapping solutions such as *OpenStreetMap* and *Bing*, and we thought that this would be a sturdy API to use.

As we said, OpenScale abstracts the map concept to apply it to any solution. If you look at the first step, we create a Map instance, but if you only do this, nothing will show up when you compile. The Map class is only a holder for visual layers that can be real maps (from other services such as Bing) or markers and indications.

After we created the Map class, we can start setting its properties. Setting the size is pretty straightforward, but setting the center of the map and the zoom level can be trickier. You can see, in the code for both those properties, a strange String value that starts with EPSG. This string tells the API what kind of unit you are using (well it is a bit more complicated than this; it actually indicates what projection you are using, but that is outside the scope of this book). The EPSG code 4326 indicates that you are using degrees and seconds for your longitude and latitudes while the code 900913 (notice how the numbers seems to spell the name of its creator, that is, GOOGLE) uses meters as unit.

To set the zoom level, use the `resolution` property as shown in the code. We use the `minResolution` and `maxResolution` methods to restrict how the user will be able to zoom.

In step 2, we added layers to our map. In the code you can see that we created three layers but that we are using just one. This was done to show you that we can use multiple maps. In this instance we use OpenStreetMap (`Mapnik` in the code) and two variations of the Bing map. You can uncomment the lines where we add the other layers to see what they look like. As a side note if you are going to use Bing maps, you should get your own API key; the following page instructs you how to do it: `http://msdn.microsoft.com/en-us/library/ff428642.aspx`.

Lastly, in step 3 we add the controls to let the user interact with the map. You don't have to do this; you could just zoom to the correct resolution and not allow the user to change the map. That way you can make sure he always sees what you want to show. In the case of our example, we let the user drag the map, use the mouse wheel to zoom in and out, and add arrows to let him pan.

There's more...

The OpenScales API offers many options such as creating your own controls and using different maps.

Custom controls

The OpenScale library comes with some basic controls implemented for panning and zooming, but they are somewhat simple and probably not styled with the proper branding. You could easily create your own controls that could animate or control the map exactly as you want it. To do so just create your own classes for those controls and use the `Map` class API to modify the map.

Using different maps

This recipe show how to use three different maps: OpenStreetMap, Bing road, and Bing Aerial. OpenScales APIs have many more maps. The following is the code to use a map from NASA:

```
var nasa:WMSC = new WMSC("Nasa", "http://openscales.org/geoserver/
ows", layers = "bluemarble")
```

Go and explore the OpenScales API to find many more.

Adding points of interest to a map

In this recipe, we will be showing points of interest on an OpenScales map. More precisely this example will display geocaches (these are containers hidden at specific locations that you search for using a GPS for a treasure hunt) in the Lower East Side in New York City. If you want to know more about geocaching, go to `http://www.geocaching.com`.

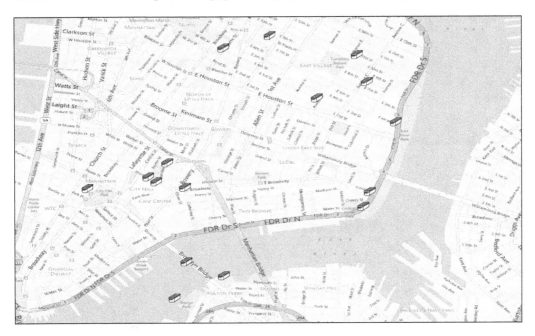

Getting ready

Having read the previous recipe about displaying a map using OpenScales' map will be useful, otherwise you can just follow along with the code provided for this recipe.

How to do it...

Follow these steps to add points of interest on a map:

1. Create a `Coordinate` class to hold the data, as shown in the following code snippet:

```
public var northSouthEastWest:String;
public var degrees:Number;
public var minutes:Number;
public function Coordinate(newNorthSouthEastWest:String,
newDegrees:Number, newMinutes:Number) {
  northSouthEastWest = newNorthSouthEastWest;
  degrees = newDegrees;
  minutes = newMinutes;
}
```

2. Create a function to convert degrees-minutes-seconds coordinate to decimal degrees:

```
public function DegreeMinuteToDegreeDecimal(direction:String,
degrees:Number, minutes:Number):Number {
  var multiplier:Number;

  switch (direction.toLowerCase()) {
    case "n":
      multiplier = 1;
      break;
    case "s":
      multiplier = -1;
      break;
    case "e":
      multiplier = 1;
      break;
    case "w":
      multiplier = -1;
      break;
    default:
  }
  return multiplier * (degrees + minutes / 60);
}
```

3. Add the `LongLat` class to hold a longitude and a latitude value.

4. Start generating the data. The following is just one `LongLat` created:

```
var data:Vector.<LongLat> = new Vector.<LongLat>();

data.push(new LongLat(new Coordinate("W", 73, 59.789), new
Coordinate("N", 40, 42.800)));
```

5. Create the OpenScale map as explained in the previous recipe.

6. Add the points of interest by creating a layer to hold them:

```
var markerLayer:VectorLayer = new VectorLayer("Markers");
_map.addLayer(markerLayer);
```

7. Create the `_createMarker` function to facilitate the addition of markers:

```
private function _createMarker(location:Location):CustomMarker {
   var geoMarker:Bitmap = new GeoMarker() as Bitmap;
   var customMarker:CustomMarker = CustomMarker.createDisplayObject
Marker(geoMarker, location, null, -15, -10);
   return (customMarker);
}
```

8. Put the data on the map by looping through it:

```
for (var i:int = 0; i < data.length; i++) {
   markerLayer.addFeature(_createMarker(new Location(data[i].
longitude.getDD(),data[i].latitude.getDD(),"EPSG:4326")));
}
```

How it works...

We are going to display points of interest on a map so we will first need to create classes to hold those coordinates. We will need two classes for this; one will hold a single coordinate, while the second will hold a longitude and latitude.

As it is easier to give decimal degrees to the OpenScales API, we created in step 2 a function to convert degrees minutes coordinate to it. As for generating the data (for step 4), we went to `http://www.geocaching.com` and searched for goecaches around the Lower East Side area in New York City.

In step 5 we create a simple map. This example doesn't need any controls, since we don't want the user to move the map around and lose the area where the markers are at.

The next step is adding the points of interest. We will do so by adding a marker at each coordinate. We didn't want to use the default style for the marker so we used the `CustomMarker` class to give it a style related to geocaching.

Now, `CustomMarkers` and `Markers` extends `Feature` and to display a feature in OpenScale, you need to add them to `VectorLayer`, which you can in turn add to the map. So step 6 creates that `VectorLayer` and we add it to the map exactly the same way you would add a `Mapnik` or a `Bing` layer.

Now all there is left to do is to loop over the data, create our markers, and add them to `VectorLayer`. When you compile, you'll get a map of New York with geocaches indicated on it.

There's more...

In this recipe we used the marker in a really simple manner, but there is way more you can do with them.

Changing the marker

In the sample code we embedded a PNG image (`Bitmap`) to be used as our marker but the `createDisplayObjectMarker` method takes `DisplayObject` as input. This means that you could also use a `Sprite` class or a `MovieClip` class as a marker, opening the way for animated markers.

A URL for image

So we used an image and we could use any `DisplayObject`, but what is really good is that you can also use a URL to load an image. This opens the door for multiple things, one of them being using the Google Chart API to generate an image or even using the service available at `http://www.googlemapsmarkers.com/` to generate custom Google Maps markers. The following code snippet shows how you would use it:

```
var customMarker:CustomMarker = CustomMarker.
createUrlBasedMarker("http://www.googlemapsmarkers.com/v1/009900/",
location, null, -15, -10);
```

Making the marker interactive

The `CustomMarker` and `Marker` classes ultimately extend the `Sprite` class. It is really to add interaction to a `Sprite` class, so it is the same for markers. Just listen to the mouse events and you can use the listener functions to add labels on rollovers or animations.

Parsing data to use as region fill

This recipe is going to be about finding and parsing data that describes regions that we might want to plot on a map. Such regions might be countries, states, provinces, and so on. The Natural Earth website at `http://www.naturalearthdata.com/`, offers geographical data about multiple subject, one of them are political geographical regions. We are going to use that data on our OpenScales map.

Getting ready

Having read the previous recipes about using OpenScales will greatly help. Also open the files downloaded from the Packt Publishing website to follow along.

How to do it...

The following are the steps required to parse data to use as region fill:

1. Head over to `https://www.google.com/fusiontables/DataSource?dsrcid=424517`.

2. Copy the column called `json_4326`; this is the data that we are going to use as source.

3. Create a class called `PolygonParser.as` that will get a JSON `String` value and return a `Polygon Vector` value.

4. Transform the JSON `String` value into an ActionScript object.

5. Loop through the data in that object to create OpenScales usable classes:

```
if (polygonObject.type == "Polygon") {
  polygonVector = new Vector.<Polygon>();
  pointVector = pointVector = new Vector.<Number>();
  for (i = 0; i < polygonObject.coordinates[0].length; i++) {
    pointVector.push(polygonObject.coordinates[0][i][0]);
    pointVector.push(polygonObject.coordinates[0][i][1]);
  }

  linearRing = new LinearRing(pointVector);
  ringVector = new Vector.<Geometry>();
  ringVector.push(linearRing);
  polygon = new Polygon(ringVector);
  polygonVector.push(polygon);

  return polygonVector;
}
```

How it works...

As we mentioned earlier, we are going to use Natural Earth's data to create a region on a map. Natural Earth offers tons of data (here is a humongous list: `https://www.google.com/fusiontables/DataSource?dsrcid=394713` compiled by `thematicmapping.org`) but we are interested in this particular spreadsheet (`https://www.google.com/fusiontables/DataSource?dsrcid=424517`) as it contains the boundaries for states in the US and Canada's provinces.

In that spreadsheet, the column `json_4236` is the one that will be useful to us. As of Flash 11.1, there is now a native API to decode JSON with super fast speed and that is what we are going to use in this case (that means that this project output a SWF that can only be player using version 11.1 of the Flash player). There is just a little problem with that: the OpenScales API uses an external library to decode JSON and that library named its class the same way as the native JSON decoder so they conflict with each other. To solve this, when the compiler is giving you errors about JSON, just paste `com.adobe.serialization.json` in front of `JSON.decode`; this will make sure it uses the library code in the OpenScales files.

Decoding the JSON is really easy; you do it in one line and it will return an object that is easily usable in ActionScript:

```
var polygonObject:Object = JSON.parse(json);
```

Now that is done, we can go over the data and create regions out of it. The goal here is to return a `Vector` object of `Polygons`. `Polygons` are complicated objects; they are made of `LinearRings`. `LinearRings` are basically multiple lines where the first one begins at the place where the last one ends; a closed cycle, an area that can be filled.

`Polygons` can use multiple `LinearRings`; the first one will define the other boundaries while the other ones will define holes in the first `LinearRing`. For this example, we are going to create `Polygons` that have no holes in them, so just one `LinearRing`. Note that these geometry concepts are used in mapping applications in general and not just in OpenScales.

In order to create a `Polygon`, we must first create a `LinearRing`. To do so we need to provide the constructor of its class a vector of `Number` values that represents all the points that the `LinearRing` will go through. The thing to notice here is that `LinearRing` doesn't take the coordinates as a `Number` pair (*x* and *y*), but just a succession of single `Number` values. It assumes that the first one is a *x* value, the second a *y* value, the third a *x* value, the fourth a *y* value, and so on. Since the JSON gives us the coordinates as `Number` pairs, we must parse it to transform it into a vector of `Number`.

The last thing to see here is that the JSON comes with the possibility that the type property be one of two values: `Polygon` or `MultiPolygon`. This will influence the way the coordinates Array is constructed. The code shown in step 5 has an `if` statement to use the proper parsing based on the type property.

Once we have our vector of `Number` values we can create all our geometry as shown in the last part of the code from step 5.

There's more...

Our parsing isn't really foolproof, and we could make it better.

Checking for errors

We parsed the JSON in a simple manner so that it would be easy to explain and it works for the provinces of Canada, but it might not work for every region provided by the Natural Earth data. By assuming less about the structure of the coordinates array we could make this more foolproof.

▸ The *Coloring a map* recipe

Coloring a map

In this recipe we will show how to fill different regions of a map with different colors. We will use the `PolygonParser` class from the previous recipe in order to get the geographical boundaries of the Canadian provinces and we are going to combine it with the crime severity index data from Statistics Canada available at `http://www.statcan.gc.ca/pub/85-004-x/2009001/t009-eng.htm`. Provinces with a darker gray (more red color in the code), will have higher crime severity index while provinces that are of a lighter gray color (more yellow in the code) will have lower crime severity index. This is illustrated in the following screenshot:

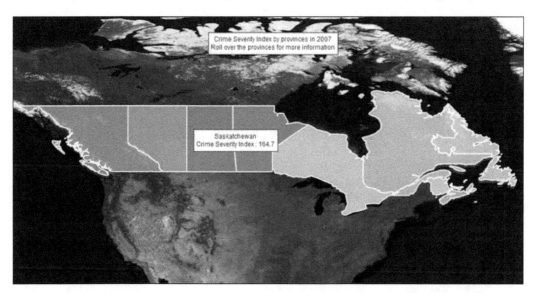

Getting ready

This recipe greatly relies on the *Parsing data to use as region fill* recipe; we suggest you read it before continuing.

How to do it...

The following steps show you how to color a map:

1. Create the `CrimeData` class that has a name, a crime severity index, and a boundaries property.

2. Combine the regional data from the Natural Earth (`https://www.google.com/fusiontables/DataSource?dsrcid=424517`) and the crime data from Statistics Canada (`http://www.statcan.gc.ca/pub/85-004-x/2009001/t009-eng.htm`) to generate our data. One entry will look like the following listing:

```
data.push(new CrimeData("Prince Edward Island", 62.8,
'{"type":"Polygon","coordinates":[[[-63.811,46.469],
[-63.784,46.455],[-63.737,46.48],[-63.681,46.562],
[-63.534,46.541],[-63.456,46.504],[-63.413,46.512],
[-63.369,46.508],[-63.286,46.46],[-63.129,46.422],
[-62.964,46.428],[-62.712,46.45],[-62.682,46.459],
[-62.423,46.478],[-62.164,46.487],[-62.074,46.466],
[-62.041,46.446],[-62.024,46.422],[-62.172,46.355],
[-62.32,46.278],[-62.526,46.203],[-62.552,46.166],
[-62.539,46.098],[-62.543,46.029],[-62.503,46.023]...)));
```

3. Create the map that we will show the data on:

```
_map = new Map();
_map.size = new Size(1000, 500);

_map.center = new Location(-95.11, 52.57, "EPSG:4326");
_map.resolution = new Resolution(10000, "EPSG:900913");

var bing:Bing = new Bing("Ar3-LKk-acyISMevsF2bqH70h21mzr_FN9AhHfi7
pS26F5hMH1DmpI7PBK1VCLBk","Aerial");
_map.addLayer(bing);
```

4. Loop over the data and find the minimum and maximum value of the crime severity index.

5. With those values in hand, compute a `scaleRatio` value that will be used to determine the color of a region.

6. Loop over the data once again to create all the regions and add their color:

```
for (i = 0; i < data.length; i++) {
  polygonVector = PolygonParser.parseData(data[i].boundaries);
  for (j = 0; j < polygonVector.length; j++) {
    polygonFeature = new PolygonFeature(polygonVector[j]);
    rule = new Rule();

    green =  240 - Math.round((data[i].crimeSeverityIndex -
minValue) * scalingFactor);
    color = (red << 16) | (green << 8) | blue;
    fill = new SolidFill(color, .8);
    stroke = new Stroke(0xffffff, 2);
    symbolizer = new PolygonSymbolizer(fill, stroke);
    rule.symbolizers.push(symbolizer);
    style = new Style();
    style.rules.push(rule);
    polygonFeature.style = style;
    polygonFeature.addEventListener(MouseEvent.ROLL_OVER, _
onFeatureOver);
    _polygonVector.push(polygonFeature);
    _crimeDataVector.push(data[i]);
    regionLayer.addFeature(polygonFeature);
  }
}
```

7. Create the class `HoveringLabel.as`, so that when a user rolls over a region we can display information about it.

8. Add `TitleSprite`, to indicate what our map is about.

9. Add a listener over the regions so that we can move the hovering label to the right place when the user rolls over a province. Here is the listener function:

```
private function _onFeatureOver(event:MouseEvent):void {
  _hoveringLabel.x = mouseX - 75;
  _hoveringLabel.y = mouseY;
  _hoveringLabel.changeText(
_crimeDataVector[_polygonVector.indexOf(event.target)].
name, _crimeDataVector[_polygonVector.indexOf(event.target)].
crimeSeverityIndex);
}
```

How it works...

A big part of the work was done in the previous recipe and we will re-use the `PolygonParser` class to get the boundaries of every province in Canada. The parsing process returns a `Polygon` instance, but in order to use it, we need to encapsulate it inside a `PolygonFeature` class so that we can add it to the `VectorLayer` class.

Let's take this moment to look in how many classes our data is encapsulated in. First we put it in a `LinearRing` class, then a `Polygon` class, then a `PolygonFeature` class, then a `VectorLayer` class, and finally into a `Map` class. It's quite a long process, but it is not that difficult once you know it.

Now we need to calculate our `scalingFactor` value. To do so we need to find our minimum and maximum crime severity index . Here is how we do it:

```
var scalingFactor:Number = 240 / (maxValue - minValue);
```

The `240` value is the range over which our color will change. With the scaling factor in hand, we can loop over the data and generate the visual for each province.

What we are going to do to get the color for each region is this: we start with the color yellow, which is no blue, maximum red (255 over 255), and a lot of green (240 over 255). Depending on whether the crime severity index is high or not, we are going to remove a lot of or a little green from our starting yellow, making our color more red (since there is no blue, removing green only leaves red). Using the `scalingFactor` variable, we can calculate how much green we remove.

```
green = 240 - Math.round((data[i].crimeSeverityIndex - minValue) *
scalingFactor);
```

Now that we computed our color, we need to assign it to the `PolygonFeature` class. This process is a bit tedious too; simple but tedious. Most of the code in step 6 is about assigning the color to the `PolygonFeature` class. We need to create instances of `SolidFill`, `Stroke`, `PolygonSymbolizer`, `Rule`, and `Style` just to assign a color to a region, but once it is done it looks really great.

There's more...

Now that we showed how to display data over regions you can modify our code to suit your needs.

Using different countries

The data from Natural Earth comprises the boundaries for all the regions of the Earth. Be it the regions of France or the prefectures of Japan, you can find the boundaries in the Natural Earth spreadsheets, available at `https://www.google.com/fusiontables/DataSource?dsrcid=394713`. Now all you need is data to be represented on a map.

Using another color range

For this recipe we used a color range of yellow going to red but you could use any color range just by using the technique we used but by modifying another color instead of the green.

What you could also do, is create the same region twice, the bottom one being white and the second one being a color of your choice. By modifying the alpha of the colored region, let's say from 0.5 to 1, you would get a range over that color (from light to dark).

See also

▸   The *Overlaying a heat map* recipe

Adding multiple layers to a map

This recipe will make use of every other recipe in this chapter and build on them. We are going to make an interactive map with four layers on it. Two maps, the Canadian provinces from the previous recipe and a layer with some Canadian cities. We will also add a control to show or hide the individual layers.

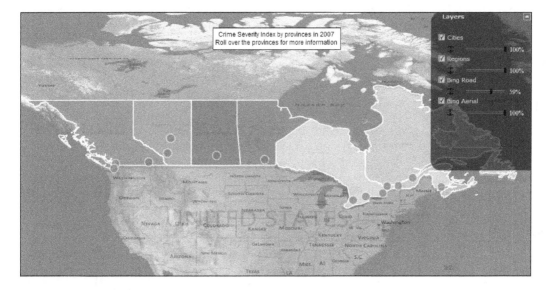

Getting ready

Since this recipe is going to make use of everything in the previous recipes, it is advised to read the beginning of this chapter.

How to do it...

The following are the steps required to add multiple layers to a map:

1. Start by generating the data. Use the region data from the previous recipe and we will create data for Canadian cities using the following site as reference, `http://www.infoplease.com/ipa/A0001796.html`. The following code snippet shows you how to store one city:

    ```
    dataCity.push( new LongLat("Calgary", new Coordinate("W", 114, 1),
    new Coordinate("N", 51, 1)));
    ```

2. Instantiate a `Map` class just as we have been doing this entire chapter.

3. Create the two `Bing` layers, one as a road map and the other as an aerial map.

4. Go over to the region data and create the visuals for the provinces that will go into our region layer.

5. Create the last layer: the city layer. Much like the *Adding points of interest to a map* recipe, where we added points of interest to a map, here our markers will represent cities. Create the class `CityMarker` to be the visual for `CustomMarkers`.

6. Add a `LayerManager` control so that we can turn on and off different layers on our map. We add it as shown in the following code snippet:

    ```
    _map.addControl(new LayerManager());
    ```

How it works...

What we want to create here is a map that has multiple layers of information that you can toggle on and off. To do so we will create four layers. The two base layers will be maps from Bing. The map that is going to be beneath all the others is the aerial one. The second map will be the road map. You should notice that we gave the road map an alpha of 0.6 so that we can see the map under it a bit. By playing with the alpha you can give a different look to your background layer.

Another point to notice is that when you create a `Bing` map layer, you don't need to give it a `layerName` value or an identifier like other layers. This will actually cause problems with the `LayerManager` control that we will add later on. To solve these problems, you can manually set the `layerName` value and the identifier yourself as shown in the following code snippet:

```
bing.layerName = "Bing Aerial";
bing.identifier = "Bing Aerial";
```

Note that you have to use "Bing Aerial" and "Bing Road" for their respective layers as other `Strings` will generate errors with the `LayerManager` control.

We are ready to add our third layer, the region layer that we created in the previous recipe.

The last layer will hold the city marker for some cities in Canada. The `CityMarker` class shows how to use `DisplayObject`, in this case a `Sprite` class, to make a marker. This marker is even interactive as it displays the name of the city as the user rolls over it. In order to make this work properly, we modified the `CustomMarker` class in its draw function. We removed the fact that it was centering the marker as it was causing problems when we added and removed the label. Instead we use the offset parameters to center our marker.

Finally step 6 shows how to add a `LayerManager` so that the user can control what data is displayed on the map.

There's more...

The `LayerManager` control is useful but you could make a better one.

Making your own LayerManager control

The `LayerManager` control provided by OpenScales is useful and quick to get on a map, but it can be quite cumbersome to use (the sliders are not that smooth). By promoting the layers to class members (now they are only local variables) you could easily create your own `LayerManager` control that could better suit you needs.

Animating turning on/off layers

And if you start playing with making your own `LayerManager` control, you should use a tweening library such as `TweenLite` or `Gtween` to animate the transitions when turning on and off layers. This will make your maps seems less twitchy.

Overlaying a heat map

For this recipe we are going to overlay a heat map over a map layer. This is a bit more challenging than what we did before but it should go smoothly as the concept is not that complex. Heat maps are used to represent density over a region by adding different colors over certain areas. In the case, we are going to display the number of animal specimens over the area of the United States using the Global Biodiversity Information Facility's data.

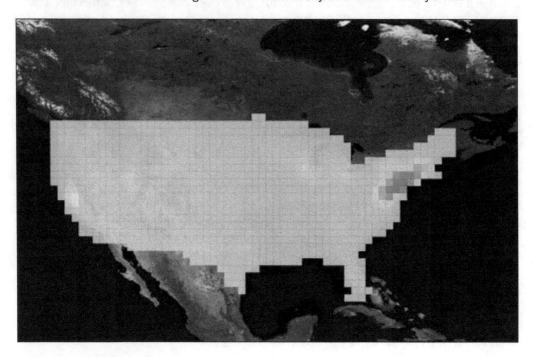

Getting ready

Open the files from the code downloaded from the Packt Publishing web site in the folder `Chapter 6` and within that, `Recipe 6`.

How to do it...

The following are the steps required to overlay a heat map on a map:

1. First get over to the `gbif.org` website to download an XML file with the US data in it. The URL is given as `http://es.mirror.gbif.org/ws/rest/density/list?originisocountrycode=US`.

2. Remove the extra markup in the XML file just so that it would be easier to parse it in ActionScript.

3. Embed the XML file in the `Main` class as shown in the following code snippet:

```
[Embed(source = "/AnimalsUS.xml", mimeType="application/octet-
stream")]
    private var XmlData:Class;
```

4. Parse the XML file and put the data in our holder class `HeatMapData`.

```
var byteArray:ByteArray = (new XmlData()) as ByteArray;
var xml:XML = XML(String(byteArray.readUTFBytes( byteArray.length
)));
var xmlList:XMLList = xml.children();

var data:Vector.<HeatMapData> = new Vector.<HeatMapData>();

var i:int;
for (i = 0; i < xmlList.length(); i++) {
  data.push(new HeatMapData(xmlList[i].count, xmlList[i].
minLongitude, xmlList[i].minLatitude));
}
```

5. Loop over every `heatMapData` instance to find its neighbors in all eight directions.

6. Loop over the data another time to calculate the average value over its neighbors and to find the maximum of those averaged values.

7. Create the map and the `VectorLayer` class to hold the heat map:

```
_map = new Map();
_map.size = new Size(800, 500);
_map.center = new Location(-93.98,40.77, "EPSG:4326");
_map.resolution = new Resolution(10000, "EPSG:900913");

var bing:Bing = new Bing("Ar3-LKk-acyISMevsF2bqH70h21mzr_FN9AhHfi7
pS26F5hMH1DmpI7PBK1VCLBk","Aerial");
_map.addLayer(bing);

var heatLayer:VectorLayer = new VectorLayer("HeatMap");
_map.addLayer(heatLayer);
```

8. Go over the data one last time to generate a polygon for each data point. Much of the work for this is done in the `createPolygon` function of the `HeatMapData` class.

How it works...

To make a heat map we need the data to be packaged in a particular way. We need one value to correspond to one area. For this recipe, the data from the Global Biodiversity Information Facility was aggregated over an area of one degree squared.

The first step is to get the data from the XML file into our holder class. Notice how using XML is a bit less straightforward than using JSON like in the *Parsing data to use as region fill* recipe.

Once we got that, we will need to loop over the data multiple times in order to calculate various values. We first need to average each value in relation to its neighbors. We do so, so that it creates more rounded regions on the heat map and also brings back values that would otherwise be too high to create a smoother range. To calculate this average we must do a double loop so that each data point can look at every other data point to check if it is one of its eight possible neighbors.

Once we got the neighbors, we loop over the data once more to create the average (we can't create the average while we are looking for neighbors, because a neighbor could use an already calculated average and that would skew the data) and find the maximum value of those averages. In this particular case we don't have to find a minimum as we know it is zero.

With the maximum found we can calculate the `scaleRatio` value:

```
var scaleRatio:Number = 495 / maximumCount;
```

495 here is our color range (255 for red and 240 for green).

Now we create the map so that we can add our polygons (they will be squares, much like pixels). We are ready for the last loop over the data. This is where we will create the `PolygonFeature` class and assign it a color depending on its averaged count value. If the averaged count value is equal to the maximum value, its polygon will be fully red, otherwise it will go from red to yellow to green. We put all the code to generate the polygon inside the `HeatMapData` class to keep the `Main` class cleaner.

The *Coloring a map* recipe has all the explanations on creating a `PolygonFeature` class and assigning it a color. Once we have all our polygons, we add them to the map. Note that since there are so many polygons on the map, it becomes a bit unresponsive when interacting with it, which is not really a problem if you want to use it as a static map.

There's more...

By using more precise data and a bigger color range we could make a better heat map.

Using more precise data

The XML file we used had data for buckets of the size of one degree squares. This made it so, that the resolution of our heat map wasn't so great. By using more precise data we could have a much smoother heat map. Everything starts from the data.

Starting from blue

Our color range went from green to yellow to red, but we could have started from blue instead and added even more depth to our visualization.

7
Animating a Graph

In this chapter, we will cover:

- ▶ Animating between two data sets
- ▶ Animating a meter
- ▶ Automatic updates
- ▶ Zooming in on specific data set
- ▶ Animating subway locations

Introduction

In this chapter we will explore how to animate graphs. We will start by revisiting graphs that we have seen in the previous chapters (bar chart, meter, line chart, and so on) and follow by showing original recipes. Three techniques will be shown, using an enter frame listener to modify a property, using the `TweenLite` library (**TweenLite** has been chosen as an animation library for this book because it is the most used and the fastest library out there; it even has a JavaScript port that performs quite well) for animation and finally erasing and redrawing the graph's every frame.

Animating between two data sets

In this recipe we will animate the transition when switching between two data sets. We will show how to animate without using any libraries. To do so we will use the bar chart as a base. We are going to start by fading in the chart. After that, we will grow the bars until they reach their desired size. In order to animate the switch between the two data sets, we will first shrink the current bars until we can't see them so that we can expand the new bars after.

Copy over the files from *Chapter 3, Creating Bar Charts*, the *Building vertical bar charts* recipe, as we will start from those.

How to do it...

The following are the steps needed to animate a bar chart:

1. In the `Bar.as` class, add the `_onEnterFrame` function:

    ```
    private function _onEnterFrame(event:Event):void {
      var distance:Number = Math.abs(height - _targetHeight);
      if (distance < 0.1) {
        height = _targetHeight;
        removeEventListener(Event.ENTER_FRAME, _onEnterFrame);
      } else {
        height -= (height - _targetHeight) / 4;
        //the 4 here impacts on the speed of the animation, higher
    being slower
      }
    }
    ```

2. Always in `Bar.as`, add the two public functions `animateIn` and `animateOut`, as shown in the following code snippet:

    ```
    public function animateIn():void {
      _targetHeight = _startingHeight;
      addEventListener(Event.ENTER_FRAME, _onEnterFrame);
    }
    public function animateOut():void {
      _targetHeight = 0;
      addEventListener(Event.ENTER_FRAME, _onEnterFrame);
    }
    ```

3. In `BarChart.as`, start by setting the `alpha` variable to `0` in the constructor.

4. After that, add the `animateIn` and `_onEnterFrame` functions:

    ```
    public function animateIn():void {
      addEventListener(Event.ENTER_FRAME, _onEnterFrame);
      setTimeout(_animateInBars, 1500);
    }

    private function _onEnterFrame(event:Event):void {
      if (alpha > .95) {
        alpha = 1;
    ```

```
    removeEventListener(Event.ENTER_FRAME, _onEnterFrame);
  } else {
    alpha += (1 - alpha) / 8;
    //the 8 here impacts on the speed of the animation, higher
being slower
  }
}
```

5. Save references to individual bars in `Vector` so that you animate them later on.

6. Add the `_animateInBars` and `_animateOutBars` functions:

```
private function _animateInBars():void {
  for (var i:int = 0; i < _barVector.length; i++) {
    _barVector[i].animateIn();
  }
}
private function _animateOutBars():void {
  for (var i:int = 0; i < _barVector.length; i++) {
    _barVector[i].animateOut();
  }
}
```

7. Create the public function `update` and its follow up function `_continueUpdate`:

```
public function update(data:Vector.<BarData>):void {
  _data = data;
  _animateOutBars();
  setTimeout(_continueUpdate, 800);
}

private function _continueUpdate():void {
  var i:int;
  for (i = 0; i < _barVector.length; i++) {
    removeChild(_barVector[i]);
  }
  _barVector = new Vector.<Bar>();

  var bar:Bar;
  for (i = 0; i < _data.length; i++) {
    bar = new Bar(_barWidth, _data[i].data * _scaleHeight);
    bar.x = 10 + _barSpacing + _barWidth / 2 + i * (_barWidth +
_barSpacing);
    bar.y = _newHeight - 10;
    _barVector.push(bar);
    addChild(bar);
  }
```

```
        addChild(_horizontalAxis);
        _animateInBars();
    }
```

8. In `Main.as`, create a second data set called `_data2`.

9. After 1.5 seconds, tell `_chart` to animate in:

```
setTimeout(_chart.animateIn, 1500);
```

10. After 8.5 seconds, change the data set to see the chart animate:

```
setTimeout(_changeData, 8500);

private function _changeData():void {
    _chart.update(_data2);
}
```

How it works...

Two tools are going to help us animate the bar chart: the enter frame listener function and the `setTimeout` function.

By adding a listener to the event `ENTER_FRAME`, we created a function that will be called every time a new frame is created. By updating a value such as `alpha` or `height` towards a target, we create an animation. Both in `Bar.as` and `BarChart.as` we use this as a stratagem (see step 1 and step 4).

Now this listener function is divided into two parts. Since we are getting closer to the value that is animated by a fraction, we first need to check if we are close enough to stop (otherwise you keep animating forever and it is not very optimal). If so, we set the value to the target and we stop animating. If not, we calculate the distance left, and we move forward by a fraction of the distance; for example, if we calculate half or a quarter of the distance left, then the smaller the fraction, the slower the animation will play. Eventually, our value is going to be very close to our target and the first condition will trigger.

You could animate differently based on time, instead of based on the distance, but in this way, you could easily get a nice easing, which means that our animation will be fast at first and slow in the end, finishing smoothly.

Another concept of animation is timing/delay. As an example to illustrate this, you may want to play another animation after the first one has played or you would want to play another animation after a certain amount of time. In ActionScript, there is a utility function called `setTimeout` that lets you do so. It takes two parameters: the first is a function to be called after some time and the second is that said amount of time in milliseconds (1000 millisecond equals to 1 second).

With those tools in hand we can animate the bar chart. The following is the sequence of events. At 1.5 seconds, we fade in the graph (alpha from 0 to 1). At 3 seconds, we animate in all the bars by making their heights go from 0 to their target values. At 8.5 seconds, we tell the chart to switch its data, so it will animate out all the bars and after 0.8 seconds, it will animate in the bars to their new heights.

There's more...

For this recipe we used `setTimeout` and the enter frame listener function but we could have just used the `TweenLite` animation library.

Using TweenLite

`TweenLite` is a very popular animation library that can be used very easily when animating one property, such as in this case the height of the bars. Here, instead of using the `animateIn` and `_onEnterFrame` functions, we could have used `TweenLite` and it would have been one line instead of 10. Another really useful feature of `TweenLite` is the `delayedCall` function, which is very similar to `setTimeout` but uses seconds instead of milliseconds. It's a small advantage, but it helps reduce confusion in the code. We chose to use `TweenLite` in this book as it is the most used and fastest animation library out there.

See also

▶ The *Building vertical bar charts* recipe in *Chapter 3*, *Creating Bar Charts*

▶ The *Animating a meter* recipe

Animating a meter

We will start from the *Drawing meters and gauges* recipe in *Chapter 4*, *Drawing Different Types of Graphs* and we will animate it using the `TweenLite` animation engine.

Getting ready

Get the code from the recipe previously mentioned and we will modify it to make it animated.

How to do it...

1. The first step would be to go to `http://www.greensock.com` and download the ActionScript 3 library.

2. Add the `greensock.swc` file to the `lib` folder in the project.

3. In FlashDevelop, right-click on `greensock.swc` and choose **Add To Library**.

4. We are now ready to use `TweenLite` in our code. In `Meter.as`, we will set `alpha` to zero so that we can animate it.

5. To do so we will add the `animateIn` and the `arrowTo` functions:

```
public function animateIn():void {

    TweenLite.to(this, 0.5, { alpha:1, delay:1 } );

    TweenLite.delayedCall(1.5, arrowTo, [percent]);

}

public function arrowTo(newPercent:Number):void {

    TweenLite.to(_arrow, 1, { rotation: _baseArrowRotation + 140 *
newPercent, ease:Bounce.easeOut } );

}
```

6. We will need to modify the `_drawArrow` function. We will first promote the arrow variable to a private variable (instead of a local one) so that we can access it outside this function.

7. After that let's create the `_baseArrowRotation` variable that will keep in memory the initial rotation of the arrow.

8. Instead of drawing the arrow at the value indicated by the user (by the percent variable), we will draw it at 0 so that we can animate it later.

```
_arrow.graphics.lineTo(outerRadius * Math.cos(0 * Math.PI / 180),
outerRadius * Math.sin(0 * Math.PI / 180));
```

9. We are done modifying `Meter.as`, so now in `Main.as` we add the following function:

```
private function _moveArrow():void {
    if (_meter.percent == 0.82) {
      _meter.percent = 0.22;
      _meter.arrowTo(0.22);
    } else {
      _meter.percent = 0.82;
      _meter.arrowTo(0.82);
    }
    TweenLite.delayedCall(3, _moveArrow);
}
```

10. All that is left to do is to call the `animateIn` function of the `Meter` class and then after some time call the `_moveArrow` function. Add the following code in the `Main.as` constructor:

```
_meter.animateIn();

TweenLite.delayedCall(4, _moveArrow);
```

How it works...

`TweenLite` is an animation platform that does all the heavy lifting of animating for you. The first few steps (steps 1 to 3) of this recipe are about getting the `TweenLite` code and adding it to the library so that we can use it in our code.

The `animateIn` function shown in step 5 is a good example of what you can do with `TweenLite`. The first use shows how to animate to alpha 1. When you want to tween (tween is often used as animate in the ActionScript jargon) something, you can use the static function `TweenLite.to`. It takes three parameters: the first one is the object you want to animate, the second one is the time you want the tween to take, and the third is an `Object` type with the properties you want to be affected. In this example, we want to tween the `meter` object (indicated by `this`) over half a second and set the final `alpha` to `1`. As you can see, there is also a special property in the third parameter called `delay`. This waits for the amount of seconds specified before starting the tween.

The second call to the `TweenLite` library is to the `delayedCall` function. This is another very useful feature of `TweenLite` which allows you to call a certain function after a determined number of seconds. You could always use the `Timer` class but we find it simpler to use the `TweenLite` class (it's just one line of code).

Next up is the `arrowTo` function, which introduces another special property called `ease`, which lets you specify an easing function for the tween. An **easing** function is a way for our animation to take place differently. It basically modifies the speed of the animation depending on the percentage of the animation completed. A typical easing function (such as the one that is used when none is provided) would make the animation start fast and end slowly. You could use `Strong.easeOut` to do so. If you would want the contrary, fast at first and slow at the end, you would use `Strong.easeIn`. The last one you could use would be slow at the beginning, fast in the middle, and slow at the end. That one would be `Strong.easeInOut`.

Now the function `arrowTo` uses a different easing function called `Bounce`. This easing function will simulate a bouncing effect on the property you are tweening. This easing doesn't always work well but for physical motion, such as our arrow rotating, it can give a good effect. Usually when you use the `Bounce` easing function (or the `Back` easing), give more time (time is the second parameter) because the property will go over more values and will seem too fast otherwise.

Finally in the `Main` class, we will create a function that will call itself after a few seconds, to move the arrow back and forth, giving the animation that you see when you compile the project.

There's more...

We briefly talked about easing but let's explore that topic a bit more.

Visualizing easing functions

We used the `Bounce` easing function because in this example it made a lot of sense, but it is not always easy to choose the right easing. This visualization will help you see the effect of the most common easing function : `http://hosted.zeh.com.br/tweener/docs/en-us/misc/transitions.html`

See also

▸ The *Drawing meters and gauges* recipe in *Chapter 4, Drawing Different Types of Graphs*

Automatic updates

In this recipe we are going to create a quotes graph that shows the value of an action, in this case the Google action, for one day. Every minute the graph is going to update itself and the update is going to be animated.

Getting ready

Open the files downloaded from the Packt Publishing website, look into the **Chapter 7 | recipe 3** folder and follow along.

How to do it...

The following are the steps required to build this graph:

1. Get the `HorizontalAxis` and `VerticalAxis` class from the *Drawing a bar chart with Flex* recipe in *Chapter 3, Creating Bar Charts*.

2. In `HorizontalAxis.as`, remove the labels; we won't be needing them.

3. In `VerticalAxis.as`, add `minimumValue` as a parameter. This axis is not going to start at 0 for this recipe but at the minimum value specified. The following is the line that needs to be modified (range is the difference between `maximumValue` and `minimumValue`).

    ```
    textField.text = String(Math.round(((i + 1) / (_numberOfMarks)) * range + minimumValue));
    ```

4. Now create `LinePart.as` and add the `createLine` function to draw the initial line:

    ```
    public function createLine():void {
      graphics.lineStyle(2, 0x4e81d4);
      graphics.moveTo(startX, graphHeight - startY);
      graphics.lineTo(endX, graphHeight - endY);
    }
    ```

5. Now create the `_onEnterFrame` function. The goal here is to draw intermediary lines that will end with the target line.

6. Add the `AnimatedLineChart` class with its `createGraph` function.

7. Add the `update` function to it, where you go over every existing line and animate it. If you don't have enough you can create new ones.

8. Create the `Main` class.

9. Instantiate `AnimatedLineChart` and add it to the stage.

10. Query the Yahoo! Finance API and once you have the data, call the update function on `AnimatedLineChart`.

11. Repeat step 10 every minute.

How it works...

In order to animate this sort of graph, we can't just tween a property like we would with a bar chart. We need to erase what is on the screen and redraw intermediate states until the animation is over. Then we can fade in the new parts using `TweenLite`.

Most of this happens in `LinePart.as`. When the data is updated, the chart tells each line segment that already exists to animate with new coordinates. If it doesn't have enough line segments, it will create new ones but fade them in just after the existing ones have finished moving.

In `LinePart.as`, the `_onEnterFrame` function does all the heavy lifting. First, it will erase the existing line by calling `graphics.clear()`, and after that it checks if the animation has run long enough. We wanted our animation to last for 0.5 seconds and our frame rate was 30 frames per second, so we need the `_onEnterFrame` function to run 15 times.

If it ran 15 times, draw the final line; if not draw an intermediary line with the current coordinates going towards the final ones.

Now we need to get our data. This is pretty simply done using Yahoo! Finance API. Using this URL: `http://bit.ly/Rzk7Cd`, you can get back a JSON string with the value of the stock of Google. In that URL, just change the GOOG for any other company symbol to get their stock value. You can query that URL every minute to get an updated value. Once you get a new value, you add it to the existing data and call an update on the graph.

There's more...

In this type of graph, it is not just the line that needs to be updated.

Horizontal axis

We didn't put markings on the horizontal axis, but it would be good to do so to give it a sense of time. As such, every time the graph updates, the horizontal axis should update too. You could even animate it to make it even better.

See also

▸   The *Creating a line graph based on a function* recipe in *Chapter 1, Getting Started with Graph Drawing*

▸   The *Zooming in on specific data set* recipe

Zooming in on a specific data set

In this recipe we are going to build a stacked area chart and allow the user to zoom in on a specific portion of it. You can view the stacked area chart as a pie chart over time. We are going to replicate the behavior of the graphics found on this page `http://flare.prefuse.org/apps/job_voyager`, but in a simplified manner.

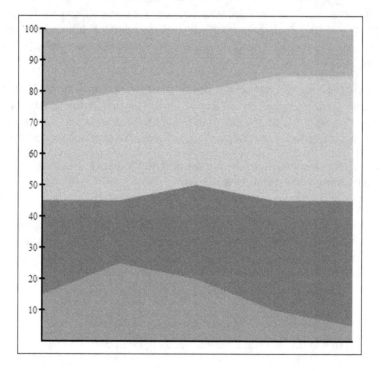

Getting ready

Open the files downloaded from the Packt Publishing website, look into the **Chapter 7 | recipe 4** folder, and follow along.

How to do it...

The following are the steps to create the animated stacked area chart:

1. Create `AnimatedAreaChartData.as` to hold your data.

2. Copy over `HorinzontalAxis.as` and `VerticalAxis.as` from the *Automatic updates* recipe in this chapter.

3. Create `Area.as`; this is where the animations are going to be.

4. Draw the initial shape in the `createArea` function of `Area.as`:
   ```
   graphics.beginFill(color);
   graphics.moveTo(0, graphHeight - 10 - scaleRatio * topLine[0]);

   var topLineLength:int = topLine.length;
   for (i = 1; i < topLineLength; i++) {
      graphics.lineTo(i / ( topLineLength - 1) * (graphWidth),
   graphHeight - 10 - scaleRatio * topLine[i]);
   }
   for (i = bottomLine.length - 1; i >= 0; i--) {
      graphics.lineTo(i / ( topLineLength - 1) * (graphWidth),
   graphHeight - 10 - scaleRatio * bottomLine[i]);
   }
   graphics.lineTo(0, graphHeight - 10 - scaleRatio * topLine[0]);
   ```

5. Save each point *x* and *y* coordinates in a vector for later uses.

6. Create the `Event.ENTER_FRAME` listener function. This function will redraw the area in every frame using intermediary points between the starting and the target points.

7. Create the public `expand` function. It recalculates the scale and computes the target points.

8. In the `expand` function, add an `ENTER_FRAME` listener to start animating.

9. Now, create the `AnimatedAreaChart.as` class.

10. In the `AnimatedAreaChart` class start recalculating the data as stacked values instead of individual values.

11. For each data set, instantiate an `area` object.

12. Add the `MouseEvent.CLICK` listener function so that when the user clicks on an area, we zoom in on it:

```
private function _onAreaClicked(event:MouseEvent):void {
  var areaIndex:int = _areaVector.indexOf(Area(event.target))
  for (var i:int = 0; i < _areaVector.length; i++) {
    if (i != areaIndex) {
      _areaVector[i].animateOut();
    } else {
      _verticalAxis.update(_areaVector[i].expand());
    }
  }
}
```

How it works...

So in this graph, we have areas that are stacked on top of each other. When we click on one, we want the other areas to disappear and the one that was clicked to expand so that it starts from 0 to its maximum, all in a smooth animation.

The hard part here is to keep track of all the points needed to make the area, the target area, and the intermediate area (animated). Since we aren't tweening only one value, we won't be able to use the `TweenLite` animation library, but we will have to use an `ENTER_FRAME` listener and erase and redraw the area's every frame.

In a stacked area chart, the data gets transformed into lines and to form an area you need two lines, yours and the one before you (if it is the first line, the one before is the horizontal axis). But you can't use the data as it is; you need the stacked values. That is the first thing we compute in `AnimatedAreaChart.as`.

So now we have a top line and a bottom line and the actual value of the data is the difference between those two (which is also represented by the area). When you zoom out, you show the stacked values. When you zoom in you show the original values.

When you create an area, in the constructor we keep the *x* and *y* coordinates of every point; those will be our starting points. When the function `expand` is called, we compute what will be the target points (the points we want to end at). This function also adds the listener to the `ENTER_FRAME` event.

In the `ENTER_FRAME` listener function, we start by looking if the animation is done playing. If yes, we remove the listener so that the function is not called any more. We then erase everything and we draw an intermediary area that is a shape between the starting and the target area. Every point is calculated from the starting point plus the difference between the starting and target points multiplied by the percentage of the animation that has played. In our case we wanted the animation to play for 15 frames (which is equivalent to half a second since the frame rate is 30 frames per seconds) so the percentage is the number of frames played divided by 15.

All that is left to do in `AnimatedAreaChart.as` is to create an area for each line in the data and to call the function `expand` if an area as been clicked (or `animateOut` for the other ones so that they are not visible anymore).

There's more...

We saw how to build the basis of this graph but we left out the back button and the reverse animation.

Adding a back button

It would be really good if once you zoomed in, on a data set, there was a way to go back. A very easy way to do so would be to simply add a back button that is only visible when you are in the zoomed in state. With that, you could really explore the data.

Reverse animation

Once you have the back button implemented, you have two ways to get back to the previous state: either you animate it or not. The easiest solution is to simply revert without animation, but it won't really be smooth and will appear twitchy. Animating it is a bit more work but it would make the graph more professional. You would just have to inverse the target points and the starting points and it would play the animation backward. After that you just fade in the other areas and you are done.

See also

▶ The *Area charts* recipe in *Chapter 1, Getting Started with Graph Drawing*
▶ The *Automatic updates* recipe
▶ The *Animating subway locations* recipe

Animating subway locations

In this recipe we are going to replicate the visualization found on http://www.mta.me, done by *Alexander Chen*. The original piece is done in HTML, but we are going to do it in Flash, without the music component.

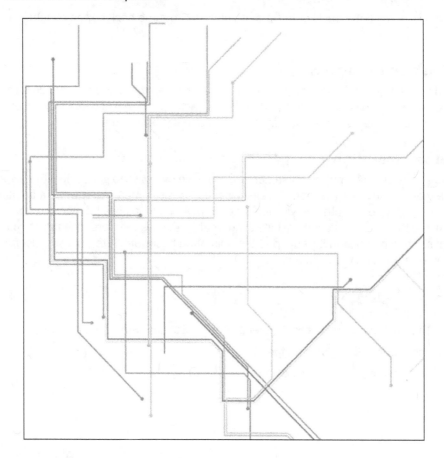

Getting ready

Open the files downloaded from the Packt Publishing website, look into the **Chapter 7 | recipe 5** folder, and follow along.

How to do it...

The following are the steps required the animate the New York City subway system:

1. Head over to `http://www.mta.info/developers/download.html` and download the *New York City Transit Subway* data.

2. From the data derive these information: line color, departures, and duration of each trip.

3. Download this map: `http://www.nycsubway.org/perl/caption.pl?/img/maps/system_1972.jpg` and open it in Photoshop.

4. In Photoshop, note the coordinates for the paths of each line.

5. Create `Main.as` and copy the data into it.

6. Create the `Subway` class.

7. In its constructor, determine the distance of each section of the path and with that information derive how many frames you must stay for on each section.

8. Create a circle to represent the subway car:

```
var totalFrames:int = Math.round(_route[3] * 4);

for (i = 0; i < _path.length; i++) {
  if (i > 0) {
    distances.push(Math.sqrt(Math.pow(_path[i][0] - _path[i - 1]
[0], 2) + Math.pow(_path[i][1] - _path[i - 1][1], 2)));
    totalDistance += distances[i - 1];
  }
}
for (i = 0; i < distances.length; i++) {
  _frames.push (Math.ceil(distances[i] / totalDistance *
totalFrames));
}
```

9. Add the `_onEnterFrame` function. Erase all the graphics and compute the new line to be drawn. Also, move the circle to the end of the path.

10. Create the `SubwayAnimation` class.

11. In it create a function that will be called every 3 seconds. This function will look at the schedule and instantiate the needed subways depending on their departure.

12. In `Main.as`, create an instance of `SubwayAnimation` and provide it with the route data and the schedule data.

How it works...

The big trouble for this recipe is getting our data. Not that it is very hard; it is just very tedious. If you head over to the MTA API development page you will find all the data you need, but not exactly in the format you want. There might even be too much data in there. Anyway, what you get is multiple text files. Some information is really easy to get such as the hexadecimal color of each line. Some will be a bit harder, such as the departure times and the duration of a trip for each lines. In any case you should build another ActionScript program (or in any other programming language you are comfortable with) just to parse the data and export it in a format you like.

Now that we got the information, we need the paths for each lines. By using the 1972 New York City subway plan, we save a bit of work as it was a bit stylized; there are fewer bumps and turns. Open the map in Photoshop and take the coordinates (x and y) of the start, the end, and every turning point for each line. There are about 27 lines; it will take some time, but not too much. Also remember that the Flash coordinate system is a bit different than Photoshop, so you will have to check the height of the picture minus the y of your coordinate in order for it to show properly in Flash. Here again you could use programming to help you in your task. You could load the image and record the coordinates of every MouseDown events.

Now that we have all our data, we can start coding. In this representation, we will make it so that 3 seconds represent one minute. So every 3 seconds we will check if there are subways departing and if so we will instantiate a Subway class for each of those departing. That happens in the SubwayAnimation class.

The Subway class has all the meat in it. Its constructor is used to calculate how many frames we must spend on each path segment. This is important because otherwise the speed wouldn't be consistent across small and large path segments. The _frameCount variable keeps track of which frame we are at in the current path segment.

The _onEnterFrame function is where we deal with the animation. We start by erasing everything. We then redraw all the completed line segments. We go on by figuring out at which point in the current segment we are at and we draw this incomplete segment. We finally place the circle at the end of the incomplete segment to represent the metro car.

We then check if we completed this segment and if yes we go on to the next segment. If all the segments were completed that means we drew the entire path. We then wait for 4 seconds and fade out the path. When the fade out is completed we make sure the Subway object is removed from the stage so that it can be destroyed, thus freeing memory.

There's more...

We stopped this visualization before doing the line collisions and adding sounds, but it wouldn't be too hard to do.

Collisions

Finding collisions can be an expensive process, so we would start by determining which line can intersect with which line so we can save a few operations. Then you check if the current path intersects with all the other paths of the other present lines. Another way you could do this is to use the `hitTestObject` function provided by ActionScript.

Playing the sounds

In `http://www.mta.me` whenever a line intersects another line, it plays a sound. So what you could do here is have a collection of 10 to 15 sounds ranging from low pitch to high pitch. The longer the line segment crossed, the lower the pitch sound of the cord will be. It is that simple.

See also

- ▶ The *Automatic updates* recipe
- ▶ The *Zooming in on a specific data set* recipe

8
Creating a Relational Network

In this chapter, we will cover:

- ▶ Preparing the data
- ▶ Creating the visual for a node
- ▶ Arranging and linking the nodes
- ▶ Navigating through the relational network
- ▶ Animating the transitions
- ▶ Adding sounds

Introduction

In this chapter we are going to create a relational network from scratch. **Relational networks** are a data visualization that is used to represent a tree data structure. They give a good idea of hierarchy and structure, and can be used in cases such as jobs hierarchy or process structure. This chapter is going to cover parsing the data, creating the nodes, arranging those nodes, navigation, animation, and sound.

Preparing the data

A relational network represents hierarchy and linkage between objects and a good data structure, such as the tree data structure. This recipe is going to show how to parse the data for it to be ready to generate a relational network.

Getting ready

Open the files downloaded from the Packt Publishing website for **Chapter 8 | Recipe 1** to follow along.

How to do it...

The following steps will show you how to parse the data for a relational network:

1. Create the data in an XML file similar to `Data.xml`. The following is what one entry looks like:

   ```
   <node name="NODE NAME" color="0x0000ff"></node>
   ```

2. In `Main.as`, add the embed code to attach the data to our project:

   ```
   [Embed(source = "/Data.xml", mimeType="application/octet-stream")]

   private var XmlData:Class;
   ```

3. Load the XML file using the `ByteArray.readUTFbytes` function:

   ```
   var byteArray:ByteArray = (new XmlData()) as ByteArray;
   var xml:XML = XML(String(byteArray.readUTFBytes( byteArray.length
   )));
   var xmlList:XMLList = xml.children();
   ```

4. Create the `Node.as` class that will hold the data. It has a name, a color, a parent, and a child field.

5. Create the recursive function, in `Main.as`, that will go through the XML data:

   ```
   private function _createNodes(parent:Node, xml:XML):Node {
     var node:Node = new Node();
     node.parent = parent;
     node.name = xml.@name;
     node.color = xml.@color;
     var children:XMLList = xml.children();
     for (var i:int = 0; i < children.length(); i++) {
       node.children.push(_createNodes(node, children[i]));
     }
     return node;
   }
   ```

6. Feed the XML data to the `_createNodes` function and keep a link to the root node:

   ```
   var data:Node = _createNodes(null, xmlList[0]);
   ```

How it works...

For this recipe, we are not going to store the data in a vector or an array, but we are going to build a tree data structure to hold it. What we are going to build is very similar to a linked list—well, actually more similar to a double linked list. Our data class will be a node. It holds the data, but it also holds pointers to its parent and to its children.

Indeed most nodes are going to be parents to other nodes and have other nodes as children. A **node** is a parent of another node if it has a link to it in its children `Vector`. The first node has no parent and is called the **root**. If a node has no children it is called a **leaf**.

JSON is always an easy solution to store the data as it is smaller and easily convertible in an ActionScript `Object` type but, for this particular recipe, XML is actually better to work with. It is very good at representing the relation between parent and child, and with a quick glance at it you get a good understanding of the structure of the tree.

Using recursion is great when dealing with trees. **Recursion** is when a function does something and then calls itself again until an end condition is met. In this case, since there is not much difference between nodes whether they are children or parents (or both), we can use the same function to parse them. The function we created for that is `_createNodes`. It creates a new node and then calls `_createNodes` for all of its children. Since the function `_createNodes` returns `Node`, we can save those in a vector. We do this until a node doesn't have a child.

There's more...

Linked lists and trees are extensive subjects. Adding these data structures to your toolkit will be extremely useful as they are used often.

Links for more theory

Wikipedia has good information about linked lists available at:

```
http://en.wikipedia.org/wiki/Linked_list
```

For more information on double linked lists, refer to:

```
http://en.wikipedia.org/wiki/Doubly_linked_list
```

For more information on trees:

```
http://en.wikipedia.org/wiki/Tree_(data_structure)
```

See also

▸ The *Parsing data to use as region fill* recipe in *Chapter 6, Mapping Geographical and Spatial Data*.

Creating the visual for a node

In this recipe, we will create the building block for our relational network: the node. This is basically a circle with a label in the middle. If it is not the center node (the parent), then it will also display how many children it has.

Getting ready

Open the files downloaded from the Packt Publishing website for **Chapter 8 | Recipe 2** folder to follow along.

How to do it...

The following are the steps required to do the visuals for a node:

1. Create the `NodeVisual.as` class where everything will happen.

2. Add in the constructor code to draw the under circle and the gradient circle:

```
_underCircle = new Shape();
_underCircle.graphics.beginFill(0xffffff);
_underCircle.graphics.drawCircle(0, 0, _radius);
addChild(_underCircle);

_circle = new Sprite();
var matrix:Matrix = new Matrix();
matrix.createGradientBox(_radius*2, _radius*2, 0, -_radius, -_
radius);
_circle.graphics.lineStyle(1, _color);
_circle.graphics.beginGradientFill(GradientType.RADIAL, [0xffffff,
_color], [0.2, 0.65], [20, 255], matrix);
_circle.graphics.drawCircle(0, 0, _radius);
addChild(_circle);
```

3. Instantiate `Textfield` and adjust its properties:

```
_label = new TextField();
_label.selectable = false;
_label.defaultTextFormat = textFormat;
_label.text = node.name;
_label.width = _label.textWidth + 3;
_label.height = _label.textHeight + 3;
_label.x = -_label.width / 2;
_label.y = -_label.height / 2;
```

4. Create the label background based on the layer height and width:

```
_labelBackground = new Sprite();
_labelBackground.graphics.beginFill(_color);
_labelBackground.graphics.drawRoundRect(_label.x - 6, _label.y -
3, _label.width + 12, _label.height + 6, 10, 10);
addChild(_labelBackground);
addChild(_label);
```

5. Create a function to show the children of this node and if this node indeed has children, call the function:

```
private function _addChildren():void {
  var circle:Shape;
  var length:int = _node.children.length;
  if (length > 26) {
    length = 26;
  }

  for (var i:int = 0; i < length ; i++) {
    circle = new Shape();
    circle.graphics.beginFill(_color);
    circle.graphics.drawCircle(0, 0, 7);
    circle.x = (_radius + 7) * Math.cos((i * 14) * Math.PI / 180
);
    circle.y = (_radius + 7) * Math.sin((i * 14) * Math.PI / 180);
    _childrenHolder.addChild(circle);
  }
  _childrenHolder.rotation = (length - 1) * 14 / -2 + _angle;
}
```

6. In `Main.as`, instantiate the root node based on the data.

How it works...

Our representation of a node will be a circle with a label on top of it. This circle will have a radial gradient in it. Now, since that gradient will have some transparency, we will actually need two circles. One will be underneath the one with the gradient with full white color just so that our node is not transparent anymore. In the code that circle is called `_underCircle`.

To create a radial gradient in ActionScript, you first have to delimit its frontiers. You do so by creating a `Matrix` object and by using its `createGradientBox` function. The next thing you need to do is to tell it how you want the colors to blend; this is done in the `graphics.createGradientFill` function. The first parameter of that function is the type of gradient you want, in our case `radial`. The second parameter is the colors that are going to be used for our gradient. Next is the transparency of those colors. After that, we will tell it, using a number from 0 to 255, where those colors meet. Finally, we will give it the matrix we created earlier to store the bounding box of the gradient. Gradients are always a bit tricky but by playing with different settings, mostly different parameters (three and four), you can achieve various effects.

Next up, we create the label and the box under it. We draw a rounded rectangle, which is mostly like drawing a normal rectangle except you need to give it information about how rounded you want it to be.

We want to give an idea of how many children a child node has. This will give more information to the user when he will eventually want to navigate to the relational network. We will display each child as a little circle around our main circle. With the size of circle we chose, we can't show more than 26 children, so we start by checking for that. After that we place these circles at radius distances from the center and spaced at an angle of 14 degrees.

There's more...

By allowing some customizable styles, we could improve on our relational network.

Styling

Indeed, right now the style for our nodes is pretty rigid; the only thing that is customizable is the color. We could allow the data to provide font and size for each node along with many other styling options. Allowing this would make our relational network more useful.

Arranging and linking the nodes

Now we are going to take the nodes created in the previous recipe and arrange them to show a level of the tree (a parent with its children). We are going to place the parent in the middle and arrange the children around it with lines showing the relationship.

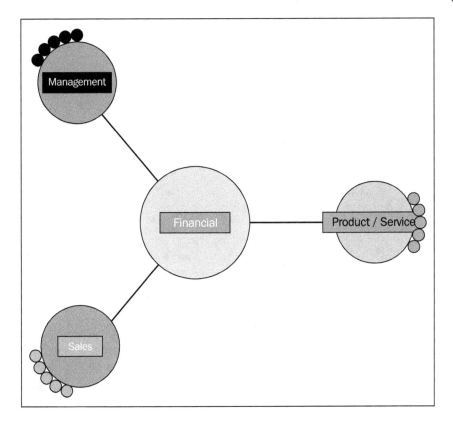

Getting ready

Open the files downloaded from the Packt Publishing website for **Chapter 8 | Recipe 3** to follow along.

How to do it...

The following are the steps necessary to put the nodes together to make a relational network:

1. Create the class `RelationalNetwork.as`.

2. Instantiate a `NodeVisual` object with the data provided; this is going to be our parent:

   ```
   _centerNode = new NodeVisual(data, 0,true);
   ```

3. Create a vector to hold all the child nodes.

4. Loop over the children of the parent node and instantiate a `NodeVisual` object for each of them:

```
for (i = 0; i < data.children.length; i++) {
  angle = 360 / data.children.length * i;
  nodeVisual = new NodeVisual(data.children[i], angle);
  if (data.children.length < 12){
    nodeVisual.x = 150 * Math.cos(angle  / 180 * Math.PI);
    nodeVisual.y = 150 * Math.sin(angle  / 180 * Math.PI);
  } else {
    if (i % 2 == 0){
    nodeVisual.x = 250 * Math.cos(angle  / 180 * Math.PI);
    nodeVisual.y = 250 * Math.sin(angle  / 180 * Math.PI);
    } else {
    nodeVisual.x = 150 * Math.cos(angle  / 180 * Math.PI);
    nodeVisual.y = 150 * Math.sin(angle  / 180 * Math.PI);
    }
  }
  nodeVisual.addLink();
  addChild(nodeVisual);
  _childrenNodeVector.push(nodeVisual);
}
```

5. In `NodeVisual.as` create a sprite to hold the link.

6. Add the `addLink` function:

```
_link.graphics.lineTo( -x, -y);
```

How it works...

To create a relational network, we take our building blocks, the nodes, and instantiate several of them. We place the parent in the middle and equally space its children around it in a circle. If there are more than 12 child nodes, they won't fit around the center node. In that case we place the first node close to the middle (at a 150 pixels distance) and the second node further away (at a 250 pixels distance), and we repeat the process for all children. All of this is done in step 4.

Now we need to show the link between the parent and each child by drawing a line between them. This line needs to be under the circles; that is why we create a sprite to hold them in step 5. We create the `addLink` function because we cannot draw the line in the constructor of `NodeVisual`. Indeed, we need to know the position of `NodeVisual` and this will only be attributed after it has been created.

There's more...

There are multiple ways we could improve on this relational network. Using Box2D and showing more than one level could be one of them.

Box2D

Box2D is a library to perform two-dimensional physics in ActionScript. We could use it to allow the user to move the nodes around. Moving one node would affect all the other ones, ensuring that none of the nodes would be overlapping and giving an organic feel to our network. There are other physics libraries out there but Box2D is the most used. Also, it is ported to many languages such as C and JavaScript, so learning it will grant you knowledge that can be used on many different projects. You can download the ActionScript version of Box2D here: `http://box2dflash.sourceforge.net/`.

Showing more than one level

Right now we are showing only one level of our tree, but we could show more. By having an `expand` button on each child node you could show more than one level. The difficulty in doing so would be arranging the newly showing node so that it doesn't overlap the ones that were already there. Also you could quickly run out of space if your tree is really big.

Navigating through the relational network

The previous recipe enabled us to show one level of a data tree; this recipe is going to allow us to navigate from one level to another, thus enabling us to explore the entire tree.

Getting ready

Open the files downloaded from the Packt Publishing website for **Chapter 8 | Recipe 4** to follow along.

How to do it...

The following are the required steps to allow the user to navigate through the relational network:

1. Create the `PlusButton` class to allow the user to navigate down the tree.
2. Create the `MinusButton` class to allow the user to navigate up the tree.
3. Add `RelationalNetworkEvent` to indicate to the relational network that the user wants to navigate.
4. In `NodeVisual`, add the `PlusButton` class if the node is a child.
5. In `NodeVisual`, add the `MinusButton` class if the node is the center node.

6. In `RelationalNetwork.as`, add a listener to the center node for the `RelationalNetworkEvent.NAVIGATE_TO_PARENT` event.

7. Still in `RelationalNetwork.as`, add a listener to each child for the `RelationalNetworkEvent.NAVIGATE_TO_CHILDREN` event.

8. In `RelationalNetwork.as`, create the listener function for the previous events. In that function remove everything from the stage and recreate the network using the node that was clicked on as the center node. If the center node was clicked use its parent.

How it works...

What we need to do here is first create the buttons (steps 1 and 2) so that the user can click on them to indicate that he wants to navigate up or down the relational network. We drew simple buttons using the Flash drawing API: a plus for the children and a minus for the center node. We located those buttons just below the label in the center of the node. The placement might not be the optimal one, but in this context, where there are not too many options, it works well (if you wanted to add more interaction possibilities, it might get crowded).

When one of these buttons get clicked, the `NodeVisual` class catches it and dispatches either a `NAVIGATE_TO_PARENT` or `NAVIGATE_TO_CHILDREN` event. The `RelationalNetwork` class then catches it. If the node that sent the event is the center node, then it recreates the network from its parent. If the node that sent the event is a child, then it recreates the network from the child node.

The code for recreating the network is found in the `_onNavigateToChildren` and `_onNavigateToParent` functions and is basically the same that can be found in the constructor of the `RelationalNetwork` class.

There's more...

By tiding up the code a bit, you could make this recipe better.

Refactoring

If you look at the code from the constructor and the functions `_onNavigateToChildren` and `_onNavigateToParent`, you will see a lot of the same code being repeated. This is not a sign of a good code (it was done like this so that we could upgrade the code for later recipes) and could be consolidated in just one function. Doing this would make the code easier to maintain.

Animating the transitions

In the previous recipe, we allowed the user to navigate through but we didn't animate the transitions, so it looks unprofessional and clunky. Animations also help the users grasp what is happening. This recipe is going to show how to animate a relational network.

Getting ready

Open the files downloaded from the Packt Publishing website for **Chapter 8 | Recipe 5** to follow along.

How to do it...

The following are the steps required to animate a relational network:

1. In `NodeVisual.as`, remove the function `addLink`.

2. Still in `NodeVisual`, add the function `_updateLine`:

```
private function _updateLine():void {
  _link.graphics.clear();
  _link.graphics.lineStyle(3, _color, 0.8);
  _link.graphics.lineTo( -x, -y);
}
```

3. Add the `animateIn` function:

```
public function animateIn():void {
  _targetX = x;
  x = 0;
  _targetY = y;
  y = 0;
  TweenLite.to(this, 0.5, {x:_targetX, y:_targetY, onUpdate:_
updateLine, ease:Back.easeOut } );
}
```

4. Also add the public function `animateOut`:

```
public function animateOut():void {
  TweenLite.to(this, 0.5, {x:0, y:0, onUpdate:_updateLine,
ease:Back.easeIn } );
}
```

5. In `RelationalNetwork`, replace calls to `addLink` by calls to `animateIn`.

6. Change the `_navigateToChildren` function definition to the following code:

```
private function _onNavigateToChildren(event:RelationalNetwork
Event):void {
  _childrenNavigateOut(NodeVisual(event.target).node);
}
```

7. Change the _navigateToChildren function definition to the following code:

```
private function _onNavigateToParent(event:RelationalNetworkEvent)
:void {
  _childrenNavigateOut(NodeVisual(event.target).node.parent);
}
```

8. Start the animation by calling _childrenNavigateOut that has the following code:

```
private function _childrenNavigateOut(centerNode:Node):void {
  var i:int;
  for (i = 0; i < _childrenNodeVector.length ; i++) {
    _childrenNodeVector[i].animateOut();
  }
      TweenLite.delayedCall(0.5, _continueNavigateToChildren,
[centerNode]);
}
```

9. After half a second, call the _continueNavigateToChildren function that holds the code to recreate a relational network.

How it works...

We first need to add the animation functions in the NodeVisual class. To animate, we are going to use TweenLite. We want to have an easing function; that is why we won't be using the ENTER_FRAME animation technique, but we still have to deal with the graphic API to draw the link. So in order to do this, we will use the onUpdate property of TweenLite to call a function every time it modifies a value. Our function for this will be _updateLine and it will remove the link and redraw it where the node is now situated, keeping it up-to-date.

Using this we will be able to use any easing from the TweenLite library. In this recipe, we used the Back easing function, but we could easily have used the Bounce easing, too. Anything that looks like a physical object, moving these two functions, works very well. For the animation in, we will use Back.easeOut so that our node goes just a bit farther than it is supposed to go and comes back after. For the animation out, we do the inverse, using Back.easeIn. The animation will start by going back a bit and then it will go to its target destination.

Once we have those animations figured out we need to time them properly to make our navigation transition. This is done in step 8 and 9. We first call animateOut on each child and wait for 0.5 seconds before we can continue. After that time, we remove everything on the stage and recreate the relational network, and then we call animateIn on each of the children.

There's more...

By having a different animation for the transition to a child node, we could enhance the user's understanding of what is happening.

Different animation for navigating to a child

Right now we have the same animation for when the user navigates to a parent or a child, but we could make the animation to a child different. You could first animate out all the other children, fade out the center node and the clicked child's link while moving the clicked node in the middle. Finally, you could recreate the network and animate in the child as we did previously. This would make it clear that we are navigating to a child.

See also

▸ The *Animating between two data sets* recipe in Chapter 7, *Animating a Graph*

▸ The *Animating a meter* recipe in Chapter 7, *Animating a Graph*

Adding sounds

To really finish off our relational network and to add strength to our animation, this recipe is going to add sounds to it all.

Getting ready

Open the files downloaded from the Packt Publishing website for **Chapter 8 | Recipe 6** to follow along.

How to do it...

The following are the steps to add sounds to a relational network:

1. In a Flash file (`.fla`), add four sounds for rollover, click, animation in, and animation out.

2. Export that file as a `.swc` file.

3. In FlashDevelop, right-click on the `.swc` file and choose **Add to Library**.

4. In `PlusButton.as`, add a listener for the `MouseEvent.ROLL_OVER` event and for the `MouseEvent.CLICK` event.

5. Add the corresponding functions:

```
private function _onMouseClick(event:MouseEvent):void {
  _soundClick.play(0,0,new SoundTransform(2));
}

private function _onRollOver(event:MouseEvent):void {
  _soundOver.play(0,0,new SoundTransform(0.75));
}
```

6. Repeat steps 4 and 5 in `MinusButton.as`.

7. In `RelationalNetwork.as`, initialize the animate in and the animate out sounds, as shown in the following code snippet:

```
_soundAnimateIn = new SoundAnimateIn();
_soundAnimateOut = new SoundAnimateOut();
```

8. In the constructor and in the function `_continueNavigateToChildren`, play the animate in sound:

```
_soundAnimateIn.play();
```

9. In the function `_childrenNavigateOut`, play the animate out sound:

```
_soundAnimateOut.play(0,0,new SoundTransform(0.5));
```

How it works...

Playing sound is not really a hard task. By adding the sounds needed to a SWC library, it makes them easily accessible and it only takes two lines of code to play them. The hard thing with sounds is to find the right ones and have them play at the right volume (choosing the right volume).

In this case we chose four sounds: one for the buttons' rollover, one for the button click, one for when the nodes animate in, and lastly, one for when the nodes animate out. The sounds for the rollover and the click should be subtle as those are not the main things we want to emphasize, but those sounds still help fill our relational network.

The main sounds are the animate in and out sounds, as they will help accentuate our animations. Contrarily to the rollover and the click sounds, which are handled by the nodes, the animation sounds will be triggered in `RelationalNetwork.as`. If they were handled by the nodes, we would be stacking one sound for every child node there is, thus creating cacophony.

There's more...

There is a way to save time and file size, using ActionScript a bit differently.

Saving space

Sounds can sometimes be hard to find, but in a case such as this recipe, we can save some time and space by playing a sound backward. Indeed, for our animate in and animate out sounds we could have used only one sound and played it backward for animate out. This can be done by using ActionScript's dynamic sound library and dealing with the sounds as raw bytes. It is a bit hard to use at first but it is a great skill to learn.

9
Creating Three-Dimensional Graphs

In this chapter, we will cover:

- ▶ Drawing in 3D: a 3D starter project
- ▶ Creating a 3D column chart
- ▶ Moving around the chart
- ▶ Beyond the cube, drawing different shapes
- ▶ Graphing tabular data in 3D
- ▶ Styling the graph with different materials
- ▶ Graphing a function in three dimensions

Introduction

If this is your very first time programming 3D, this chapter is going to be a challenge. There's no way around it, but programming 3D involves a lot more than drawing in two dimensions.

Not only do you have an additional coordinate, but you also need to convert the 3D drawing into a 2D image that can be shown on the screen.

There are models, cameras, scenes, views, and much more that you usually don't need to understand for 2D programming. But even the smallest 3D program requires you to at least understand the basic concepts and know how they fit in the larger picture.

Luckily, there are many tutorials online to get started with 3D and ActionScript. For instance, the following link provides a good overview of the basics: `http://www.flashmagazine.com/Tutorials/detail/flash_3d_basics/`

In this chapter and the next, we will focus solely on Away3D (http://away3d.com/). This is one of the most popular and open source 3D libraries for ActionScript. We use only this library to keep the explanation as simple as possible, but you can perfectly apply the same techniques using any other 3D library available.

We have chosen to opt for Away3D Version 4. Although still in beta, we are convinced this is the future of 3D in ActionScript. This has a few implications: you will need Flash 11 or newer to create and view the programs. Flash 11 added Stage3D, a hardware-accelerated way of drawing in 3D. The major advantage is that the 3D display will be much faster and will allow for many more elements on the screen.

Drawing in 3D: a 3D starter project

This first recipe will give a quick overview of the different components of a 3D engine. It will show you the minimal program you need to know to draw your first cube in three dimensions.

Although not strictly necessary we also show how to add a light to your 3D scene. Adding even the simplest light will create a much more vivid and impressive image.

Getting ready

Start by downloading the Away3D library from http://away3d.com/. We are going to use Version 4, currently in beta. By using this beta version, we run the risk of small changes that might break some of the code (check the site for updates), but it will also make sure you are prepared for the future. There are some major incompatible changes between Away3D Version 3 and Version 4, so it's best to immediately learn the latest.

Extract the Away3D download to a folder.

Now create a new FlashDevelop project and copy everything from the Away3D src folder into the src folder of the project. If you open any of the files inside the Away3D package you should *not* see an error that the package name is incorrect.

Copy the pb folder that came with Away3D into the root of your project (at the same level as the src folder). These PixelBender files are necessary for the correct functioning of Away3D.

Right-click on the project and choose **Properties**. Change the Flash player version (in the Platform section) to at least 11. If you pick the latest one and you get errors later on, it may be that you don't have that Flash version installed. As long as you can run Version 11, you should be fine. If you cannot, you will need to download and install the latest Flash player. The example projects use Version 11.1.

How to do it...

Create or re-use the existing `Main` class. The recipe code uses a separate package for each recipe to keep things tidy. As with pretty much all previous recipes, the `Main` class will extend `Sprite`. That's about where the similarities with previous recipes end.

Start by adding a view property to the `Main` class:

```
private var _view:View3D;
```

In the `Main` class' constructor we will set everything up:

1. Create a view of the 3D world and add it to the display list:

```
_view = new View3D();
_view.backgroundColor = 0x666666;
_view.antiAlias = 4;
addChild(_view);
```

2. Create and configure a light by using the following code snippet:

```
var light:DirectionalLight = new DirectionalLight(-0.5, -1, 0.7);
light.ambient = 0.5;
light.specular = 0.45;
light.diffuse = 0.5;
_view.scene.addChild(light);
```

3. The following code snippet creates a cube:

```
var cubeGeometry:CubeGeometry = new CubeGeometry(50,50,50);
var cubeMaterial:ColorMaterial = new ColorMaterial(0xff9933);
cubeMaterial.lightPicker = new StaticLightPicker([light]);
var cube:Mesh = new Mesh(cubeGeometry, cubeMaterial);
_view.scene.addChild(cube);
```

4. Point the camera towards the cube with the following code snippet:

```
_view.camera.x = 100;
_view.camera.y = 200;
_view.camera.z = -200;
_view.camera.pitch(45); //around x-axis
_view.camera.yaw(-20);  //around y-axis
```

5. Add an enter frame listener that will render the scene:

```
addEventListener(Event.ENTER_FRAME, onEnterFrame);
```

The final ingredient is the `onEnterFrame` implementation that will make sure that the 3D world is drawn to the screen:

```
private function onEnterFrame(ev : Event) : void
{
    _view.render();
}
```

Run the program. Congratulations, that was your first 3D application.

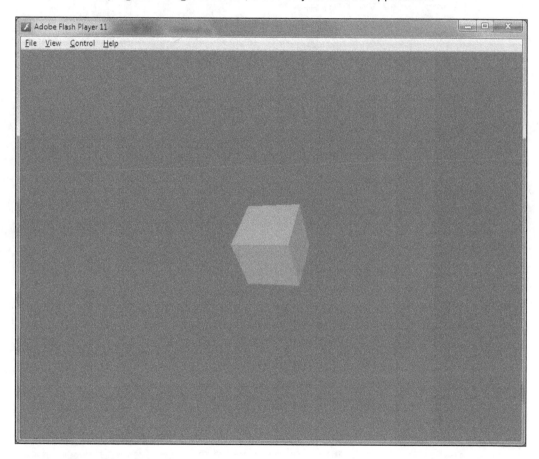

How it works...

In this recipe we've used some of the most important elements of any 3D engine:

- ▶ The **scene** is somewhat comparable to the display list. It is a hierarchical structure of all the elements inside the 3D world. Although inside it is the view class in this recipe, it is actually the very core of any 3D program.

► A **view**, as it says, offers a view into the 3D world. Although we won't show it in this book, you can connect multiple views to a scene. For instance, a 3D drawing program shows the view from the top, left, and front of the project.

► A **light** is also pretty self-explanatory. You can have multiple lights in a scene, but they must always be connected to the material you want lit by them. This is done through a `light picker`.

► A **material** describes what an object will look like. We'll be revisiting different kinds and options for materials in the later recipes and in the next chapter.

► A **geometry** describes the form of the object. For instance, a cube's geometry consists of six faces.

► A **mesh** is the basic 3D element in the scene. It combines a geometry with a material.

► The **camera** describes how the view will render the scene. That is pretty abstract, but if you look at the code, you will see that you can put the camera in a certain place, using the (*x,y,z*) coordinates and you can point it in a certain direction, using the `pitch` and `yaw` properties. There are other ways to point the camera, usually involving a **controller** that controls the camera. We'll see one such controller in the recipe on moving around the scene.

► **Rendering** is the process of calculating a view based on the current state of the scene and camera. Without rendering the scene, we'd just see a blank screen.

That's a lot of information, and no one will grasp everything at once. For now, you should know that we place objects (meshes) inside a 3D scene and look at them through a camera.

If you want to create graphs in three dimensions, the most important elements are the meshes and the camera. We'll look at those in this chapter and let you explore the Internet to get an understanding of everything else. For instance, we won't be discussing shadows or effects such as `depth of field` (that will make the image in the distance blurry)

There's more...

Undoubtedly, you've come to realize that we can only show you the tip of the iceberg when it concerns 3D drawing. The following are a few resources to get a deeper understanding.

The maths

Everything in a 3D engine is based on maths. Most of that is hidden for you by your 3D video card, by the drivers of that card, by Flash's Stage3D, and by the Away3D engine. Sometimes, however, you'll want to understand what is going on.

In the very final recipe of this chapter, we'll look at how all 3D objects are built with triangles. Check the recipe if you want to start your journey through the 3D engine internals.

3D and games

If you start investigating 3D, you'll soon discover that it is most often linked with games. Many 3D engines offer additional features that ease game development (such as management of player characteristics, multiplayer network code, and so on).

In most cases, you can just ignore that part of the code and still use it perfectly for any graph drawing you want to do. Away3D is almost entirely focused on 3D, so you'll find very little other code in the library. There are some companion applications, such as Prefab3D (`http://www.closier.nl/prefab/`) that are more aimed at 3D games.

Away3D 3

If you search the Internet, you'll find that most current tutorials and documentation are aimed at Away3D 3, and not 4. Be warned that these versions are not compatible. Although the concepts are still exactly the same and many class names are identical, you will not be able to just copy the code.

After finishing these two chapters on drawing in 3D, you'll have a better understanding of the basics, and you should be able to convert most of the code for Version 3 to Version 4.

Creating a 3D column chart

Now that we know how to draw a cube in 3D, it's time to convert that cube into a bar and draw a 3D bar chart. To keep things simple, we'll start with just one set of data.

Getting ready

Start by creating a new `Main` class inside a new package. We'll start from a setup similar to the previous recipe. For now, we've left out the mesh definition and the camera setup, as these will differ:

```
package com.graphing.graph
{
    import away3d.containers.View3D;
    import away3d.lights.DirectionalLight;
    import away3d.materials.lightpickers.StaticLightPicker;
    import com.graphing.Graph3D;
    import flash.display.Sprite;
    import flash.events.Event;
    public class Main extends Sprite
    {
        private var _view:View3D;
        private var _data:Array = [[0,20],[50,70],[100,0],[150,150],[2
00,300],[250,200],[300,400],[350,20],[400,60],[450,250],[500,90],[550,
400],[600,500],[650,450],[700,320]];
```

```
    public function Main():void
    {
        _view = new View3D();
        _view.backgroundColor = 0x666666;
        _view.antiAlias = 4;
        addChild(_view);

        var light:DirectionalLight = new DirectionalLight(-0.5, -1,
0.7);
        light.ambient = 0.5;
        light.specular = 0.45;
        light.diffuse = 0.5;
        _view.scene.addChild(light);

        addEventListener(Event.ENTER_FRAME, onEnterFrame);
    }

    private function onEnterFrame(ev : Event) : void
    {
        _view.render();
    }
  }

}
```

Running this should give no errors, but will also give a blank screen, as we haven't placed anything in the scene.

How to do it...

Just as in previous chapters, we will place the graph code inside a separate class. This is shown in the following steps:

1. Create a Graph3D class:

```
package com.graphing
{
    import away3d.containers.ObjectContainer3D;
    import away3d.entities.Mesh;
    import away3d.materials.ColorMaterial;
    import away3d.materials.lightpickers.LightPickerBase;
    import away3d.materials.MaterialBase;
    import away3d.primitives.CubeGeometry;

    public class Graph3D extends ObjectContainer3D
    {
```

```
        public var material:MaterialBase = new
ColorMaterial(0xff9933);

        private var _data:Array;

        public function Graph3D(lightPicker:LightPickerBase)
        {
            material.lightPicker = lightPicker;
        }

        public function set data(value:Array):void {
            _data = value;
        }

        public function createGraph():void {
            drawDataPoints();
        }
    }
}
```

2. The `ObjectContainer3D` class functions similarly to the `Shape` class in a 2D setting. So now we need to fill it with our graph.

3. First we create a method to draw a single cube, one bar from our graph:

```
private function drawCube(x:Number, y:Number, z:Number):void
{
    var cubeGeometry:CubeGeometry = new CubeGeometry(40, y , 40);
    var cube:Mesh = new Mesh(cubeGeometry, material);

    cube.x = x;
    cube.y = y/2;
    cube.z = z;

    addChild(cube);
}
```

4. Next we use this method to draw the graph:

```
private function drawDataPoints():void {
    for (var i:int = 0; i < _data.length; i++)
    {
        drawCube(_data[i][0], _data[i][1], 0);
    }

}
```

5. Now it's a matter of connecting the dots.

6. In the `Main` class' constructor, create the `Graph3D` object and add it to the scene, as given in the following code snippet:

```
_graph = new Graph3D(new StaticLightPicker([light]));
_graph.data = _data;
_graph.createGraph();
_graph.x = -350; // center the graph
_graph.y = -250;
_view.scene.addChild(_graph);
```

7. Finally, point the camera in the right direction:

```
_view.camera.y = 700;
_view.camera.z = -500;
_view.camera.pitch(45);
```

How it works...

The graph consists of multiple cube meshes. Although mathematically speaking we are actually drawing cuboids, Away3D calls them cubes. For simplicity, we will also stick to this naming convention.

These cubes are drawn one-by-one and collected in an `ObjectContainer3D` object. This class is a container class that can contain any number of other 3D objects or containers. If you understand how the display list works for drawing in two dimensions, then you should feel right at home.

The `CubeGeometry` constructor will place the center of the cube at the origin (0,0,0). By manipulating the x, y, and z coordinates, we can move it to our desired position.

Since all individual cubes have positive x coordinates, the graph is on the positive side of the x-axis. To center it, we need to change the x coordinate of the graph. This moves all the cubes to the left. Again this works exactly like the display list.

There's more...

The later recipes will expand on this example, yet there are quite a few things that we can't cover in detail.

View3D

The `View3D` object itself extends `Sprite`. What this means is that we can manipulate it just like any other object in the display list. You can scale it, move it around, or limit its size.

By default it will take up the entire screen, but if you want to incorporate it in a Flash application, you will probably want to give it a specific size and move it to the location where you want to draw the graph.

Two views

This was already mentioned in the previous recipe, but now is the perfect time to experiment with this: if you take a look at the `View3D` constructor, you'll notice that it can accept a `Scene3D` parameter. So you can use the scene from one view and create a new view with the same scene.

In effect, this allows you to create two views that look at the same scene from different angles. When combined with resizing and moving the view, you can have two side-by-side views looking at the same graph,or you could create a picture-in-picture effect.

Shadows

In all the recipes, you'll notice one strange omission: there is a light source, but none of the objects cast shadows. We're not covering shadows for a few reasons:

- Not all graphs will be better with them
- It's an even more advanced topic
- The documentation for shadows in Away3D 4 is currently nonexistent, which could mean that the API might still change

If you would like to try your hand at shadows, start with this example:

```
https://github.com/away3d/away3d-examples-broomstick/blob/master/src/
SoftShadowTest.as
```

and the forum is also very helpful, such as in this thread:

```
http://away3d.com/forum/viewthread/862/
```

Moving around the chart

Being able to move around a 3D chart is one of the more spectacular features of 3D graphing. It really shows off the advantages of using a 3D engine and it will allow your users to see the same data in many different ways.

Getting ready

We'll use the previous recipe and add mouse interaction to it. So start by making a copy of the previous recipe's code and either copy it to a different package, or give it a different name. Don't forget to change the document class.

How to do it...

We'll need to store a few bits of data to calculate the mouse movements and convert them to camera changes:

1. We will start by adding a number of variables to the `Main` class:

```
private var _cameraController:HoverController;
private var _moving:Boolean = false;
private var _lastPanAngle:Number;
private var _lastTiltAngle:Number;
private var _lastMouseX:Number;
private var _lastMouseY:Number;
```

2. Now in the constructor method, remove the code that set up the camera and replace it with the following code snippet:

```
_cameraController = new HoverController(_view.camera, null, 180,
0, 500);
_view.addEventListener(MouseEvent.MOUSE_DOWN, onMouseDown);
_view.addEventListener(MouseEvent.MOUSE_UP, onMouseUp);
```

3. Now implement the event listeners:

```
private function onMouseDown(event:MouseEvent):void
{
    _moving = true;
    _lastPanAngle = _cameraController.panAngle;
    _lastTiltAngle = _cameraController.tiltAngle;
    _lastMouseX = stage.mouseX;
    _lastMouseY = stage.mouseY;
    stage.addEventListener(Event.MOUSE_LEAVE, onStageMouseLeave);
}

private function onMouseUp(event:MouseEvent):void
{
    _moving = false;
    stage.removeEventListener(Event.MOUSE_LEAVE,
onStageMouseLeave);
}

        private function onStageMouseLeave(event:Event):void
        {
    _moving = false;
    stage.removeEventListener(Event.MOUSE_LEAVE,
onStageMouseLeave);
}
```

That's all there is to it. Run the program and if you click-and-drag the mouse you will be able to pan around the graph, as shown in the following screenshot:

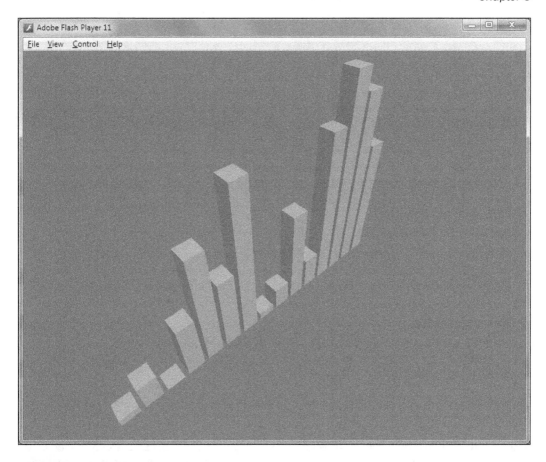

How it works...

We attach a `HoverController` object to the camera. This controller will restrict the camera movement, so that it only follows certain allowed paths.

Once a controller has been defined, it is best not to directly change the camera. Except for maybe setting up the initial position, you should let the controller do its work; otherwise you might end up with unpredictable results.

The `HoverController` object has many optional arguments. In this recipe, we only set the initial pan and tilt angle, and the distance. There are other arguments that allow you to limit the movement, for instance, when there's no reason to look at the underside of the graph.

Check the following documentation for full details:

```
http://away3d.com/livedocs/away3d/4.0/away3d/controllers/
HoverController.html#HoverController%28%29
```

With the controller attached, we now need to have something that changes the status of the controller. You can use keyboard events, but in this recipe we chose to listen to mouse-drag gestures: move the camera as long as the mouse button is pressed.

We've seen a similar technique used in *Chapter 5, Adding Interaction*, when selecting and interacting with the graph. This recipe adds one more element: listening to the MOUSE_LEAVE event. This is a safeguard for when the user moves the mouse cursor outside the stage.

There's more...

As with previous recipes, we've only scratched the surface. There are many ways to move around a 3D world although some won't be of much use for displaying graphs. For instance, in first-person shooters, players use the cursor keys to simulate walking through the world.

Other controllers

We've only shown HoverController, but Away3D has two more controllers. LookAtController is a more general version; it also fixes the camera so it looks at one point, but it has more degrees of freedom.

FirstPersonController was previously described and will probably be of little use for most graph programmers.

You can always implement your own controller, starting from the ControllerBase class. The code will revolve around implementing the update method. This method is responsible for enforcing whatever limits you want to put in place.

Lenses

Although not directly related to moving around the scene, it is related to the camera and interesting enough to mention: cameras can have lenses. These allow you to control the field of view and the projection type.

The following article has a few examples and shows how to use lenses:

```
http://www.flashmagazine.com/tutorials/detail/away3d_4_
basics_-_the_cameras/
```

Other ways of moving

In this recipe, we've moved the camera around. But you could just as well move the scene around and leave the camera fixed.

Keep in mind that if you change the 3D world, it will change for all cameras looking at that scene, so this could have unintended side effects if you have multiple views.

So in general this is not advised, but there might be situations where it's just easier to manipulate the scene instead of the camera.

Controllers not just for cameras

If you look at the code of the controllers in Away3D, you may have noticed that they are attached to an entity, not a camera. While a camera is an entity, entities are the highest level class that is part of the scene.

This means that a cube and a light are also entities, so you can also define controllers on them. This can be useful if you want to move around multiple objects along set paths.

This is typically used for games, so it will probably not be used as much in graph applications, but it's good to keep in mind when your 3D graphs become a little more complicated, or you want to add some advanced movements.

Beyond the cube, drawing different shapes

Up until now, we have only drawn cubes. It's about time we looked at some other forms. In this recipe, we look at how you can use Away3D's built-in shapes to create different visualizations. We will replace the cubes from the previous recipe with cylinders.

Getting ready

We will adapt the previous recipe. So create a copy of it and move it to a new package or rename it. Finally, set it as the document class.

How to do it...

First let's make the `Graph3D` class a little more generic:

1. Create a member variable inside the `Graph3D` class:

   ```
   public var drawFunction:Function = drawCube;
   ```

2. Update the `drawDataPoints` method so it uses the new variable:

   ```
   private function drawDataPoints():void {
       for (var i:int = 0; i < _data.length; i++)
       {
           drawFunction(_data[i][0], _data[i][1], 0);
       }
   }
   ```

Now we can put our new drawing function inside the main program (although in a real program, you may want to keep it in the `Graph3D` class):

1. Create a new member variable inside the `Main` class:

    ```
    private var _lightPicker:LightPickerBase;
    ```

2. Change the graph initialization so that it uses a custom drawing function:

    ```
    _lightPicker = new StaticLightPicker([light]);
    _graph = new Graph3D(_lightPicker);
    _graph.data = _data;
    _graph.drawFunction = drawCylinder;
    _graph.createGraph();
    _graph.x = -350;
    _graph.y = -250;
    _view.scene.addChild(_graph);
    ```

3. And implement the `drawCylinder` function:

    ```
    private function drawCylinder(x:Number, y:Number, z:Number):void
    {
        var cylinderGeometry:CylinderGeometry = new
    CylinderGeometry(20, 20, y);
        var cylinderMaterial:ColorMaterial = new
    ColorMaterial(0xff9933);
        cylinderMaterial.lightPicker = _lightPicker;
        var cylinder:Mesh = new Mesh(cylinderGeometry,
    cylinderMaterial);

        cylinder.x = x;
        cylinder.y = y/2;
        cylinder.z = z;

        _graph.addChild(cylinder);
    }
    ```

If you run the program now, you should see the same graph, but now drawn with cylinders instead of cubes.

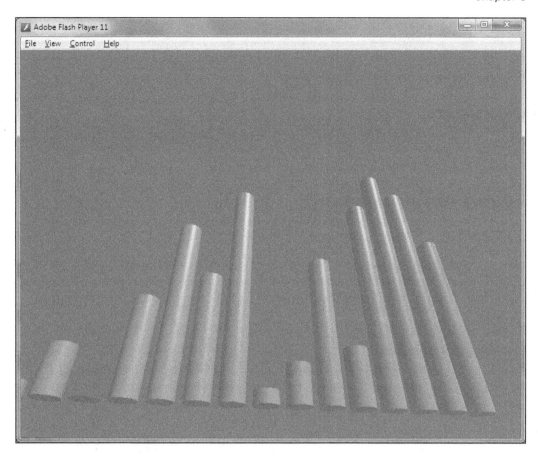

How it works...

ActionScript allows you to store pointers to functions inside variables. We use this to make the drawing function customizable. We can create whatever function we want to draw the data points, but it only has to accept three parameters.

Next we build up a mesh based on a cylinder geometry. This piece of code is exactly the same as drawing a cube, only now we create a different geometry that takes different parameters.

The parameters for the cylinder geometry are the radius at the top and bottom, and the height. Most of the additional parameters that the cylinder geometry takes will be of little use when creating graphs.

There's more...

This short recipe showed only one different shape that you can use. The shape of the graph elements can be adjusted in a number of ways.

More shapes

Apart from the cube and cylinder, Away3D also has a `ConeGeometry` shape that will be of use for this type of graph. If you draw different types of graphs, you may also find a use for `CapsuleGeometry` and `SphereGeometry`.

Defining your own geometry

If you're not happy with the existing shapes, it is possible to define your own geometry and draw whatever you desire.

We'll take a closer look at this in the *Graphing a function in three dimensions* recipe of this chapter; however, keep in mind that this is a very advanced topic and should not be attempted by first-time 3D developers. You're often better off creating a shape in the 3D editor and loading that one.

Loading 3D shapes

Away3D comes with a number of parsers that can load 3D models from 3D editors, such as 3D Studio Max and Wavefront. This is, by far, the easiest way to get a custom model into your application.

An example can be found at `http://www.allforthecode.co.uk/aftc/forum/user/modules/forum/article.php?index=6&subindex=8&aid=328`.

Graphing tabular data in 3D

In this recipe, we expand on drawing in multiple dimensions. For now, we've only shown a 2D graph translated to 3D. Now we will show how to draw two separate data sets and get a real three-dimensional graph.

Getting ready

Start by creating a copy of the *Moving around the chart* recipe. This will be the basis for the current recipe.

Now replace the data set with the following one:

```
private var _data:Array = [[0, 20, 40], [50, 70, 60], [100, 0, 10],
[150, 150, 170],
[200, 300, 280], [250, 200, 210], [300, 400, 350], [350, 20, 50],
[400, 60, 70], [450, 250, 230], [500, 90, 110], [550, 400, 350],
[600, 500, 400],[650, 450, 380],[700,320, 350]];
```

It's basically the same set as before, plus an additional one.

How to do it...

The current code should work as it is, but it will only display the first data set:

1. To also display the second one, we only need to extend the Graph3D class. Replace the drawDataPoints method with the following code (remember drawFunction is the method responsible for drawing individual datapoints):

```
private function drawDataPoints():void {
    for (var i:int = 0; i < _data.length; i++)
    {
        for (var j:int = 1; j < _data[i].length; j++) {
            drawFunction(_data[i][0], _data[i][j], j*50);
        }
    }
}
```

   Re-running the program will show both sets side-by-side. If you want to take a closer look at the second set, you can hover around the graph by dragging the mouse.

2. Now let's draw the second data set in a different color. Replace the material variable with an array:

```
public var materials:Array = [new ColorMaterial(0xff9933), new
ColorMaterial(0x3399ff)];
```

   In the constructor we need to apply the light picker to all materials:

```
for (var i:int = 0; i < materials.length; i++) {
    materials[i].lightPicker = lightPicker;
}
```

3. The material will now be passed to the drawCube function as a parameter, so we add a parameter to the function declaration:

```
private function drawCube(x:Number, y:Number, z:Number,
material:MaterialBase):void
```

4. And finally, we add that parameter to the function call in the `drawDataPoints` function:

```
drawFunction(_data[i][0], _data[i][j], j*50, materials[j-1]);
```

The program will now show both the data sets in different colors, as shown in the following screenshot:

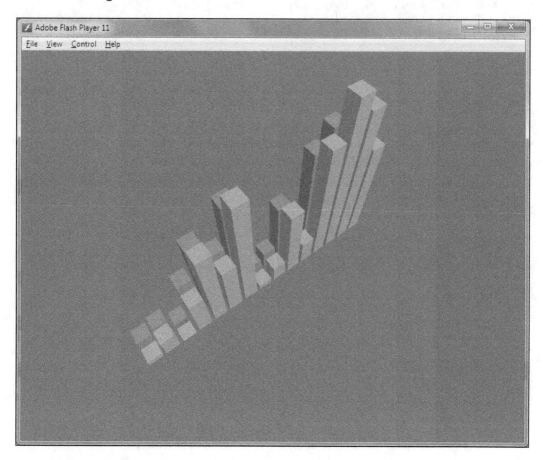

How it works...

Once you got this far in the chapter, you must've noticed that this is probably the easiest recipe of the entire chapter.

Instead of having one loop over the individual points, we now have two loops. The outer loop is still the same, while the inner loop makes sure that we draw both sets.

To make a distinction between the two sets, the z-coordinate is different for each set. The z-coordinate controls how close or far away the object is from the viewer.

In a similar vein, we also switch the material (and thus the color) based on the data set. If you have more data sets, make sure you have a material for each one, otherwise your dataset won't be displayed.

There's more...

Now that we have code to create full 3D graphs, you can start to extend it in various ways.

Transparent materials

Just like `Sprite`, `materials` also has an `alpha` channel and can be made transparent. For instance, add this to the `Graph3D` constructor:

```
materials[i].alpha = 0.8;
```

This will result in slightly transparent cubes. This can be useful if one data set hides another one.

A more generic Graph3D class

Our data set has points exactly 50 units apart from each other. We use that fact in the `Graph3D` class on two separate occasions:

▶ In the `drawCube` function, the size of our cubes is 40. This results in nicely spaced cubes.

▶ In the `drawDataPoints` function, the data sets are spaced 50 units apart.

If you want a more generic function to draw data sets where you don't know the distance between points, you will need to obtain that value some way.

One option is to subtract the largest from the smallest value and divide by the number of datapoints. This will give a good approximation.

Another option is to add this as a parameter to the function so that you can change it on a case-by-case basis.

Other shapes and materials

Of course, you can change the entire look of the different data sets even more. You can have one drawn with cubes and another one with cylinders.

In the next recipe we'll see even more ways to style and customize the look of the graph. All of these can be applied to individual data sets, or even individual points if you want to.

Styling the graph with different materials

Up until now, we've always used the solid color `ColorMaterial` to draw our graphs. However, to get the most out of your 3D world, you'll need to know `TextureMaterial`. This recipe introduces how to use it with a bitmap. The next chapter will show a few practical examples of the techniques learned here.

Getting ready

As in the previous recipe, start by creating a copy of the *Moving around the chart* recipe.

You'll also need a bitmap image. For instance, you can download open source textures that are free to use from `http://opengameart.org/textures/all`. There is only one requirement: the bitmap's size, both height and width, should be powers of two.

This is a limit inside Away3D that stems from the limits of the graphical card that renders the image to the screen.

How to do it...

Put the bitmap image inside the `lib` folder and embed it in the main application. Do this by right-clicking and selecting **Generate Embed Code**. Next, attach it to a class name and create an instance. Your code should look like the following code snippet:

```
[Embed(source = "../../../../lib/TiZeta_parsley.jpg")]
private var BitmapClass:Class;
private var bitmap:Bitmap = new BitmapClass();
```

We now create `BitmapTexture` and `TextureMaterial`. The code belongs in the constructor of the main class, before creating the graph:

```
var bitmapTexture:BitmapTexture   = new BitmapTexture(bitmap.
bitmapData);
var bitmapMaterial:TextureMaterial = new
TextureMaterial(bitmapTexture, true, true);
bitmapMaterial.lightPicker = lightPicker;
```

This new material can now be used to overwrite the default material (in this case, we're only providing material for one data set):

```
_graph.materials = [bitmapMaterial];
```

If you run the code now, you'll see the bitmap applied to the graph. This is shown in the following screenshot:

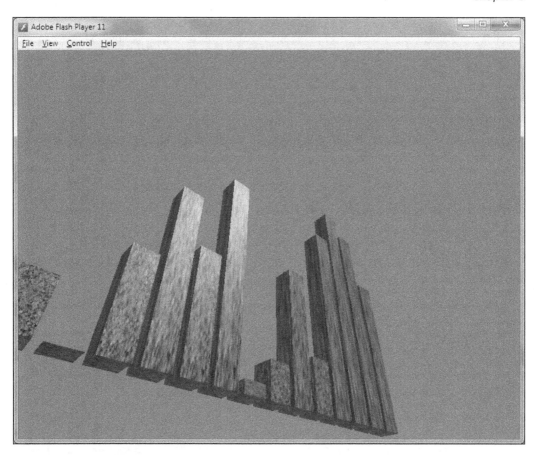

How it works...

`BitmapTexture` is the most basic texture around. If you want to create an over-the-top presentation, take a look at `VideoTexture`.

`TextureMaterial` combines the bitmap inside `BitmapTexture` with a number of other parameters and forms a material. This material will be applied to the geometry.

The constructor parameters are all fairly technical and you won't need them until you are looking for them. An important one is the third one, which indicates whether or not the texture is repeated when it is too small to cover the entire object. Although the default is not to repeat, you'll probably want to change this in many cases.

In the next chapter, we'll look in more detail at some of the `TextureMaterial` properties, such as the ability to create bumpmaps that give the impression of a rough surface.

With the texture created, we can now combine it with a geometry object to form a mesh. This mesh is a 3D object that we can add to the 3D world. In this example, we just use the default values, but there are also quite a few things that can be changed, such as how exactly the texture is applied to the geometry.

There's more...

Texture mapping is a very broad subject, one that also requires a bit of background and understanding of how 3D engines work. Therefore, we've only been able to introduce the very basics.

Different image on each cube face

To keep things simple, we've deliberately chosen an image where this is not clear: but by default Away3D will map different parts of the texture to different faces of the cube. Imagine that you split the texture in a two-by-three grid. Each part will be mapped to a different side of the cube.

Currently, there is a bug in Away3D, which prevents this from working as you would expect. A fix can be found here:

`http://jansensan.net/apply-a-texture-on-a-cube-in-away3d-4-0`

If you'd like for each face to have the same image repeated, you can turn this off by specifying `false` as the seventh parameter to the `CubeGeometry` constructor.

Text

We haven't talked about displaying text yet. And it is with good reason. Sadly, there is no easy way to display text in Away3D at this point. This will probably change as helper classes and add-on libraries are written.

Right now, if you want to display text inside the 3D world, your best bet is to use the `Sprite3D` class. Such an entity will always be facing the user, so the text will always be legible.

You can combine this with `BitmapTexture` and `TextureMaterial`. The bitmap data for the texture can in turn be obtained from creating a `BitmapData` object and using the `draw` method to draw `TextField` on there.

It's a very convoluted way, which is why it's almost certain that there will appear easier ways in the not-too-distant future.

Fine-tuning texture mapping

The way two-dimensional textures are put onto three-dimensional objects (mapped) is pretty complex and is a chapter of its own. A good starting point is Wikipedia: `http://en.wikipedia.org/wiki/Texture_mapping`.

If you want to manipulate the position where the texture is applied to the object, you can change the UV coordinates and their scaling. Again, see Wikipedia for an introduction: http://en.wikipedia.org/wiki/UV_mapping.

Since texture mapping is specific to a geometry, you can reach these properties through the geometry object. `scaleUV` controls the size of the texture on the object (make sure repeating textures is turned on if you want to scale down). The `UVData` vector that is part of each subgeometry of the geometry object controls the position.

In many cases, if you need to manipulate these variables, you are usually better off creating the shape and mapping it in a 3D editor and loading it. See the *Beyond the cube, drawing different shapes* recipe.

Graphing a function in three dimensions

This last recipe in the chapter is probably also the most advanced in the entire book, but it can be used to create an impressive effect.

In this recipe, we define our own generated 3D object, not based on cubes or other existing shapes. To obtain this result, we define a very basic geometry that we used to build a custom shape.

Getting ready

The starting setup is similar as before. We will define a new class to hold our graph. So copy any of the previous recipes, but remove all references to `Graph3D` and the data from it.

How to do it...

The idea here is to plot a three-dimensional function:

```
y = (sin(x)² . cos(z)²) / (5 . x² . z²)
```

1. We will use Flash's built-in `Vector3D` class to clean up some of the code. `Vector3D` is an object that simply holds the tree's *x*, *y*, and *z* values of a point in the 3D world.

2. We will work from the bottom up. First create a new class called `RectangleGeometry`, as shown in the following code:

```
package com.graphing
{
    import away3d.core.base.SubGeometry;
    import away3d.primitives.PrimitiveBase;

    import flash.geom.Vector3D;
```

```
public class RectangleGeometry extends PrimitiveBase
{
    private var _v0:Vector3D;
    private var _v1:Vector3D;
    private var _v2:Vector3D;
    private var _v3:Vector3D;

    public function RectangleGeometry(v0:Vector3D,
v1:Vector3D, v2:Vector3D, v3:Vector3D)
    {
        super();

        _v0 = v0;
        _v1 = v1;
        _v2 = v2;
        _v3 = v3;
    }

    override protected function buildGeometry(target:SubGeomet
ry):void
    {
        var rawVertices:Vector.<Number> = Vector.<Number>([_
v0.x, _v0.y, _v0.z, _v1.x, _v1.y, _v1.z, _v2.x, _v2.y, _v2.z, _
v3.x, _v3.y, _v3.z]);
        var rawIndices:Vector.<uint> = Vector.<uint>([0, 1, 2,
0, 2, 3]);

        target.autoDeriveVertexNormals = true;
        target.autoDeriveVertexTangents = true;
        target.updateVertexData(rawVertices);
        target.updateIndexData(rawIndices);
    }

    override protected function buildUVs(target:SubGeometry):v
oid
    {
        //TODO if you want to use textures
    }
}
}
```

This class is responsible for drawing individual rectangles out of the function's surface.

3. Now create a `Function3D` class that will combine data points into a 3D surface, using the `RectangleGeometry` class:

```
package com.graphing
{
```

```actionscript
import away3d.containers.ObjectContainer3D;
import away3d.entities.Mesh;
import away3d.materials.ColorMaterial;
import away3d.materials.lightpickers.LightPickerBase;
import away3d.materials.lightpickers.StaticLightPicker;
import away3d.materials.MaterialBase;
import away3d.primitives.CubeGeometry;
import away3d.primitives.PlaneGeometry;
import away3d.tools.commands.Merge;
import flash.geom.Vector3D;

public class Function3D extends ObjectContainer3D
{
    private var _data:Array;
    private var _lightPicker:LightPickerBase;

    public function Function3D(lightPicker:LightPickerBase)
    {
        this._lightPicker = lightPicker;
    }

    public function set data(value:Array):void {
_data = value;
}

    public function createGraph():void {
        var material:ColorMaterial = new
ColorMaterial(0xff9933);
        material.lightPicker = _lightPicker;

        for (var i:int = 1; i < _data.length; i++) {
        for (var j:int = 1; j < _data[i].length; j++) {
            var v1:Vector3D = _data[i][j];
            var v2:Vector3D = _data[i][j - 1];
            var v3:Vector3D = _data[i - 1][j - 1];
            var v4:Vector3D = _data[i-1][j];

            drawRectangle(v1, v2, v3, v4, material);
        }
    }

    }

private function drawRectangle(v1:Vector3D, v2:Vector3D,
v3:Vector3D, v4:Vector3D, material:MaterialBase):void
```

```
        {
            var rectangleGeometry:RectangleGeometry = new
    RectangleGeometry(v1, v2, v3, v4);
            var rectangle:Mesh = new Mesh(rectangleGeometry,
    material);
        addChild(rectangle);
            }
        }


    }
```

4. In the `Main` class, add the following helper functions to calculate the surface values:

```
    private function calculateData():Array {
        _data = [];
        for (var x:Number = -5; x <= 5; x += .25) {
            var line:Array = [];
            for (var z:Number = -5; z <= 5; z += .25) {
                line.push(new Vector3D(x*100, surface(x, z) * 2000,
    z*100));
            }
            _data.push(line);
        }
        return _data;
    }


    private function surface(x:Number, z:Number):Number {
        return (Math.pow(Math.sin(x), 2) * Math.pow(Math.cos(z), 2)) /
    (5 + x * x + z * z);
    }
```

5. And finally, we use these calculated functions to construct the 3D representation of the function. Add the following last bit of code to the constructor of the class:

```
    _graph = new Function3D(new StaticLightPicker([light]));
    _graph.data = calculateData();
    _graph.createGraph();
    _view.scene.addChild(_graph);
```

The result is as shown in the following screenshot:

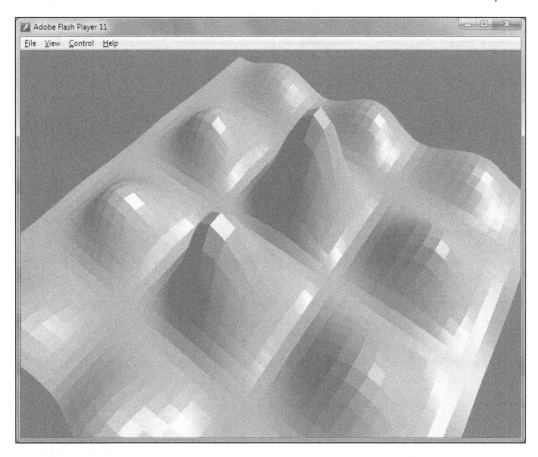

How it works...

Our approach is similar to the *Creating a line graph based on a function* recipe in *Chapter 1, Getting Started with Graph Drawing*. We calculate the value of the function at discrete intervals and draw straight lines between those values. If the gap between values is small enough, the end result is a smooth function graph.

In this example, computer processing and graphic's power will be the limiting factor. Depending on your computer speed, you may need to increase the gap between values. If the end result is too slow, you should increase the value inside the loops. It's currently at 0.25, but even at 1 it will still give you an idea of the function's shape.

As a base, we use rectangles, because that is the form in which we calculate the coordinates. We've deliberately kept the class as simple as possible. The main thing to notice is that there are four vertices, but six indices. That is because we need to construct every item in the 3D world out of triangles.

Take a look at the following diagram of a random quadrilateral.

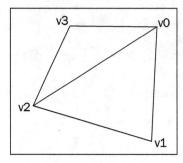

To draw one rectangle, we need to draw two triangles: a triangle between vertices 0, 1, and 2, and one between vertices 0, 2, and 3.

The indices point into the array of vertices, so we can re-use vertices multiple times to create our geometry.

When looking at the `Function3D` code, it is important to notice that we are using a different data structure than in the previous recipes. This change was made to make the code easier to read and adapt.

We now store the `Vector3D` points inside a 2D array (one dimension for *x*, one for *z*). This allows us to easily build up the `RectangleGeometry` instances and add these to the scene.

In the `Main` class, we've moved the function we want to plot into its very own `surface` function. This allows you to easily plug in other formulas and see how these look.

The `calculateData` function will calculate a datapoint at set distances. We've also added a little bit of scaling code (multiplication by 100 and 2000), so that we don't need to reconfigure the camera and controller.

There's more...

If you experiment a little with the application, you'll notice that there are many improvements or changes that can be made. The following are a few.

One geometry

If you look closely at the individual rectangles, you'll notice that, even though they aren't flat, they are rendered perfectly smooth, similar to how a sphere is rendered.

Between rectangles you can see a hard edge.

The reason for this edge is that the different rectangles are individual geometries. If you want a perfectly smooth surface, you will want to create one big geometry. This would involve moving the loops within the `createGraph` function inside the `RectangleGeometry` class.

It's a fairly simple tweak that will have an impressive visual effect.

Color change based on height

The surface now has one uniform color. Due do the lighting, it is possible to clearly see the peaks. However, you may also want to experiment with changing the color based on the height of the rectangle. This will give the higher peaks a different color than the lower areas.

Two-sided surfaces

If you spin around the surface, you'll notice that it disappears. That's because we only defined the top surface and not the bottom one.

The top of a rectangle is defined by the direction in which the coordinates are entered. They should always be entered in a clockwise direction, when looking directly at the rectangle.

So you can draw a second down-facing surface, by adding a second rectangle, but with the coordinates in counterclockwise order.

See also

This recipe has used the very basis of a 3D engine, namely triangles. If you want to fully understand what's happening, your best starting point is reading up on how 3D engines work. The Gamedev website has a large section on technical books: `http://www.gamedev.net/page/books/index.html/_/technical/graphics-programming-10/`.

10
Working with Various 3D Graph Types

In this chapter, we will cover:

- ▸ Mapping keyboard usage in 3D, part 1: The model
- ▸ Mapping keyboard usage in 3D, part 2: The data
- ▸ 3D world population chart, part 1: The globe
- ▸ 3D world population chart, part 2: Dressing up
- ▸ 3D world population chart, part 3: The data

Introduction

Now that we have covered the basis of 3D drawing and creating graphs, it's time to look at more advanced examples. This chapter covers only two examples, but due to their complexity they are spread out over different recipes and each highlights one or more subjects related to 3D drawing.

As mentioned previously, you'll quickly notice that there's a lot to it. However, the result can be spectacular.

Mapping keyboard usage in 3D, part 1: The model

In the next two recipes, we want to create a better way of representing the data found in this Wikipedia article: `http://en.wikipedia.org/wiki/Letter_frequency`.

The idea is to create a 3D graph of the frequency with which letters are used in various languages and to overlay this graph on an actual keyboard image, so the letters that are used the most are represented by keys that stick out more from the base keyboard, as shown in the following screenshot:

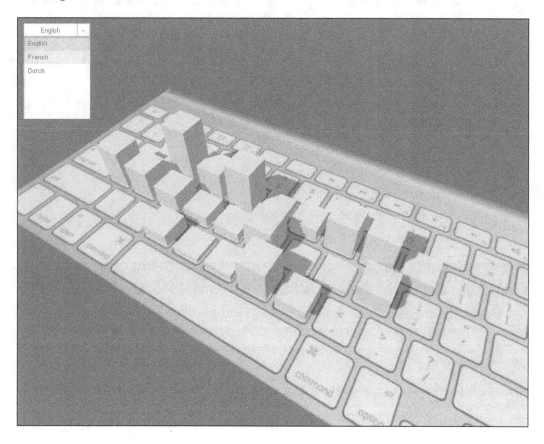

We will create this in two steps: in the first recipe, we'll look at how to create the 3D model of the keyboard and the bars. In the second recipe, we'll add the actual data to the chart.

Getting ready

This chapter will use the Away3D 4 library. So to get started, you should set up your workspace, exactly as in the previous chapter. Also copy over the `Main` and `Graph3D` classes from the *Graphing a function in three dimensions* recipe in *Chapter 9, Creating Three-Dimensional Graphs.*

How to do it...

We will replace the `Graph3D` class with a similar class, but specialized for displaying the keyboard object:

1. First replace the `Graph3D` class in the constructor of the main program with the new `Keyboard3D` class we will implement:

```
_keyboard = new Keyboard3D(light);
_view.scene.addChild(_keyboard);
```

2. Right now, this program will not run, so create a `Keyboard3D` class:

```
package
{
    import away3d.containers.ObjectContainer3D;
    import away3d.entities.Mesh;
    import away3d.lights.DirectionalLight;
    import away3d.materials.ColorMaterial;
    import away3d.materials.DefaultMaterialBase;
    import away3d.materials.lightpickers.StaticLightPicker;
    import away3d.materials.methods.FilteredShadowMapMethod;
    import away3d.materials.TextureMaterial;
    import away3d.primitives.CubeGeometry;
    import away3d.textures.BitmapTexture;
    import flash.display.Bitmap;

    public class Keyboard3D extends ObjectContainer3D
    {
        public function Keyboard3D(light:DirectionalLight)
        {
        }
    }
}
```

3. That should make the program run. For the keyboard image, we used one of the many available images of the latest Apple keyboards. It was resized to 1024 by 512 pixels to comply with the texture limitations (see the *Styling the graph with different materials* recipe from *Chapter 9, Creating Three-Dimensional Graphs*, for a full explanation). Embed the image using the following code:

```
[Embed(source = "../lib/keyboard.png")]
private var KeyboardImageClass:Class;
private var _keyboardImage:Bitmap = new KeyboardImageClass();
```

4. In the constructor, create a simple cube and map the keyboard image onto it:

```
var keyboardTexture:BitmapTexture = new BitmapTexture(_
keyboardImage.bitmapData);
var keyboardMaterial:TextureMaterial = new TextureMaterial(keyboar
dTexture);
keyboardMaterial.repeat = true;
keyboardMaterial.lightPicker = new StaticLightPicker([light]);
keyboardMaterial.shadowMethod = new
FilteredShadowMapMethod(light);

var keyboardGeometry:CubeGeometry = new CubeGeometry(1024, 6,
512);
var keyboard:Mesh = new Mesh(keyboardGeometry, keyboardMaterial);
keyboard.rotationY = 180;
keyboardGeometry.scaleUV(3, 2);

addChild(keyboard);
```

    At this point you should be able to run the application and rotate around a flat keyboard.

5. Next we add the cubes on the keys that will hold the information. For now we'll just assign them random numbers. First add the coordinates of the different keys as a private variable in `Keyboard3D`:

```
private var _keyData:Array = [
["A", 139, 283], ["B", 451, 355], ["C", 312, 355], ["D", 277,
283], ["E", 259, 211], ["F", 346, 283],
["G", 416, 283], ["H", 485, 283], ["I", 606, 211], ["J", 554,
283], ["K", 624, 283], ["L", 693, 283],
["M", 589, 355], ["N", 519, 355], ["O", 675, 211], ["P", 745,
211], ["Q", 121, 211], ["R", 329, 211],
["S", 208, 283], ["T", 398, 211], ["U", 536, 211], ["V", 381,
355], ["W", 190, 211], ["X", 242, 355],
["Y", 467, 211], ["Z", 173, 355]
];
private var _keyMeshes:Array = [];
```

6. Next create a method for drawing individual keys:

```
private function addKey(x:Number, z:Number, usage:Number):Mesh
{
    var keyGeometry:CubeGeometry = new CubeGeometry(54,usage,54);
    var key:Mesh = new Mesh(keyGeometry, _material);

    key.x = -1 * (x + 27 - 512);
    key.y = usage / 2 + 3;
    key.z = z + 27 - 256;

    addChild(key);

    return key;
}
```

7. And finally draw all the keys in the constructor of `Keyboard3D`:

```
for (var i:int = 0; i < _keyData.length; i++) {
    var key:Array = _keyData[i];
    _keyMeshes.push(addKey(key[1], key[2], 300*Math.random()));
}
```

How it works...

In this recipe, we've introduced very little new content. If you read the previous chapter, you should be familiar with almost everything demonstrated here.

The only new item here is the display of shadows. As you can see, Away3D 4 makes it very easy to have objects cast shadows on other objects.

Since calculating shadows is fairly processor-intensive, all shadow calculations are off by default. There are two parts to turning on shadows:

1. Lights must be enabled to cast shadows. Currently, only directional lights support casting shadows.

2. The objects that will cast and receive shadows must have a method attached that will calculate the shadows. This method will be responsible for calculating what regions of the object should be drawn as shaded.

The `_keyData` object and the `addKey` method use coordinates and sizes that were obtained in a drawing program (such as Adobe Photoshop). The selection tool was used to select the key and the resulting coordinates were copied into the program. In Photoshop, the coordinates of the keyboard image run from (0,0) in the top-left corner to (1024,512) in the bottom-right corner.

In the 3D world, the keyboard is centred in the middle of the coordinate system, so its coordinates go from (-512,-256) to (512,256). We could have used an additional `ObjectContainer3D` class to perform the translation, similar to what we did in the *Drawing in two dimensions* recipe in *Chapter 1, Getting Started with Graph Drawing*. To keep the code concise, we chose to keep this basic transformation in the code of the `addKey` method.

The `usage` variable will hold the number of times a key is used and will dictate the height of the key. Since the cube mesh is place at the center, we need to move half of the height of the key upward, plus three more units, which is the thickness of the base keyboard.

There's more...

This recipe shows one way of solving the problem, but of course there are many ways to obtain the same effect.

External 3D editor

Using a graphics program to obtain every individual key coordinate is a lot of work. An easier way is to create the object in a 3D editor and import this into the program.

But there are a few hurdles that you'll have to jump:

> ▶ The import functionality in Away3D 4 is fairly limited. The Wavefront OBJ format, which can be created by most editors, is supported but with every conversion between formats you risk breaking something.

> ▶ There are still a few bugs and missing features in the Away3D library's import code. For instance, textures are imported, but are not applied to the correct geometries. You will need to do that manually.

Manipulating the shadows

If you look closely at the shadows, you may notice that they aren't cast perfectly. In the current implementation of the filtered shadow method, there seems to be a slight bug that may already be resolved by the time you try this recipe.

You can manipulate the exact placement of a shadow by changing the `epsilon` property of the method.

A good exercise, if you want to learn more about shadows, is to try the other, different shadow methods available at:

`http://www.away3d.com/livedocs/away3d/4.0/away3d/materials/methods/ShadowMapMethodBase.html`

For instance, `HardShadowMapMethod` will create shadows with a very sharp edge.

Right now, there is very little documentation on shadows in Away3D 4, so your best bet is the forum:

`http://away3d.com/forum/.`

Mapping keyboard usage in 3D, part 2: The data

In this recipe, we'll replace the random data that we added to the keyboard object with the actual data taken from:

`http://en.wikipedia.org/wiki/Letter_frequency.`

We will only add three languages, but you'll see that you can add as many as you want.

Getting ready

To display a combobox that lets the user pick the language to show, we will use the *minimalcomps* library. It can be downloaded from `https://github.com/minimalcomps/minimalcomps/downloads`. This library is, as the name implies, an extremely basic implementation of many graphical components. Due to its simplicity, it is also very easy to use in any ActionScript program.

To use it in your project, download it and place the SWC file in the `lib` directory of the project. Inside FlashDevelop, right-click on the file and choose **Add to library**. This will make all the classes inside the file available to your programs.

We'll, of course, continue from the previous recipe.

How to do it...

In the previous recipe we constructed the model; this recipe is about applying the data to it:

1. In the main program, add the letter frequencies:

```
private var _letterFrequencies:Object = {
"English" : [163.34,29.84,55.6,85.06,254.04,45.76,40.44,121.88,
139.46,3,14.94,80.5,50.34,134.98,150.14,38.58,1.96,119.74,126.66,
181.12,55.16,20.74,49.3,3.06,39.42,1.48],
"French"  : [152.72,18.02,65.2,73.38,294.3,21.32,17.32,14.74,
150.58,10.9,0.98,109.12,59.36,141.9,107.56,60.42,27.24,131.06,
158.96,144.88,126.22,32.56,2.28,7.74,6.16,2.72],
"Dutch"   : [149.8,31.6,24.8,118.6,378.2,16.2,68,47.6,130,29.2,45,
71.4,44.2,200.6,121.2,31.4,0.18,128.2,74.6,135.8,39.8,57,30.4,0.8,
0.7,38.6]
}
```

2. In the constructor, add a default language that is shown when the program starts up:

    ```
    _keyboard.data = _letterFrequencies["English"];
    ```

3. Add a combobox from the minimal components library:

    ```
    var choice:ComboBox = new ComboBox(this, 10, 10, "English");
    choice.addItem("English");
    choice.addItem("French");
    choice.addItem("Dutch");
    choice.addEventListener(Event.SELECT, onSelect);
    ```

    The final piece of code in the main program is the `onSelect` listener:

    ```
    private function onSelect(ev: Event):void {
    _keyboard.data = _letterFrequencies[ev.target.selectedItem];
    }
    ```

4. Now we still need to implement the setting of data inside the `Keyboard3D` class. Start by removing the random data that we set and replace the starting height with 1:

    ```
    _keyMeshes.push(addKey(key[1], key[2], 1));
    ```

5. And then add the data setter:

    ```
    public function set data(value:Array):void {
        for (var i:int = 0; i < value.length; i++) {
            var key:Mesh = _keyMeshes[i];
            key.scaleY = value[i];
            key.y = value[i] / 2 + 3;
        }
    }
    ```

    The resulting code will now generate the image that was shown at the start of the previous recipe, *Mapping keyboard usage in 3D, part 1: The model*.

How it works...

The letter frequency data is not the raw data from Wikipedia, but a bit of preprocessing was done in Excel. We converted the percentage values to absolute values that fit and show up nicely for the size of the keyboard that we used.

If you want to make this part of the code more reusable, there's nothing that says this operation must be done in Excel. It can just as well be done in ActionScript code.

The constructor of the combobox immediately adds it to the stage (the `this` reference in the argument list) so that there's no need to add an extra `addChild` call.

Because our `View3D` class is just as well a part of the (2D) display list, there's nothing holding us back from mixing and matching it with any other ActionScript components, such as, in this case, the combobox.

Selection of an item in the combobox follows the traditional ActionScript model. You attach an event listener to the select event. Inside the listener, you can use the event itself to see what exactly was selected.

By setting the height of the keys to `1`, we can use the `scale` value to easily change the height. Another more complicated option would be changing the geometry itself, but this would involve a lot more code.

There's more...

The end result is already a great and engaging graph, but there are still a few more things that you can do to improve it.

Key material

Currently the keys are just plain gray. It would be very nice if they showed the actual key on top.

We've skipped this step because it is a little more complicated than you might think at first. In the previous recipe, we've shown how to use materials on cubes. If you'd like to use this option, you would have to create a different image for each and every key. Although it's not impossible, it's a pretty time-consuming process.

A different option is to re-use the existing keyboard image and use the UV coordinates to map just the right part of the image on top of the key. However, here you'll run into the limits of the default cube, which make it pretty hard to address only the top face of the cube. If you want to go this route, you'll probably be better off creating two meshes for every key, one plane for the top and one cube for the rest of the body.

Read data directly from Wikipedia

A good test of everything you've learned in this book is to obtain the data directly from the Wikipedia page. You can use the data-importing techniques discussed in the *Loading data with XML* in *Chapter 2*, *Working with Data*, to read the XHTML file and use the XML processing capabilities of ActionScript to extract the data.

This will also allow you to quickly add many more languages to the display.

Showing labels on hover

Similar to what we have shown in the *Making the points interactive: Hovering* recipe in *Chapter 5*, *Adding Interaction*, it is also possible to show additional information when the user hovers over a certain key.

If you want to receive mouse events on any 3D object, you first need to enable the mouse events. You do this by setting the `mouseEnabled` property to `true` on the mesh.

Next you can add listeners to the mesh that listen to the various `MouseEvent3D` events. And finally, see the note in the previous chapter on displaying text.

3D world population chart, part 1: The globe

This demonstration is based on the Chrome globe experiment that can be seen at `http://www.chromeexperiments.com/globe`. We will re-use the data and recreate it in ActionScript with a few changes here and there.

The end result will look like the following screenshot:

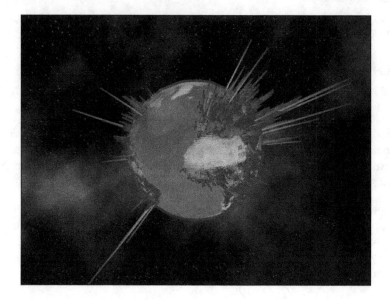

Lines represent the population at that location on the earth.

The work has been split into three recipes:

- A first, fairly short, recipe that looks at showing a globe and applying a texture
- A second recipe that goes into a few techniques for making the globe look more attractive
- And a final recipe that will display the actual data

All images used within these recipes are the free version available on `http://planetpixelemporium.com/earth.html`, unless otherwise noted. We use the small size images, but if you really want to use this in a finished work, you may want to purchase the higher resolution images.

Getting ready

We will start from a similar project as before. We will re-use the existing code for moving around the 3D world and plug in our own 3D object.

Download the color, bump, and cloud map. You may need to resize some of the images so their lengths and widths are in a power of two. When they are correctly sized, place them in the lib folder of your project.

How to do it...

The changes to the main application are minimal:

1. Add a private variable (we will define the World3D class in a moment):

   ```
   private var _world:World3D;
   ```

2. Replace all the constructor code related to the previous graph drawing with this new object:

   ```
   _view.scene.addChild(_world = new World3D(new
   StaticLightPicker([light])));
   ```

3. Now create a World3D class, that extends ObjectContainer3D. This should solve all compiler issues and allow you to run the program (although you'll see no output).

4. We'll now draw the globe, using the provided color map, and embed the color map in the class. You can type in the embedded part manually, or you can right-click on the image and pick **Generate Embed Code**. Both work equally well.

   ```
   [Embed(source = "../lib/earthmap1k.jpg")]
   private var WorldImageClass:Class;
   private var _worldImage:Bitmap = new WorldImageClass();
   ```

5. Now create a sphere material, geometry, and mesh in the constructor of World3D:

   ```
   var worldTexture:BitmapTexture    = new BitmapTexture(_worldImage.
   bitmapData);
   var worldMaterial:TextureMaterial = new
   TextureMaterial(worldTexture);
   worldMaterial.lightPicker = lightPicker;
   var worldGeometry:SphereGeometry = new SphereGeometry(300, 64,
   64);
   var world:Mesh = new Mesh(worldGeometry, worldMaterial);
   addChild(world);
   ```

   Running the program will display a globe that you can pan around using the mouse.

How it works...

This is the warm-up recipe for what's about to come, so it's a little new in here. You'll notice that the supplied texture maps perfectly to a globe. Most, if not all, 3D engines use the same method of projecting a texture onto a sphere, so almost all textures for the spheres you'll find will also work with Away3D.

One interesting thing to note is the `SphereGeometry` constructor. It takes up to four arguments. The first one is the radius and works as you would expect.

The second and third parameters define how many segments Away3D will use to draw the sphere. This requires a bit of explanation.

As we have seen before, Away3D's basic building block is a flat triangle. With only triangles, it is impossible to draw a perfect sphere. So Away3D uses the same technique that we used to draw functions.

It calculates the coordinates of the sphere at discrete points and connects these points with triangles. The more triangles it uses, the more the end result will look like a sphere. But also, the slower the program will become. Therefore, Away3D gives you the choice of how many triangles you would want to use to draw a sphere.

In this case, the sphere is the focal point of the application, so we pick a fairly large number. If you would use spheres in the background, it's probably better to go with the default values.

See also

If you want to read more on approximating spheres and other objects with triangles, there are quite a few articles to be found on the Internet. The following link will give you a good start: `http://en.wikipedia.org/wiki/Sphere`.

Apart from approximating with triangles, another trick is used to make you believe that you are looking at a perfect sphere, while you are not. The material itself is drawn using **phong shading**, which adds to the impression of a perfect curve. More information on shading in 3D engines in general and phong shading in particular can be found on the Wikipedia and in various books on 3D engines:

- `http://en.wikipedia.org/wiki/Phong_shading`
- `http://en.wikipedia.org/wiki/Shading`

3D world population chart, part 2: Dressing up

Now that we have our base globe, we will look at a few options that are available to make it look better. We'll go into the three techniques in this recipe:

- Adding an animated cloud layer
- Adding bump mapping to give the impression of relief on the globe
- Adding a skybox to fill the background skies

Getting ready

This recipe's starting code is the code from the previous recipe.

We will introduce a skybox. Many previously made skybox images can be downloaded from the Internet. The one that is included with the source files was found on the Unity3D forums (`http://forum.unity3d.com/threads/99258-Space-Skybox`), but you can also use Spacescape to create your own: `http://alexcpeterson.com/portfolio/spacescape`.

No matter how you obtain the skybox images, in the end you should have six images of equal size, one image for each direction. Place all the images in the `lib` folder of the project and give them a name so you can easily remember which is which (top, bottom, left, right, back, front).

How to do it...

To add an animated cloud layer, follow the next steps:

1. In `World3D`, embed the cloud image, as shown in the following code snippet:

```
[Embed(source = "../lib/earthcloudmap.jpg")]
private var WorldCloudImageClass:Class;
private var _worldCloudImage:Bitmap = new WorldCloudImageClass();
```

2. Add a cloud private member field:

```
private var _clouds:Mesh;
```

3. In the constructor, create a translucent cloud sphere:

```
var cloudTexture:BitmapTexture    = new BitmapTexture(_
worldCloudImage.bitmapData);
var cloudMaterial:TextureMaterial = new
TextureMaterial(cloudTexture);
cloudMaterial.lightPicker = lightPicker;
cloudMaterial.alpha = 0.2;
```

```
var cloudGeometry:SphereGeometry  = new SphereGeometry(310, 64,
64);
_clouds = new Mesh(cloudGeometry, cloudMaterial);
addChild(_clouds);
```

4. Finally, add a method to animate it:

```
public function animate():void {
    _clouds.rotationY += 0.1;
}
```

5. You run the animation from within the enter frame listener of the main class. So in the Main class, in the onEnterFrame method, add the following:

```
_world.animate();
```

6. Run the program, and you should see a cloud layer slowly moving across the globe.

7. Now, let's add bump mapping to the globe. Embed the bump map image inside the World3D class:

```
[Embed(source = "../lib/earthbump1k.png")]
private var WorldNormalImageClass:Class;
private var _worldNormalImage:Bitmap = new
WorldNormalImageClass();
```

8. In the constructor, add it to the world material:

```
worldMaterial.normalMap = new BitmapTexture(_worldNormalImage.
bitmapData);
```

That's all there is to it. You should now see a globe with much more depth.

9. The final effect we will add is a skybox to fill the background of the display. Create a new World3DSkybox class:

```
package
{
    import away3d.primitives.SkyBox;
    import away3d.textures.BitmapCubeTexture;
    import flash.display.Bitmap;
    public class World3DSkybox extends SkyBox
    {
        [Embed(source = "../lib/Skybox360 001 Right +x.png")]
        private var _PosXClass:Class;
        private var _posX:Bitmap = new _PosXClass();

        [Embed(source = "../lib/Skybox360 001 Left -x.png")]
        private var _NegXClass:Class;
        private var _negX:Bitmap = new _NegXClass();
```

```
[Embed(source = "../lib/Skybox360 001 Up +y.png")]
private var _PosYClass:Class;
private var _posY:Bitmap = new _PosYClass();

[Embed(source = "../lib/Skybox360 001 Down -y.png")]
private var _NegYClass:Class;
private var _negY:Bitmap = new _NegYClass();

[Embed(source = "../lib/Skybox360 001 Front +z.png")]
private var _PosZClass:Class;
private var _posZ:Bitmap = new _PosZClass();

[Embed(source = "../lib/Skybox360 001 Back -z.png")]
private var _NegZClass:Class;
private var _negZ:Bitmap = new _NegZClass();

public function World3DSkybox()
{
    var cubeMap:BitmapCubeTexture = new BitmapCubeTexture(
        _posX.bitmapData,
        _negX.bitmapData,
        _posY.bitmapData,
        _negY.bitmapData,
        _posZ.bitmapData,
        _negZ.bitmapData
    );
    super(cubeMap);
}
}
}
```

10. In the main program's constructor, add the skybox to the scene:

    ```
    _view.scene.addChild(new World3DSkybox());
    ```

11. Also in the constructor, increase the camera draw distance:

    ```
    _view.camera.lens.far = 100000;
    ```

How it works...

The cloud layer is a fairly simple illusion that can be used to great effect. You can adjust the `alpha` value and the distance from the earth to whatever values you like best. The enter frame listener is called every time Flash draws a new frame in the animation. It is the perfect place to put any animation code you may have.

Bump and normal mapping is a trick used by 3D engines to simulate tiny height differences in materials. It does not change the object itself, but it gives the impression that the material has wrinkles, bumps, or height differences.

You can read up on it on Wikipedia: `http://en.wikipedia.org/wiki/Bump_mapping`.

A **skybox** is a very large cube that you look at from the inside. It is drawn at a distance, farther than any other object in the scene, and it will always stay in that location. You cannot move to the edge of the box. It's a good way to fill out the otherwise boring empty background of a 3D scene.

You don't have to define a new class for the skybox, but it is an easy way to put all the embeds together and keep a tidy workspace.

We needed to increase the distance up to which the 3D engine will render objects. If not, the earth would disappear into the skybox when moving around it.

There's more...

3D engines offer an incredible amount of different filters, effects, and other tricks to simulate the real world. When you're creating graphs, you probably won't need most of them, but it is good to know that they're there in case you want to spice up your display.

Adding effects

The material's `addMethod` function allows you to add additional post-process effects, such as fog and cartoon rendering.

The `EffectMethodBase` documentation gives an overview of the different possibilities: `http://away3d.com/livedocs/away3d/4.0/away3d/materials/methods/EffectMethodBase.html`.

Still more effects

The Away 3D example repository at `https://github.com/away3d/away3d-examples-broomstick/tree/master/src` holds examples for even more ways of changing the look of materials.

For instance, environment mapping is another trick in the 3D engine's arsenal that will make objects look as if they reflect their surroundings. In some graphs, this can be used to great effect.

3D world population chart, part 3: The data

Now that the globe is finished, it's time to start adding the data. We will use the data format as it is provided by the original inspiration for this recipe: `http://code.google.com/p/webgl-globe/`.

Data sets come in series of repeating (latitude, longitude, magnitude) tuples. The latitude and longitude map to a place on the globe. The magnitude represents the actual data we want to show, in this case, the population at that location.

Getting ready

We will start from the end result in the previous recipe.

The data set can be downloaded from `http://code.google.com/p/webgl-globe/source/browse/globe/population909500.json`.

Click on the **View raw file** link to download the actual JSON file. Store that file in the `lib` folder of the project.

How to do it...

All code for this recipe will be added to the `Graph3D` class:

1. Embed the JSON object:

   ```
   [Embed(source = "../lib/population909500.json", mimeType = "application/octet-stream")]
   private var PopulationData:Class;
   ```

2. Add a segment set private variable that will hold the different lines that represent the population:

   ```
   private var _lines:SegmentSet;
   ```

3. In the constructor, initialize the set and add it to the 3D container:

   ```
   _lines = new SegmentSet();
   addChild(_lines);
   ```

4. Now we can load and parse the JSON file (we use the year 2000 population data for this recipe):

   ```
   var json:Object = JSON.parse(new PopulationData());
   var data:Array = json[2][1];
   trace(data.length);
   for (var i:int = 0; i < data.length; i+=3) {
       addLine(data[i+0], data[i+1], data[i+2]);
   }
   ```

5. And finally we need to draw the actual lines:

```
private function addLine(latitude:Number, longitude:Number,
amount:Number):void
{
    var phi:Number    = (90.0 - latitude) * Math.PI / 180.;
    var theta:Number = (180.0 - longitude) * Math.PI / 180.;
    var r:int         = 300 + 500 * amount;

    var x:Number = r * Math.sin(phi) * Math.cos(theta);
    var y:Number = r * Math.cos(phi);
    var z:Number = -r * Math.sin(phi) * Math.sin(theta);

    var line:LineSegment = new LineSegment(new Vector3D(0, 0, 0),
new Vector3D(x, y, z), 0x99eeff, 0x002233, 5);
    _lines.addSegment(line);
}
```

If you run the application, you should see the result that we showed in the first recipe of this series, *3D world population chart, part 1: The globe*.

How it works...

The data is read from an existing JSON file. In *Chapter 2, Working with Data*, we already saw that Flash makes this exceptionally easy. We select the 2000 dataset by picking the third element in the list (offset 2) and taking the second from that.

Ideally, you'd want to check that this is really the 2000 dataset, just in case the content of the JSON file changes.

The data comes in a combination longitude, latitude, and population density. Longitude/latitude coordinates are called **Geodetic**. This coordinate system describes locations on a sphere and is a spherical coordinate system (at least approximated, which is good enough for this application).

You can read up on it on Wikipedia at the following links: `http://en.wikipedia.org/wiki/Geodetic_system` and `http://en.wikipedia.org/wiki/Spherical_coordinate_system`. Be prepared for a lot of maths and a lot of confusion, because there are many ways of representing coordinates on earth.

When we draw in 3D on a computer screen, we need Cartesian coordinates (the traditional *x,y,z* coordinates). The conversion consists of a trigonometry formula that converts angles into distances. It falls outside the scope of this book, but if you want to understand it, Wikipedia is, again, an invaluable resource: Check `http://en.wikipedia.org/wiki/Trigonometry` and the previously linked pages.

Away3D has a special type for drawing lines, called **segments**. These are grouped in a segment set. Usually they are used for drawing wireframes, the outlines of a 3D object, useful for debugging complex 3D scenes. However, in this case we use them to draw the dataset.

A `LineSegment` variable has a starting point and an endpoint, represented by a vector. It also has a color at the start and end of the line. The color in between is a gradual transition between the two. The final parameter is the thickness of the line.

There's more...

We've now seen the basics of working with 3D and data, and hopefully you've noticed that the only limitation is your imagination.

Data set picker and loader

Just as in the keyboard recipe, you can add a combobox that allows the user to select which dataset to display. The JSON file we used contains population data for the years 1990, 1995, and 2000.

You can also add code to load the file from the Internet (see *Chapter 2, Working with Data*). When that is in place, you can point to other datasets. And you can even add automatic updates that reload data regularly.

See also

In the last two chapters, we've only shown the basics of creating 3D graphs and 3D engines. If you want to learn more about Away3D, take a look at the many examples on their GitHub repository (`https://github.com/away3d/`) and ask your questions in the forum (`http://away3d.com/forum/`).

Index

Symbols

A

CubeGeometry constructor 222
curveTo function 23, 109, 110
CustomMarker class 166
cylinder geometry
    drawing 227-229

D

data
    attaching, to points 143, 144
    exporting, as CSV 75-77
    exporting, to PDF file 78-80
    keyboard usage, mapping in 3D 251, 252
    loading, from Excel files 68-71
    loading, in Excel 75-77
    loading, with XML 66, 67
    parsing, for use as region fill 166-168
    preparing 54-57
    preparing, for relational network generation
        197-199
    reading, directly from Wikipedia 253
    storing, in two arrays 31
    tree, using as 128
databases 57
DataClass property 61
data.csv file 56
data display
    enriching 139-143
data file
    loading, from Internet 60, 61
data points
    dragging, to new values 151-154
    selecting, in graphs 144-146
data points, selecting in graphs
    ways, for improvements 147
dataProvider attribute 51
data range 96
data set
    zooming in 188-190
data set loader 263
data set picker 263
datasets, 3D World Population Chart 261-263
data updates
    sending, to graph 135-138

data updates, sending to graph
    ways, for improvement 138
data visualization 113
delayedCall function 183
display list 9
DisplayList object 5
donut charts
    about 106
    as pie charts 110
    creating, steps 107-109
    labels, adding 109
double linked list
    URL, for info 199
drawArea method 34, 38, 39
drawAxisLine method 26
drawBitmapPoint method 41
drawCube function 233
drawCylinder function 228
drawDataPoints function 233
drawDataPoints method 152, 227
drawGraph method 17
drawHorizontalAxis method 26
drawLine method 34
drawPoint method 14, 17, 23, 136, 141
drawRect method 46
dynamic graphs
    about 135
    based on editable table 147-150

E

easing function 185
    visualizing 186
EditTable class 148
EffectMethodBase documentation 260
endingPercent property 120
enterFrame method 153
Event.CANCEL event 66
events
    dispatching 139
    listening for 139
Excel
    data, loading 75-77

graphs, zooming
  ways, for improvements 134

H

HardShadowMapMethod 250
heat map
  about 176
  overlaying, over map layer 176-178
HeatMapData class 177
histograms
  about 94
  building, ActionScript 3 used 94-96
hitTestObject method 146, 195
horizontal axis
  adding, to sine graph 24-28
HorizontalAxis class 92, 96
horizontalAxis tag 86
hover
  labels, displaying on 253
HoverControllerobject 225
HoverInfo class 144
HTTPStatusEvent.HTTP_STATUS event 62

I

images
  adding, to PDF 81
import function 55
Internet
  data file, loading from 60, 61
IOErrorEvent.IO_ERROR event 62
iText PDF library 81

J

Java 57
JavaScript 205
JSON
  about 71, 169, 199
  URL, for info 72

K

keyboard usage
  mapping, in 3D 246-252
key material 253

L

labelPosition argument 106
labels
  displaying, on hover 253
LayerManager control 175
leaf 199
legend
  about 45, 120
  adding, to chart 93
  background, adding 48
  creating 45-47
  working 47, 48
Legend class 45
LibreOffice 54
light 217
LinearRing class 172
lineBitmapStyle method 44
line graph
  creating, based on function 17-23
lineStyle method 44
linked list
  about 199
  URL, for info 199
local hard drive
  file, loading from 63-66
LongLat class 164
LookAtController 226

M

Main.as file 49
Main class 215
Main.mxml file 49
map
  coloring 169-172
  displaying, OpenScales API used 160-162
  multiple layers, adding to 173, 174
  points of interest, adding on 163-166
Map class 161
map layer
  heat map, overlaying over 176-178
marker
  chaning 166
  interactive, making 166
Marker class 166

R

radius property 110
real 3D engine
  using 102
RectangleGeometry class 238, 242
recursion 199
RegExp class
  URL, for info 60
regular expression handling
  URL, for info 60
relational database 57
relational network
  animating 207, 208
  data, preparing for 197-199
  navigating through 205, 206
  nodes, arranging 202-204
  nodes, linking 202-204
  sounds, adding to 209, 210
  styling options 202
  visual, creating for node 200-202
relational networks 197
relative URL 62
rendering 217
resolution property 162
REST service
  about 57, 71
  consuming 72-74
RFC 4180 standard 60
root 199
row 68

S

save method 80
scene 216
Scene3D parameter 222
screen coordinates
  about 10
  versus graph coordinates 28
script tag 85
segments 263
setSelected method 147
setters
  using 120
setTimeout function 182
shadows
  about 223

manipulating 250
Shape class 220
showDataTips attribute 51
sine graph
  horizontal axis, adding to 24-28
  vertical axis, adding to 24-28
SOAP service
  about 57
  using 75
sounds
  adding, to relational network 209, 210
Sparkline class 97
sparklines
  about 97
  area, adding under line 98
  creating, for text content enrichment 97, 98
  data, averaging 98
SphereGeometry constructor 256
spreadsheet
  graphing 29-31
Sprite child 9
Sprite class 166
startingPercent property 120
stopPropagation method 157
StringHelper class 57
strokeWidth property 110
subway locations
  animating 192-194
SweetiePlus icons
  URL 41
switch statement 109

T

tabular data
  graphing, in 3D 230-233
tag clouds
  about 123
  alpha, modifying 125
  creating, steps 123, 124
  embedded fonts, using 125
Taytay
  URL 60
test files
  setting up 54-57
textField class
  customization 48

Thank you for buying
ActionScript Graphing Cookbook

About Packt Publishing

Packt, pronounced 'packed', published its first book "*Mastering phpMyAdmin for Effective MySQL Management*" in April 2004 and subsequently continued to specialize in publishing highly focused books on specific technologies and solutions.

Our books and publications share the experiences of your fellow IT professionals in adapting and customizing today's systems, applications, and frameworks. Our solution based books give you the knowledge and power to customize the software and technologies you're using to get the job done. Packt books are more specific and less general than the IT books you have seen in the past. Our unique business model allows us to bring you more focused information, giving you more of what you need to know, and less of what you don't.

Packt is a modern, yet unique publishing company, which focuses on producing quality, cutting-edge books for communities of developers, administrators, and newbies alike. For more information, please visit our website: www.packtpub.com.

Writing for Packt

We welcome all inquiries from people who are interested in authoring. Book proposals should be sent to author@packtpub.com. If your book idea is still at an early stage and you would like to discuss it first before writing a formal book proposal, contact us; one of our commissioning editors will get in touch with you.

We're not just looking for published authors; if you have strong technical skills but no writing experience, our experienced editors can help you develop a writing career, or simply get some additional reward for your expertise.

Adobe Flash 11 Stage3D (Molehill) Game Programming Beginner's Guide

ISBN: 978-1-84969-168-0   Paperback: 412 pages

A step-by-step guide for creating stunning 3D games in Flash 11 Stage3D (Molehill) using AS3 and AGAL

1. The first book on Adobe's Flash 11 Stage3D, previously codenamed Molehill

2. Build hardware-accelerated 3D games with a blazingly fast frame rate.

3. Full of screenshots and ActionScript 3 source code, each chapter builds upon a real-world example game project step-by-step.

4. Light-hearted and informal, this book is your trusty sidekick on an epic quest to create your very own 3D Flash game.

Away3D 3.6 Essentials

ISBN: 978-1-84951-206-0   Paperback: 400 pages

Take Flash to the next dimension by creating detailed, animated, and interactive 3D worlds with Away3D

1. Create stunning 3D environments with highly detailed textures

2. Animate and transform all types of 3D objects, including 3D Text

3. Eliminate the need for expensive hardware with proven Away3D optimization techniques, without compromising on visual appeal

4. Written in a practical and illustrative style, which will appeal to Away3D beginners and Flash developers alike

Please check **www.PacktPub.com** for information on our titles

Learning Adobe Muse

ISBN: 978-1-84969-314-1   Paperback: 268 pages

Create beautiful websites without writing any code

1. A step by step guide to using Adobe's latest design tool to build websites

2. A thorough coverage of all the features introduced in Adobe Muse

3. Design tips and advice for new designers

Mastering Adobe Captivate 6

ISBN: 978-1-84969-244-1   Paperback: 476 pages

Create professional SCORM-compliant eLearning content with Adobe Captivate

1. Step by step tutorial to build three projects including a demonstration, a simulation and a random SCORM-compliant quiz featuring all possible question slides

2. Enhance your projects by adding interactivity, animations, sound and more

3. Publish your project in a wide variety of formats enabling virtually any desktop and mobile devices to play your e-learning content

4. Deploy your e-Learning content on a SCORM or AICC-compliant LMS

Please check **www.PacktPub.com** for information on our titles

www.ingramcontent.com/pod-product-compliance
Lightning Source LLC
LaVergne TN
LVHW062309060326
832902LV00013B/2120